GLOBALIZATION, GROWTH
AND MARGINALIZATION

Also by A. S. Bhalla

BLENDING OF NEW AND TRADITIONAL TECHNOLOGIES
(*co-editor*)

ECONOMIC TRANSITION IN HUNAN AND SOUTHERN CHINA

ENVIRONMENT, EMPLOYMENT AND DEVELOPMENT (*editor*)

FACING THE TECHNOLOGICAL CHALLENGE

NEW TECHNOLOGIES AND DEVELOPMENT (*co-editor*)

REGIONAL BLOCS: Building Blocks or Stumbling Blocks?

SMALL AND MEDIUM ENTERPRISES: Technology Policies and
Options (*editor*)

TECHNOLOGICAL TRANSFORMATION OF RURAL INDIA
(*co-editor*)

TECHNOLOGY AND EMPLOYMENT IN INDUSTRY (*editor*)

TOWARDS GLOBAL ACTION FOR APPROPRIATE TECHNOLOGY
(*editor*)

UNEVEN DEVELOPMENT IN THE THIRD WORLD

Globalization, Growth and Marginalization

Edited by

A. S. Bhalla

David Thomson Senior Research Fellow
Sidney Sussex College
University of Cambridge

and

formerly Special Adviser to the President of the
International Development Research Centre
Ottawa

First published in Great Britain 1998 by
MACMILLAN PRESS LTD
Houndmills, Basingstoke, Hampshire RG21 6XS and London
Companies and representatives throughout the world

A catalogue record for this book is available from the British Library.

ISBN 0–333–72814–9 (hardcover)

First published in the United States of America 1998 by
ST. MARTIN'S PRESS, INC.,
Scholarly and Reference Division,
175 Fifth Avenue, New York, N.Y. 10010

ISBN 0–312–21278–X (clothbound)

Library of Congress Cataloging-in-Publication Data
Globalization, growth and marginalization / edited by A.S. Bhalla.
p. cm.
Includes bibliographical references (p.   ) and index.
ISBN 0–312–21278–X (cloth)
1. Income distribution—Developing countries.   2. Developing
countries—Economic conditions—Regional disparities.
3. Competition, International.   4. International economic relations.
I. Bhalla, A. S.
HC59.72.I5G55 1998
338.9'009172'4—dc21

97–41070
CIP

First published in Canada 1998 by
INTERNATIONAL DEVELOPMENT RESEARCH CENTRE
PO Box 8500, Ottawa, ON
Canada K1G 3H9

Canadian Cataloguing in Publication Data
Globalization, growth and marginalization
Includes bibliographical references and index.
ISBN 0–88936–839–2 (paperback)
ISBN 0–88936–850–3 (hardback)
1. Income distribution—Developing countries.
2. Developing countries—Economic conditions—Regional disparities.
3. Competition, International.
4. International economic relations.
I. Bhalla, A. S.
II. International Development Research Centre (Canada)
HC59.72.I5G55 1998   338.9'009172'4   C98–980009–1

This book is printed on paper suitable for recycling and made from fully managed and sustained forest sources.

10   9   8   7   6   5   4   3   2   1
07   06   05   04   03   02   01   00   99   98

Printed and bound in Great Britain by Antony Rowe Ltd, Chippenham, Wiltshire

Contents

Contents

List of Tables and Figures

Tables

List of Tables and Figures

Figures

Preface

The genesis of this volume lies in consultations I had over lunch in Toronto with Professor Gerald Helleiner of the University of Toronto in October 1995. Caroline Pestieau, the IDRC Vice-President for Programmes, had kindly offered to support my research in a form that would be mutually beneficial. So a modest grant was made available to commission a selected number of papers for this volume.

While the issue of globalization is receiving considerable attention, not enough work is being done on the social costs involved (in terms of poverty, inequality, unemployment and exclusion) in the era of globalization, nor on the interrelationships between the information highway, the process of globalization and the growing marginalization of people in poor developing countries. These topics were finally chosen in view of their particular interest to the IDRC and developing countries. Globalization and information technology may be having an adverse effect on poor developing countries with an inadequate national capacity. On the other hand, with the rapidly declining utilization cost of high technology, this technology is becoming more and more accessible even to the poorer developing countries. However cost is not the only barrier to access to information technology and integration into the global economy. As this volume shows, institutional and infrastructure barriers are equally if not more important.

Globalization is defined in economic terms, that is, in terms of trade liberalization, including the breaking down of tariff and non-tariff barriers, and the freer flow of capital, technology, finance, goods and services across national boundaries. While the non-economic aspects of globalization are no doubt important, they are not considered here. We have opted for focus and depth rather than breadth of coverage.

What is studied is the impact of globalization on growth and productivity, poverty, income distribution and unemployment. Apart from a global analysis in Chapter 1, special emphasis is placed on the regional dimensions of this impact. Variations across different regions and subregions in terms of degree of integration into the global economy receive particular attention. Separate chapters are devoted to Africa, South Asia, East and South-East Asia and Latin America.

I owe a debt of gratitude to a number of people, notably Gerald Helleiner of the University of Toronto for suggesting the topic; Albert Berry of the University of Toronto, Ha-Joon Chang of the University of Cambridge and Azizur Rahman Khan of the University of California at Riverside for useful comments on the research outline for the project; and Caroline Pestieau, Réal Lavergne and Rohinton Medhora of the IDRC and Professor Sir Hans Singer of the Institute of Development Studies at the University of Sussex for critical comments on selected chapters. Albert Berry's contribution to the volume is particularly significant: as well as his work in Chapters 3 and 7, he willingly and voluntarily offered constructive comments and suggestions on most of the chapters of the volume. For skilful editing of the various chapters, I am grateful to my wife Praveen Bhalla. Finally, I would like to express my appreciation to Eshete Hailu of the IDRC and Degol Hailu of the School of Oriental and African Studies (SOAS) of the University of London for research assistance and data compilation.

Ottawa and Cambridge   A.S. BHALLA

Acknowledgements

The editor and publishers wish to thank the following for permission to use copyright material: Edward Elgar Publishers and MERIT, University of Maastricht for Table 2.5, taken from J. Hagedoorn (ed.), *Technical Change and the World Economy* (1995); The International Finance Corporation (IFC) for Table 6.3, taken from *Trends in Private Investment in Developing Countries 1990–94* (Discussion Paper no. 28, 1995), The United Nations and the Economic Commission for Latin America and the Caribbean, for Tables 3.1, 3.4 and 3.5, taken from *Economic Survey of Latin America and the Caribbean 1994–95*, and Table 3.2, taken from *Statistical Yearbook for Latin America and the Caribbean 1995*; The United Nations Development Programme (UNDP) for use of their data base to compile Table 1.3. The World Bank for Table 1.1, taken from its *Annual Report 1995*, Table 2.1, taken from *Global Economic Prospects and Developing Countries 1996*, and Table 4.3, taken from *Managing Capital Flows in East Asia 1996*; Organization for Economic Cooperation and Development (OECD) for Table 2.2, taken from *The International Diffusion of Advanced Telecommunications: Opportunities for Developing Countries* (1991), and Table 7.9, taken from *Globalisation and Linkages to 2020: Challenges and Opportunities for OECD Countries* (1997).

List of Abbreviations

ACIS	Advanced cargo information system
ADP	Automatic data processing
ADR	American depository receipts
APC	Association for Progressive Communications
APEC	Asia Pacific Economic Cooperation
ASYCUDA	Advanced system for customs data
BBS	Bangladesh Bureau of Statistics
BCCI	Bank of Commerce and Credit International
CAD	Computer-aided design
CAM	Computer-aided manufacture
CIFEG	International Centre for Exchange in the Geosciences
CNMT	Computer numerically-controlled machine tool
COMESA	Common Market of Eastern and Southern Africa
CTC	Centre for Transnational Corporations (UN)
DNA	Deoxyribonucleic acid
DSR	Debt service ratio
ECCAS	Economic Community of Central African States
ECOWAS	Economic Community of West African States
ESEA	East and South-East Asia
EU	European Union
FDI	Foreign direct investment
GATT	General Agreement on Tariffs and Trade
GDP	Gross domestic product
GDR	Global depository receipts
GNP	Gross national product
HDI	Human development index
HES	Household Expenditure Surveys
HIC	High-income country
ICT	Information and communications technology
IDB	Inter-American Development Bank
IDRC	International Development Research Centre
IFC	International Finance Corporation
IFIs	International financial institutions
IMF	International Monetary Fund
INTECH	Institute for New Technologies (UNU)
ISDN	Integrated services digital network
ISI	Import-substituting industrialization
IT	Information technology

JASPA	Jobs and Skills Programme for Africa (ILO)
KP&T	Kenya Post and Telecommunications
LDC	Less developed country
MERCOSUR	Common Market of the Southern Cone
NAFTA	North American Free Trade Agreement
NCC	National Computer Centre
NCMT	Numerically controlled machine tool
NIC	Newly industrializing country
NIE	Newly industrializing economy
OECD	Organization for Economic Cooperation and Development
PANGIS	Pan-African Geological Information System
PC	Personal computer
PEI	Portfolio equity investment
PIT	Poverty income threshold
PREALC	Regional employment programme for Latin America and the Caribbean (ILO)
PTA	Preferential trade area
R&D	Research and development
RMCs	Regional member countries
SADC	Southern African Development Community
SAP	Structural adjustment programme
SMEs	Small and medium enterprises
SSB	State Statistical Bureau (China)
TFP	Total factor productivity
TINET	Trade Information Network
TNCs	Transnational corporations
UNCTAD	United Nations Conference on Trade and Development
UNDP	United Nations Development Programme
UNECA	United Nations Economic Commission for Africa
UNECLAC	United Nations Economic Commission for Latin America and the Caribbean
UNIDO	United Nations Industrial Development Organization
UNRISD	United Nations Research Institute for Social Development
UNU	United Nations University
VCR	Video cassette recorder
WIDER	World Institute for Development Economic Research (UNU)
WTO	World Trade Organization

Notes on the Contributors

Albert Berry is Professor of Economics and Director of the Latin American Programme at the Centre for International Studies at the University of Toronto. Formerly he was Professor of Economics at Yale University and Assistant Director of the Economic Growth Center, Yale University. Professor Berry has been a consultant to the Ford Foundation, the ILO, the World Bank and the Planning Commission of Colombia. His publications include *Agrarian Structure and Productivity in Developing Countries* (with William Cline), *Success in Small and Medium Enterprises: Evidence from Colombia* (with Mariluz Cortes and Ashfaq Ishaq) and *Poverty, Economic Reforms and Income Distribution in Latin America*.

A.S. Bhalla is David Thomson Senior Research Fellow, Sidney Sussex College, University of Cambridge. At the time of editing this volume, he was Special Adviser to the President, International Development Research Centre (IDRC), Ottawa. Prior to joining the IDRC he held various senior management positions at the International Labour Office in Geneva, Switzerland. Dr Bhalla has been Pearson Fellow at the IDRC; Hallsworth Professorial Fellow in Economics at the University of of Manchester; Visiting Research Associate at the Economic Growth Centre, Yale University; Research Officer at the Institute of Economics and Statistics at the University of Oxford; and University Tutorial Fellow at the University of Delhi. Dr Bhalla is the author of several books, including *Regional Blocs: Building Blocks or Stumbling Blocks?* (with P. Bhalla), *Facing the Technological Challenge* and *Uneven Development in the Third World*, now in its second edition.

Jeffrey James is Professor of Development Economics and Director of the Center for Graduate Studies in Economics and Management, Tilburg University, the Netherlands. Formerly he was Assistant Professor of Economics at Boston University; staff member of the Technology and Employment Division, ILO, Geneva; and Research Fellow, Queen Elizabeth House, Oxford. Professor James is the author of several major publications, including: *Consumption and Development, The State, Technology and Industrialization in Africa, Transition to Egalitarian Development* and *Technological Behaviour of Public Enterprises in Developing Countries*.

Azizur Rahman Khan is Professor of Economics, University of California at Riverside. He has also served as Senior Economist at the World Bank; Director of the Asian Employment Programme of the ILO; Chief of the

General Economics Division, Planning Commission of Bangladesh; Research Director of the Pakistan Institute of Development Economics and the Bangladesh Institute of Development Studies; and Lecturer at the London School of Economics. Professor Khan's publications include *Overcoming Unemployment, Structural Adjustment and Income Distribution, Globalisation and the Developing World* (with Keith Griffin) and the *Economy of Bangladesh*.

Flora Musonda is a Research Fellow at the Economic and Social Research Foundation, Dar es Salaam, Tanzania. She holds a PhD in economics from the University of Lund, Sweden, and a BA in economics from the University of Dar es Salaam. Her fields of specialization include regional integration, international trade policy, aid and debt and economic reforms.

Paul Streeten is Professor Emeritus of Economics at Boston University, a consultant to the UNDP on the Human Development Report and to UNESCO on the Report on Culture and Development. He is editor and Chairman of the Board of *World Development*. He is an Honorary Fellow of Balliol College, Oxford (where he was a Fellow from 1948 until 1978), and of the Institute of Development Studies, Sussex (where he was a Fellow from 1966 until 1968). He has honorary degrees from the Universities of Aberdeen and Malta. Professor Streeten's recent books are *Development Perspectives, First Things First, What Price Food?, Beyond Adjustment, Mobilizing Human Potential, Strategies for Human Development, The UN and the Bretton Woods Institutions*, and *Thinking about Development*.

Samuel Wangwe is Executive Director of the Economic and Social Research Foundation, Dar Es Salaam, Tanzania. Formerly he was a Senior Research Fellow at the UNU Institute for New Technologies (INTECH), Maastricht, the Netherlands; and Professor of Economics, University of Dar Es Salaam, Tanzania. He possesses over twenty years' experience in academic, research and consultancy work with both local and international institutions in the fields of education, industrialization, trade, technology and structural adjustment. Professor Wangwe's publications include *Alternative Development Strategies in African Development* (co-editor) and *Exporting Africa: Technology, Trade and Industrialization in Sub-Saharan Africa* (editor).

Introduction

A.S. Bhalla

Globalization means different things to different people. The term, which is used to describe the shape of the world economy today, has become fashionable but its meaning and implications, particularly for developing countries, are far from clear. The phenomenon is not new since trade and foreign direct investment (FDI), the most commonly used indicators of globalization, grew rapidly even in the nineteenth and early twentieth centuries. The geographical dispersion of economic activitiy has been taking place for decades if not centuries. This volume therefore considers globalization as a continuum, with the latest phase (the 1980s and early 1990s) representing the acceleration of globalization (see Chapter 1 for a discussion of globalization in a historical perspective).

If globalization is not a new phenomenon, does the current phase of globalization differ from the earlier phases? Today's information and communications technologies have led to an unprecedented growth of trade in services and the replacement of Fordist mass production by flexible production systems or specialization (the new organizational innovations as distinct from technological ones). These are the two distinguishing features of the present phase.

Both the economic and the non-economic features of globalization are the subject of current debate. Apart from the economic features in terms of growth in trade, investment, finance and technology flows, growing uniformity in social values resulting in part from the standardization of consumer tastes and loss of national sovereignty are noted as some of the non-economic features.

KEY FEATURES OF GLOBALIZATION

Below we discuss five economic features and two non-economic features of globalization.

Economic Features

Growth in Trade

World trade has been expanding rapidly since the nineteenth century. As Chapter 1 by Streeten notes, world trade increased 540-fold between 1820 and 1992. During the pre-First World War period (1870–1913), the annual

1

percentage growth rate of world trade was about 3.5 per cent; this rate increased to 5.8 per cent during the post-Second World War period (1950–90). The period between the two World Wars witnessed a dip in the growth rate, as could be expected (see Kitson and Michie, 1995, p. 7). Trade as a share of GDP is a commonly used indicator of globalization. The growth in this ratio in the post-Second World War period has been significant, but as Chapter 1 shows it has not been higher than the pre-1914 values.

What has been new in the postwar period (from the 1950s onwards) is a shift in the exports of developing countries from primary products to manufacturing, and faster growth of trade in services than in manufacturing. Trade in commercial services (transport, travel and other private services, including financial, communication, construction, information, professional and personal services) grew particularly rapidly in the 1980s and early 1990s. Between 1980 and 1993 trade in these services grew at nearly 8 per cent per annum, and trade in goods at about 5 per cent (see Braga, 1996).

Growth in trade is presented by the protagonists of globalization as an unmixed blessing. However, as Streeten (Chapter 1) and Berry (Chapter 3) warn us, *laissez faire* and free trade can be harmful at the country level. Rapid expansion of trade can expose countries to the vagaries of external shocks and competition, which may not always be desirable. Furthermore, benefits from exports may not be generalized if the elasticity of demand for the exports of developing countries is too low. Finally, these benefits may occur only after a long period of import-substitution policies, as shown by the record of East Asian economies (see Chapter 3).

Growth in FDI and Capital Flows

Growth in FDI has been much faster than both trade and output growth. According to the UNCTAD (1996), between 1980 and 1994 FDI stock to GDP doubled, FDI flows to domestic investment doubled and outflows of FDI to world GDP nearly doubled. FDI is the largest component of total resource flows, exceeding net private loans.

But the importance of FDI is being overshadowed by the growth of portfolio investments. There is a growing shift from longer-term FDI to more short-term and volatile investments in stocks and bonds. In the past decade the composition and mix of resource flows (that is, FDI, commercial bank loans and equities and bonds) have been changing. Global firms require finance for production in different country locations, which has increased the importance of international finance. Between 1983 and 1993 the value of the cross-border assets of banks more than tripled; between 1986 and 1992 global foreign exchange transactions also tripled. The stock of global financial assets is equivalent to twice the GDP of the OECD countries (see Oman, 1996). It has grown much more rapidly than world trade.

Financial globalization has been facilitated by the internationalization of production and the growth of global industries, the rapid pace of technological change and financial deregulation by numerous countries. New information technologies enable an around-the-clock, cross-border flow of financial data. The difficulty of controlling the flow of such information has led governments to lift restrictions and regulations on international financial flows (see Agosin and Tussie, 1993). New technology has also made many financial services more tradable across national boundaries.

The consequence of this integration of financial markets is that trade, employment, production and national economic policies in general have become more exposed to volatile fluctuations in the financial market. Private capital flows generally respond to short-term interest rates and exchange rate changes, which may not be conducive to longer-term development. Instability in one country (for example the financial crisis in Mexico, Thailand and Indonesia and Clinton's failure to obtain fast-track authority from the US Congress for future trade negotiations) tend to spill over into neighbouring and distant countries alike when financial markets are internationalized. Writing on Latin America, Berry (Chapter 3) notes the negative effects of short-term flows in terms of macroeconomic instability, slowing down the rate of growth and inhibiting export production.

Global Production and Consumption

Another feature of globalization is the 'increasing internationalisation of the production, distribution and marketing of goods and services' (Harris,1993). This is the result of the globalization of financial and capital markets, increased flows of FDI, the rapid diffusion of information by new communications technologies and the adoption by transnational enterprises of new organizational forms of production. Today these enterprises are a major driving force behind FDI in manufacturing and services. The trend towards downsizing by these enterprises has led to international subcontracting (for example IBM is subcontracting software tasks to firms in Bangalore, India), which is now part of the new globalization process. Similarly, industries linked to information technology lend themselves more easily to globalization than other industries (service industries or functions such as accounting, banking, insurance and so on are more easily relocated to low-wage economies). In the case of textiles and garments, the miniaturization of information technology (such as computer-aided design and manufacturing – CAD and CAM) and instantaneous transmission of design and marketing information across the globe, have led to the fragmentation of production and distribution worldwide in order to cater to local tastes and preferences.

The relocation of assembly production offshore, mainly by the United States, in the 1960s may be considered as the beginning of the internationalization of production (Grunwald and Flamm, 1985). Developing countries with low labour costs became competitive in the production and exportation of labour-intensive manufactures. This increasing competition from developing countries led the industrialized countries to erect protection barriers, move out of the production of labour-intensive goods into the production of high-technology goods or shift to skill-intensive industries. Traditional labour-intensive, low-skill industries thus moved from the indus- trialized countries to low-wage developing economies. Assembly production is generally concentrated in the electronics and garments industries, both of which are labour-intensive with high value-to-weight ratios (which keeps transportation costs low).

The new international division of labour and the fragmentation of produc- tion (its dispersal across national boundaries) was in part made possible by the developments in process technology. These developments made possible the fragmentation of tasks (Fröbel *et al.*, 1980). This changing pattern of international comparative advantage promoted intra-industry trade among transnational firms.

The globalization of production is increasingly being accompanied by the globalization of consumption, thanks to the convergence of consumer tastes in certain goods and services. The opening up of most developing economies today (see below) and the widespread use of information technology have contributed to the homogenization of demand. On the other hand the con- vergence of consumer tastes across national boundaries may, in some instances, conflict with gains from trade. Bhagwati (1994, p. 239, note 12) notes that harmonization of consumer tastes (or endowments) 'reduces gains from trade by reducing the diversity that produces trade'.

Global Competition

Global production, discussed above, is accompanied by growing global com- petition among the producers and suppliers of goods and services. By provid- ing information to buyers and sellers worldwide, information technology has contributed to the globalization of demand, and as a consequence it has led to the globalization of competition (see Oman, 1994).

The globalization of competition involves both the *price* and the *quality* of goods and services. Some firms operate in markets where demand changes slowly and where price may be a more dominant factor than product diversi- fication. James (1993, p. 419) raises a pertinent question about whether the new forms of global competition will erode the competitive advantage of those firms that 'cater primarily to markets in which demand changes relat- ively slowly and in which price rather than product differentiation is domin- ant'. Therefore it is useful to distinguish between specialized niche markets and standardized product markets. It is mainly in the former that quality is more important than price (Perez, 1994). In high-volume standard products, delivery and price are likely to remain important factors.

Transnational enterprises are under increasing pressure to capture increasing shares of the global market in order to amortise fixed production costs over a shorter time period (shorter product cycles). Their responses to global competition include downsizing and increasing reliance on overseas suppliers, 'strategic alliances' to spread the high costs of R&D and product development, global advertising, and mergers and acquisitions. These new strategies of corporations are intended to create global competitive advantage, reap greater economies of scale in new technology development and reduce risk and uncertainty about market shares.

Trade and Investment Liberalization Policies

The GATT Uruguay Round accord, which has been ratified by a large number of countries, has led to a successive reduction of average tariffs in all OECD countries and many newly industrializing countries. The Uruguay Round brought the first multilateral trade negotiations on banking and financial services. Industrialized countries, particularly the United States and the United Kingdom, are urging the liberalization of trade in banking services within a multilateral framework. Presumably this is motivated by the two countries' belief that such liberalization will allow them to regain some of their lost competitiveness through their superiority in financial services (see Akyüz, 1995). The first ministerial meeting of the WTO, held in Singapore in December 1996, agreed on tariff reductions on information technology goods, and on negotiating the liberalization of telecommunications. Finally, the liberalization of FDI and an international investment code are being promoted within the framework of the OECD. These areas are also being addressed by various regional arrangements such as APEC, NAFTA and the EU.

But the 1980s witnessed an increase in non-tariff barriers in agriculture, steel, electronics, footwear and textiles and clothing. Referring to developing countries, Agosin and Tussie (1993, p. 1) note that 'while they continued to espouse officially a free-trade doctrine, in practice the governments of developed countries...continued to make use of non-tariff barriers to manage imports from developing countries'. The increasing application by industrialized countries of antidumping measures against developing-country exports shows a clear trend in this direction. Although so far this has not retarded growth in world trade, in future it is possible that the effect of protectionist tendencies on trade will be negative. It is not clear whether this possible negative effect will more than offset the positive effect of lowering tariffs.

The process of globalization has also been accelerated by economic reforms and the liberalization of trade and investment policies, undertaken even by developing countries. Most developing countries have replaced the old import-substitution policies by export promotion and openness. Both domestic and international factors account for these changes. Domestic factors include the need to increase exports to overcome a decline in domestic demand, to pay for debts and to ease balance of payments constraints. A UNU/WIDER study (Helleiner, 1995) shows that growth of exports was a major source of industrial growth in the 1980s in many developing countries, including Malaysia, Mexico, Turkey and possibly Brazil and Thailand. To the extent that developing countries unilaterally adopted these new export-oriented policies, they could be considered to have induced the process of globalization, or at least its most recent phase. This is particularly true of the East and South-East Asian (ESEA) economies, which have been export-oriented for much longer than many South Asian and Latin American economies. International factors include the process of globalization already underway, which necessitated developing countries to open up their economies in order to take advantage of exports and inflows of FDI for upgrading technology, management and international competitiveness; and pressure from bilateral trading partners, aid donors or multilateral agencies such as the World Bank to introduce structural adjustment programmes, including trade, investment and financial liberalization. The UNU/WIDER study shows how FDI helped developing-country firms to overcome the problems of switching from domestic production to exports.

But the convergence and harmonization of domestic policies is not yet complete. At the first ministerial meeting of the WTO in Singapore in December 1996, developing countries (supported by Germany and the UK) rejected such harmonization in the case of environmental and labour standards. These countries fear that 'fair trade' is an excuse for greater protectionism by the industrialized countries in sectors where they are unable to compete internationally, for example labour-intensive manufactures.

Non-Economic Features

Loss of National Sovereignty

Besides economic transformation, globalization involves changes in the social and political structures and status of societies. Politically, globalization entails the loss of national sovereignty or, as some like to dramatize, the demise of the nation state. It is believed that in the global economy transnational or global corporations are becoming all powerful. The state will play a lesser and different role in serving the business interests of these corporations. Hirst and Thompson (1996, p.176) note that 'the job of nation states is like that of municipalities within states heretofore: to provide the infrastructure and public goods that business needs at the lowest possible cost'.

Admittedly the role of the nation state is changing, and it is less autonomous in the sense that national economic and monetary policies are also affected by what happens outside the national boundaries. Global competition is increasingly being governed by market forces rather than national governments. The policy autonomy of governments has been reduced by two important factors, namely the unprecedented and rapid cross-border flows of information and the global integration of financial markets, discussed above. While these phenomena reduce the autonomy of all national economies, the smaller, more open economies are likely to be worst hit since they are more vulnerable to external shocks. Global financial integration can improve the scope of the private sector to circumvent the various restrictions imposed by national monetary authorities.

But even as the forces of globalization and international economy are eroding the unchallenged power of the state, the opposite tendencies – nationalism, and ethnic and local loyalties – are also growing, as witnessed in Bosnia, in many of the former states of the Soviet Union and in Rwanda and Burundi. The experience of the European Union is a further reminder of nationalist resistance to the growth of supranational institutions in Europe. The implementation of the Maastricht Treaty, the creation of a European currency, Central Bank and so on are seen by many EU members as an unnecessary encroachment on national sovereignty. The resort to 'subsidiarity' (decisions may be taken at the national and local levels where they can be best implemented) in the European Union was intended to pacify these nationalist and local sentiments.

Standardization of Values and Cultures

The new information technology and advances in telecommunications have tended to erode the heterogeneity of national life styles, social and economic values and even cultures. This is visible in the standardization of consumer tastes in favour of fast foods (evidenced by the omnipresence of McDonald's and Coca Cola) and American films and soap operas. The promotion of consumerism through global marketing, the media and advertising is widely viewed as an inevitable accompaniment to global competition and the search for global markets.

This phenomenon seems to be confined mainly to the expanding middle classes in most countries. With few exceptions, the so-called global 'products' are largely beyond the reach of the poor.

The different dimensions of globalization discussed above may occur simultaneously or sequentially. For example export expansion and foreign investment may go together, as shown by the recent experience of China. We argue below that the process of globalization is the result of an interplay of different forces.

In the interest of coherence and focus, this volume is confined to the *economic* features of globalization. But this is in no way intended to belittle the relevance and importance of the non-economic and cultural implications of globalization. In this volume globalization is analysed in terms of export expansion, growth in foreign direct investment (FDI), and the trade and investment liberalization policies of developing countries. The focus is mainly on the impact of globalization on developing as opposed to the industrialized countries. To explore variations in the degree to which developing countries are becoming globally integrated, a regional rather than a country approach is adopted.

The world of today is a very different place from the world of thirty years ago. Institutional and structural responses to the new phase of globalization and management of the global economy according to new rules of the game are therefore essential to an equitable sharing of the fruits of globalization (see Chapter 1). This volume argues that free and unmanaged globalization can cause economic and social hardship by exacerbating poverty and income inequalities (Chapters 1 and 3).

WHAT DRIVES GLOBALIZATION?

The seven features and forces of globalization discussed above show both complementarity and conflict. Some people believe that unilateral liberalization of the developing countries' trade, investment and financial sectors has contributed strongly to the acceleration of globalization. In other words, the phenomenon is seen as *endogenous*. To others, the unprecedented pace of technological change and the spread of new information technology and telecommunications are *exogenous* factors that are causing globalization. It is difficult to disentangle the various forces at work, but it may be fair to say that both endogenous and exogenous factors have a role to play and that each influences the other.

We believe that globalization is driven by the interaction of trade, FDI, technology and policies (that is, liberalization policies, particularly those of developing countries). Growth in trade alone induces less 'functional integration' than FDI and information technology. Since the reduction of tariff barriers under successive GATT rounds, 'tariff jumping' FDI has become much less important than FDI that complements trade. This is evident in the operations of transnationals in China and the rest of East Asia. Bhagwati (1978) argued that export-oriented countries attracted more FDI than others since they catered for larger regional and international markets. A cross-section study by Balasubramanyam *et al.*, (1996) has provided some empirical support for this hypothesis.

The current phase of globalization is induced by both technological change and organizational innovations such as flexible production systems (for a discussion of the interrelationship between the two, see James and Bhalla, 1993). The new information and telecommunications technologies have 'shrunk' the world and enabled 'functional integration' of transnational strategies of production, marketing, outsourcing and so on. The increase in intrafirm trade is a measure of this phenomenon.

While the current phase of globalization is no doubt driven by the liberalization of trade and investment policies, particularly by developing countries, it is not always clear whether such liberalization is the cause or the effect of globalization. If considered a cause of globalization, then one can argue that the process is endogenous to a particular country which can in principle, control the pace of globalization.[1] However, since most countries have liberalized and opened up their economies, any country following the route of import substitution is likely to do so at its own peril (see Chapter 4 for this argument). Thus some inevitability is attached to the need for convergence.

THE IMPACT OF GLOBALIZATION

In this volume, our main concern is to analyse the impact of globalization on (1) growth and productivity, (2) poverty and inequality, and (3) employment. Poverty and income distribution are given particular attention, since these aspects of globalization are relatively neglected in the current literature. The bulk of the literature on globalization is concerned with its growth implications. Yet for both industrial and developing countries alike, the other two aspects noted above are important.

The impact of globalization is generally deemed to be positive since it is often assumed that economic liberalization will improve market efficiency and accelerate economic growth. We show in this volume that this did not happen in the 1980s and early 1990s. There are also costs involved in integrating into the global economy, and these need to be taken into account. Globalization may intensify existing uneven development within countries, between countries and between regions, particularly between low-wage assemblers in developing countries and high-skill producers in industrialized countries.

The costs of globalization take several forms. At the global level, globalization may reinforce or aggravate 'income gaps' and technology gaps between nations since not all countries are equally prepared or endowed to take advantage of it. Also, during the late 1970s and early 1980s (before the latest phase of globalization) the initial conditions were not equally favourable for all countries. In industrialized countries the process of globalization, combined with the emergence of an information and knowledge-based society, is likely to widen the gap between skilled and unskilled members of society (the so-called 'knowledge gap') and exacerbate wage and income inequalities. In developing countries too, the existing wage and income inequalities are likely to widen (see Chapters 3 and 4). Only the modern industrial sectors of these countries are likely to be able to integrate successfully into the global economy.

The above social costs of globalization need to be weighed against the benefits in terms of higher growth and productivity. As several chapters in this volume show, the social costs are likely to be significant. However it is not clear whether the increase in wage and incomes inequality during the 1980s (particularly in South Asia and Latin America) was due to globalization or to the domestic policies of developing countries.

THE STUDIES IN THE VOLUME

This volume is divided into eight chapters, the first two of which are conceptual analyses. Chapters 3 to 6 deal with the economic situation in four different regions (South Asia, East and South-East Asia, Latin America and Africa) during the 1980s and 1990s. Chapter 7 provides a regional overview of the impact of globalization and information technology on growth, inequality and employment. The final chapter outlines specific areas in which further research is needed before any definitive conclusions can be drawn about the positive or negative impact of globalization and the information highway.

Chapter 1 examines globalization (defined in terms of an increase in the ratio of exports to GDP and foreign investment to GDP) in a historical perspective. It shows that while the process accelerated and became more multidimensional from the 1980s onwards, it started much earlier. The chapter also examines the particular benefits and costs involved in the process of globalization. It identifies the winners and losers and outlines policies that may be required to minimize the costs.

In tracing the influence of information technology on patterns of global integration, Chapter 2 examines trade-induced and foreign-investment-induced mechanisms of technological influence. Three main types of information technology (IT) are considered: (1) IT in industrial production (computer-aided design, CAD, and computer numerically controlled machine tools, NCMT), (2) telecommunications infrastructure, and (3) electronic communications technology (the Internet and electronic mail). Based on this information, a taxonomy is developed that combines the forms of IT with mechanisms of influence, and identifies firms in developing countries that are likely to benefit or suffer from the process of global integration.

The regional chapters (3–6) discuss problems of growth and productivity, inequality and employment generation during the process of globalization in the 1980s and 1990s. Chapter 7 presents a regional overview, drawing partly on the individual regional chapters. It notes that growth has been slow in all regions except ESEA, and that poverty and income inequality have increased in all regions except ESEA. The employment situation is less clearcut. Employment expansion has taken place in ESEA, but there is no clear evidence of a net employment increase in Latin America during the 1980s and 1990s. In this region and in Africa, employment has shifted towards informal employment during periods of severe economic recession. In general employment has grown faster in countries where economic growth has been rapid.

The global distribution of jobs between North and South in the era of globalization is also briefly discussed in Chapter 7. Despite the growing literature, it is still not clear whether the increase in unemployment of the unskilled in the North is trade- or technology-determined. Partial explanations attributing the cause to a single factor are misleading. There is no clearcut evidence that either trade or technology is necessarily job-destroying. The experience of East and South-East Asia shows that rapid absorption of information technology can increase employment as well as competitiveness in conditions of rapid economic growth. Thus the problem of unskilled unemployment in the North may be due more to slow growth and lack of demand than to trade or technology.

Policy and appropriate international action to manage globalization are discussed in Chapters 3–7. Depending on the circumstances, *managed* trade may be more beneficial to countries than *free* trade. Chapter 3, on Latin America, shows that complete trade liberalization, accompanied by overvalued currencies (due to surges of capital inflows) can be harmful to small and medium firms, which employ a substantial proportion of the working population. Careful *management* of trade and capital flows is therefore necessary to keep at bay the threats arising from globalization.

Chapters 4 and 5 underline the fact that appropriate incentive systems, infrastructure and human capital are vital to beneficial integration into the global economy. The East Asian experience shows that these important ingredients, plus good governance, have been lacking in other regions, particularly South Asia and Africa.

Finally, Chapter 8 outlines areas for further research and policy analysis on the impact that globalization and information technology are having on growth, employment and income distribution. First, further work is needed on why globalization is not leading to faster growth in industrial and most developing countries, with the exception of those in East and South-East Asia. Second, what is the precise impact of globalization on inequality *between* nations and *within* nations? Third, the impact of globalization on the non-trading sectors and on small and medium-size enterprises needs to be examined empirically. For example, what is the extent of the international competitiveness of these enterprises? What kinds of small enterprise have been most vulnerable to import surges under globalization during the 1980s and 1990s. Fourth, the relationship between globalization and the nature and location of innovations needs serious examination. For example is the globalization of production being accompanied by the globalization of technology? Finally, the part played by government in globalization is another fruitful area for further research.

Note

1.   This point is due to Albert Berry of the University of Toronto.

1 Globalization: Threat or Salvation?

Paul Streeten[1]

Globalization is transforming trade, finance, employment, migration, technology, communications, the environment, social systems, ways of living, cultures and patterns of governance. The growth of technology and globalization mutually reinforce each other. Much of the process of globalization is historically not unprecedented, but the technology, the setting and certain features are new. International interdependence is growing, and to some extent, and partially, so is international integration. But it is accompanied by the disintegration and fragmentation of other parts. Is globalization a threat to humanity, or its salvation? Markets have to be embedded in a framework that enables their productive energies to flourish and to be used for socially and ecologically sustainable development. The reduced power of national governments combined with the spread of worldwide free markets and technological innovation without a corresponding authority to regulate them and hold them accountable has contributed to the marginalization of large regions and groups of people. Unemployment, poverty, inequality and alienation are increasing, partly (though not solely) as a result of this process. Crime, drugs, terrorism, violence, civil wars, diseases and environmental destruction are becoming globalized. Under international competition, capital, technology and advanced skills dominate the more readily dispensable factors: unskilled labour and the environment. Cost reductions are carried out and labour and nature suffer.

This chapter analyses the implications of these trends for the international movement of ideas, technology, firms (small and large, national and multinational, public and private), money and people. The first section deals with the notions of integration and interdependence between nations. It briefly discusses the main aspects of globalization, namely trade, global financial flows, technology and transnationals, and the international convergence of real wages. The second section is concerned with the beneficial and harmful aspects of globalization. It examines the impact of globalization on growth and productivity, unemployment, income distribution, technology and institutions. The third section deals with the role of government in the era of globalization. One generally expects the scope of government to be diminished as globalization proceeds. Instead I argue that globalization and

13

markets imply not less government but more. The fourth section warns against the dangers of *laissez faire*, and shows that adjustments to free trade and globalization are costly and may not always be desirable. The final section outlines the implications of globalization for research and analysis and for international action.

INTEGRATION AND INTERDEPENDENCE

We read everywhere that international integration is proceeding rapidly as the result of the increased flow of trade, capital, money, direct investment, technology, people, information and ideas across national boundaries. International integration implies the adoption of policies by separate countries as if they were a single political unit. Measurement of the degree of integration is often based on whether interest rates, share prices or the prices of goods are the same in different national markets. Integration, however, can be a term loaded with positive connotations. Although there may be some objections to the unwanted imposition of uniformity, and although the disintegration of a pernicious system may be desirable, it is generally regarded as improper to advocate 'disintegration'. But it is possible for integration to be defined either with or without such value premises. The value premise can be that all members of the integrated area should be treated as equals, either with respect to certain opportunities, such as access to the law, jobs, trade, credit, capital flows and migration, or with respect to certain achievements, such as a minimum standard of life, of education and health services. In this sense of integration, common taxation and social services are implied. If we omit this particular value premise and define integration as equal economic opportunities, however unequal the initial endowment of members of the integrated area, the world was more integrated at the end of the nineteenth century than it is today.[2] Although tariff barriers in countries other than the UK were higher then (20–40 per cent compared with 5 per cent in 1990), non-tariff barriers were much lower; capital and money movements were freer under the gold standard (that is, without the deterrent of variable exchange rates); and the movement of people was much freer; passports were rarely needed and citizenship was granted easily. Today, international migration is strictly controlled. Between 1881 and 1890 the average annual rate of immigration into the United States was 9.2 per 1000 of the US population, reaching over 10 per 1000 in the first decade of this century. Between 1981 and 1990 the average annual rate of immigration was 3.1 per 1000 of the US population (see US, 1991, pp. 9, 54).

The four components of an integrated international system to promote development are today fragmented (Streeten, 1989). These are (1) the generation of current account surpluses by the centre; (2) the financial institutions that convert these surpluses into loans or investments; (3) the production and sale of producer goods and up-to-date technology; and (4) the military power to keep peace and enforce contracts. Before 1914 these came under the jurisdiction of the dominant power, Great Britain. Between the wars there was no international order, as Britain was no longer able and the United States not yet willing to take responsibility. For quarter of a century after the Second World War they were exercised and coordinated by the United States. But today we live in a schizophrenic, fragmented world, without coordination. Non-tariff barriers to trade, imposed by the OECD countries, and restrictions on international migration have prevented fuller global integration. The result has been deflation, unemployment and slow or negative growth in many countries of the South.

Between 1870 and 1914 the world was integrated unwittingly. By imposing fewer objectives on government policy (for example, full employment, economic growth, price stability and so on), and by accepting what in retrospect appear to be irrational constraints – such as the Gold Standard, and consequently fixed exchange rates, the lack of freedom to pursue expansionist monetary policies, and the constraint of balanced budgets – different countries were integrated into a single world economy dominated by one power, Great Britain. Domestic policies were severely constrained by the need to adhere to the gold standard. Integration, however, was no guarantee of peace. It did not prevent the First World War. Today the constraints on national policies consist in the activities of multinational companies and banks.

Later, many objectives of government policy were added to the nightwatchman state's duty to maintain law and order: among them full employment, economic growth, price stability, wage maintenance, reduced inequality in income distribution, regional balance, protection of the natural environment, greater opportunities for women and minorities and so on. The rejection of constraints on policy such as fixed exchange rates, and limits on discretionary monetary and fiscal policies, led to the greater integration of national economies by permitting policies for full employment and the welfare state; but at the same time they led to international disintegration. Such disintegration was, however, entirely consistent with a high degree of international *interdependence*. For interdependence exists when one country, by unilateral action, can inflict harm on other countries. Competitive protectionism, devaluation, deflation and pollution of the air and sea beyond national boundaries are instances. A nuclear war would be the ultimate form of interdependence resulting from international disintegration. Today global market forces can lead to conflict between states, which contributes to international disintegration and weakens governance.

Interdependence is measured by the cost of severing the relationship. The higher the cost to one country, the greater the degree of dependence of that country. If a small country benefits more from the international division of labour than a large country, its dependence is greater. If severing economic links results in high costs being incurred by both partners to the transaction, there is interdependence.

It is quite possible to have extensive and rapidly growing international relations without a high degree of interdependence. This is the case if the relations can be abandoned at low cost. There could, for example, be a large and rapidly growing trade in slightly different models of motor car, produced at similar costs, but there would be little deprivation or loss if buyers had to substitute home-produced models for imported ones. The index of inter-dependence would be consumer and producer surpluses, not the volume, value or rate of growth of international trade.

There is a different sense of 'interdependence', whereby 'dependence' merely means 'influenced by', and there are neither great benefits from main-taining nor costs from severing the relationship. In this attenuated sense there can be interdependence even though the cost of cutting off relations is low or even negative. But this is not a useful sense for our purposes.

Trade

International trade is taken to be an indicator of interdependence, and its high and, with some interruptions, rapidly growing values are accepted as evid-ence. Between 1820 and 1992 the world population increased fivefold, income per head eightfold, world income fortyfold and world trade 540-fold (Maddi-son, 1995; Streeten, 1989; Wade, 1996b). But three important qualifications are necessary

First, if we consider the ratio of international trade to national income, the rapid growth of the postwar decades can be seen as a return to pre-1914 values after the interruptions of two world wars, the Great Depression and high protection. The share of world exports in world GDP rose from 6 per cent in 1950 to 16 per cent in 1992. For the industrial countries, the propor-tion increased from 12 per cent in 1973 to 17 per cent in 1992. For 16 major industrial countries the share of exports in GDP rose from 18.2 per cent in 1900 to 21.2 per cent in 1913 (Bairoch, 1993; Maizels, 1963; Nayyar, 1995). This was largely the result of a dramatic reduction in transport costs and the ratios were very similar for particular countries.[3]

The total ratios of trade to GDP are, however, misleading. Over the postwar decades the share of services, including government services, in GDP increased enormously. Many of these are, or were until recently, not tradable. If we were to take the ratio of international trade to the production of goods only, it would show a substantial increase not only compared with the interwar period, but also compared with the period before 1913.

The second qualification to the notion that unprecedented globalization is now taking place is that the developing countries, and the groups within these countries that have participated in the benefits from the growing trade (and also from foreign investment, which is highly concentrated among East Asia, Brazil, Mexico and now China) have been few, not more than a dozen, though their number has grown. The large, poor masses of the Indian subcontinent and Sub-Saharan Africa have (at least so far) not participated substantially in the benefits to be had from the growth of international trade and investment. In fact the bulk of the international flow of goods, services, direct investment and finance is between North America, Europe and Japan. The least developed countries accounted for only 0.1 per cent of total global investment inflows and for 0.7 per cent of inflows to all developing countries. Africa in particular has been almost completely bypassed (OECD, 1992, p. 233).

The third qualification is the abovementioned fact that it is not the volume, value or rate of growth of trade that should be accepted as an indicator of economic interdependence, but the damage that would be done by its elimination, that is, consumer and producer surpluses. These are difficult to measure. But we know that much trade is conducted in only slightly differentiated goods, which could readily be replaced by similar domestic products without great loss to buyers or great increases in costs.

On the other hand a small and slowly growing volume of trade could be of great importance and lead to substantial losses if it were cut off. Like a link in a bicycle chain, it could, though small itself, make a big difference to the working of the whole system. The United States, for example, depends heavily on quite small imports of manganese, tin and chromium. Before the First World War trade largely took the form of an exchange between raw materials and manufactured products, for which consumer and producer surpluses are large. Today the bulk of trade is intra-industry or even intrafirm trade in manufactured products, for which these surpluses are much smaller.

The process of globalization, according to some definitions, means opening up to trade or liberalization. In the past decade such liberalization has mainly been followed by the ex-socialist countries, which have turned away from central planning in order to link up with the world economy, and by the developing countries, which have replaced import-substituting industrialization with export orientation accompanied by a partial dismantling of the state. This move has not been entirely due to free choice, but partly a response to global forces and pressure by the World Bank and the International Monetary Fund in connection with their stabilization and structural adjustment programmes. Additional influences have been the rich countries' words and doctrines of state minimalism, and the hope of benefiting from global gains.

Some OECD countries, on the other hand, have put up additional non-tariff barriers, such as so-called voluntary export restraints, procedural protection, most notably in the form of antidumping actions, and specific subsidies to exports of goods and services competing with imports. The Multifibre Arrangement and the Common Agricultural Policy of the European Union are blatant protectionist devices. Other barriers have been raised against steel, electronics and footwear.

Trade is of course just one (and not the most important) of the many manifestations of economic interdependence, including the flow of factors of production, capital, technology, various types of labour and foreign exchange across frontiers. These factors are discussed below.

Global Financial Flows

Global financial flows have increased enormously, and on an average day they now amount to more than $1 trillion. This represents a ratio of foreign exchange dealings to world trade of nearly 70:1 and equals the world's total official gold and foreign exchange reserves. In 1971 about 90 per cent of all foreign exchange transactions were to finance trade and long-term investment, and only 10 per cent were speculative. Today these percentages are reversed: well over 90 per cent of all transactions are speculative (Eatwell, 1995, p. 277). The enormous growth of these flows is the result of the collapse in 1973 of the Bretton Woods system of fixed exchange rates combined with the deregulation and liberalization of capital flows, and the opportunities this has provided for speculation on variable exchange rates.

The 24-hour international capital market has given rise to the fear that the international financial system is unstable. But the recent difficulties point to the strength, rather than the weakness, of the international system. The effects of the different crises – the Latin American debt crisis, the US savings-and-loan fiasco, the BCCI scandal, Mexico, Barings, Daiwa – did not spread internationally. Many individuals were hurt, including taxpayers, but these were mainly residents of the areas concerned and the rest of the world was sheltered. The system did not break down, but of course this does not mean that it cannot do so in the future.

The globalization of financial flows, as of trade, has been partial: there are hardly any flows to low-income countries; and while private flows to middle-income developing countries have increased enormously, official development assistance has stagnated (Table 1.1). The bulk of the flows is between OECD countries; and there is some foreign investment in a selected group of developing countries, mostly in Latin America, East Asia and China. These intra-OECD flows contradict neoclassical theory, according to which capital should flow from capital-abundant to capital-scarce countries. In fact the United States, one of the richest of the capital-rich countries, has attracted the most capital. And among developing countries it is those with substantial human capital and good government policies that attract financial capital.

Table 1.1   Long-term financial flows to developing
countries ($ billions)

	1987	1994
Long-term aggregate net resource flows	68.5	227.3
Private flows	25.1	172.9
of which:		
net private loans	9.8	55.6
foreign direct investment	14.6	77.9
portfolio equity investment	0.8	39.5
Official development assistance	43.4	54.4
of which:		
official grants	16.9	30.5
net official loans	26.4	23.9

Source: World Bank (1995b) p. 214.

In the light of this large increase in financial flows, it is a puzzle to find that, in most countries, domestic savings and investment are more closely aligned than they were before 1914. This means that net flows are much smaller than gross flows. As we have seen, many explanations have been offered for this paradox, among them the possible obstacles that fluctuating exchange rates impose on long-term real investment. As we shall discuss below, deregulation and liberalization have not accelerated investment or growth, nor have they resulted in higher levels of employment, better income distribution or lower borrowing costs. They have also increased the volatility of asset prices. While they have brought some benefits, they have also led to greater risks for investors and the financial system. In the 1980s the task of stabilizing against high inflation, the debt crisis and structural adjustment preoccupied many governments. In the 1990s the problems associated with coping with rapid swings in capital flows have become more pressing, highlighted by Mexico's financial crisis in 1995. Suddenly government was called upon to bail out financiers who had previously preached the virtues of free markets. This raises the question of whether a return to control of capital markets is indicated.

There is a need for the reregulation and harmonization of legislation. The more free-enterprise-oriented a country is, the greater the need for official supervision. Deregulation has resulted in higher and less stable interest rates, less stable exchange rates, boom and slump in property prices, and gambling on asset values, interest and exchange rates. The danger of business failure is high. If we wish not to have to bail out financial institutions, deregulation has to be supported by close and well-coordinated supervision.

The Bretton Woods system was based on the premise that currency convertibility, multilateral trade and stable exchange rates require constraints on international capital mobility. Financial liberalization, carried too far, can damage the more important trade liberalization. For example when a country ought to devalue because its prices have risen more than foreign prices, it may be unable to do so because of speculative short-term capital inflows. Or changes in capital flows can produce large swings in the exchange rate, which are detrimental to trade.

Technology

In addition to economic interdependence (trade, finance, direct investment) technological impulses are being rapidly propagated throughout the world. When the global satellite communications system was established, instantaneous communication from any part of the world to any other became possible. Advances in technology such as the jet engine, telex, satellite TV, container ships, super tankers, super ore carriers and other technical progress in transport, travel and, above all, communication and information have shrunk the world. By reducing the cost of communication, technology has helped to globalize production and finance. In turn globalization has stimulated technological progress by intensifying competition and competition has forced the introduction of new technology. Globalization has spread its results widely through foreign direct investment. The barriers erected by geography, if not eradicated, certainly matter less. And the interaction of technology and globalization has presented new problems.

We hear much of the creation of a borderless world and the end of the nation state. It is true that satellites and the Internet have greatly increased the speed at which the communication of cultural and informational impulses is propagated throughout the globe. But here again, as in trade and investment, vast areas in the poor South are either being left out (subsistence farmers are not affected by global forces) or are suffering the backwash effects of globalization (for more details on information technology, see Chapters 2 and 3).

Transnationals

Transnational corporations are said to be one of the main driving forces of globalization. Whereas at the end of the nineteenth century the main agents on the international scene were states, dominated by Britain until 1913 and by the United States for a quarter of a century after the Second World War, today transnational corporations and international banks have to some extent replaced states as the main agents. The world's 37 000 transnational corporations and their 20 0000 affiliates control 75 per cent of world trade. One-third of this trade is intrafirm (UNRISD, 1995, p. 27). The principle guiding their action is profit. At the same time, very few of these firms are genuinely transnational or even international (Shell and Unilever are exceptions in that they are genuinely duo-national: British and Dutch). Most of the other companies that operate in many countries bear the stamp of the country of their headquarters. As we have seen, the prediction that sovereignty would be held at bay and that the nation state, confronted with ever larger and more powerful transnationals, would wither away, was, like the reports of Mark Twain's death, somewhat exaggerated. Many countries have successfully dealt with, regulated and taxed these firms.

Transnationals are more domesticated than some observers suggest. Most of them hold most of their assets and have most of their employees in their home country and conduct the bulk of their R&D there. This is confirmed by the fact that in the second half of the 1980s 89 per cent of US patents taken out by 600 of the world's largest firms listed the inventor as a resident of the home base (Wade, 1996b). Hence strategic decisions and innovations come from the home country. This may, however, be replaced by a wider global spread of R&D as a result of telematics, the convergence of computer, communication and control technology.

Convergence of Real Wages

The convergence of real wages in different countries is another aspect of globalization (see Williamson, 1995). Since the 1950s the gap between US and European wages has shrunk markedly. Similarly, in the second half of the nineteenth century European wages caught up with US ones. In Europe, some countries closed the gap with Britain, then the Continent's leader. Williamson (1996b) argues that economic integration (rather than, say, better education in the low-wage countries) was the main cause of this narrowing. As a result of the growth of international trade the prices of traded goods became more alike in different countries, and the relative prices of the abundant factors of production in each country rose (land in the United States, labour in Europe), while those of the relatively scarce factors fell (labour in the United States, land in Europe). A recent study by O'Rourke *et al.* (1996) confirms this. Emigration from Europe to the United States also helps to explain the rise in wages in Europe and their containment in the United States.

Global Mobility

Views differ on the benefits and costs of the global mobility of items such as trade, finance, technology, ideas and labour. In a much-quoted passage, Keynes wrote 'Ideas, knowledge, art, hospitality, travel – these are things which should of their nature be international. But let goods be home-spun whenever it is reasonably and conveniently possible; and, above all, let finance be primarily national' (Keynes, 1933; *Collected Writings of John Maynard Keynes*, 1982, p. 237). Today it is more fashionable to deplore 'cultural imperialism' or the homogenization of television and the mass media and the global spread of mass culture, and to attempt to confine culture to local knowledge, activities and products, while advocating free trade in goods and services. Neoliberals advocate *laissez faire* but not the free movement of people, or *laissez passer*, perhaps because they fear it will accelerate population growth in low-income, emigration-oriented countries and therefore inhibit an increase in their welfare, or that it will interfere with economic objectives (especially the level and distribution of income), cultural values, social stability or security in countries receiving migrants.

UNEVEN BENEFITS AND COSTS OF GLOBALIZATION

Globalization has helped to create undreamed of opportunities for some people, groups and countries. Human indicators such as literacy, school enrolment, infant mortality and life expectancy have enormously improved in the last few decades. In low- and middle-income countries life expectancy increased from 46 years in 1960 to 63 years in 1990; in the same period infant mortality per 1000 live births fell from 149 to 71; adult literacy rates rose from 46 to 65 per cent; and real GDP per head rose from $950 to $2170 (UNDP, 1993, p. 143). The Cold War has ended and the prospect of peaceful settlement of old disputes has improved from West Asia to South Africa and Northern Ireland. Democracy has spread throughout the world and replaced autocratic regimes. Globalization has been particularly good for Asia, for the global growth of production, for profits and for the owners of capital and sophisticated skills (Table 1.2).

At the same time the economic restructuring, liberalization, technological change and fierce competition – in both the goods market and the labour market – that went with globalization have contributed to increased impoverishment, inequality, work insecurity, a weakening of institutions and social support systems, and the erosion of established identities and values. Liberalization and reduced agricultural protection, by reducing agricultural supplies, have raised the price of food (compared with what it would otherwise have been), and food-importing countries have suffered as a result. Globalization has been bad for most of Africa, and in many parts of the world for employment (see the later section on unemployment), for those without assets or with rigidly fixed, unadaptable skills. International competition for markets and jobs has forced governments to reduce taxation and with it the social services that had protected the poor,[4] and cut those public services and regulations that had protected the environment. Between 1972 and 1986, social expenditure

Table 1.2   Balance sheet of globalization (rough approximations)

Good for	Bad for
Japan, Europe, North America	Many developing countries
East and South-East Asia	Africa (exceptions: Botswana, Mauritius)
Output	Employment
People with assets	People without assets
Profits	Wages
People with high skills	People with few skills
The educated	The uneducated
Professional, managerial and technical people	Workers
Flexible adjusters	Rigid adjusters
Creditors	Debtors
Those independent of public services	Those dependent on public services
Large firms	Small firms
Men	Women, children
The strong	The weak
Risk takers	Human security
Global markets	Local communities
Sellers of technologically sophisticated products	Sellers of primary and standard manufactured products

as a proportion of total government expenditure for developing countries as a whole declined from 35 per cent to 29 per cent, and for industrial market economies, from 58 per cent to 56 per cent (see World Bank, 1988). In the Philippines, between 1980 and 1993 health expenditure fell from 4.5 per cent to 3.0 per cent, and in Kenya from 7.8 per cent to 5.4 per cent (World Bank, 1995a). In Latin America, despite the recovery of social expenditure in 1991, per capita expenditure on health and education services was lower than in 1980–81 (see IDB, 1996, p. 47). Globalization has also forced governments and firms to 'downsize', 'restructure' and 'reengineer' and has made necessary all kinds of steps to ensure that the cost of labour is kept low.[5] Just as at the height of the welfare state in the quarter century after the Second World War, when it was thought that government could steer the economy towards full employment, national integration has been accompanied by international disintegration. Similarly, after the early 1970s (partial) international integration led to national disintegration.

   The share of developing countries in the global distribution of wealth has shrunk. UNDP data on the global distribution of wealth between industrial countries, developing countries and the former USSR and Eastern Europe (Table 1.3) show that wealth distribution has become more unequal. Between

Table 1.3   Global distribution of wealth, 1960–94 (percentages)

	Industrial countries	Developing countries	Former USSR & Eastern Europe
1960	67.3	19.8	12.9
1970	72.2	17.1	10.7
1980	70.7	20.6	8.7
1989	76.3	20.6	3.1
1994	78.7	18.0	3.3

Source: UNDP data base.

1960 and 1994 the share of developing countries, and particularly that of the former socialist countries of Central and Eastern Europe, shrank while that of Western industrial countries increased.

In the poor countries, poverty, malnutrition and disease have increased, despite improvements in living conditions. Nearly one third of the populations of developing countries and more than one half of Africans live in absolute poverty. In 1992 six million children aged five or less died of pneumonia or diarrhoea; 23 million people are classified as refugees. The dissolution of the extended-family system, together with the increasing reliance on market forces and the dismantling of state institutions, has left many victims of the competitive struggle stranded and helpless.

Globalization and the economic progress that goes with it have proceeded unevenly in time and in space. The rise in income per head has differed widely between countries and regions, so that income gaps have widened. Income disparities between rich and poor nations have doubled over the last thirty years.

It does not follow that developing countries would have been better off if they had closed themselves off from the process of globalization and become autarkic. As Joan Robinson once said, there is only one thing that is worse than being exploited by capitalists, and that is not being exploited by them. The same goes for participation in globalization. Those with skills and assets open up to globalization, those without them get left behind. But there are better options than to allow these people to become the victims of the blind forces of globalization. Measures such as social safety nets, guaranteed employment schemes and training provisions to cushion poor people in low-income countries against being battered by these forces should be built into the system of international relations. This is necessary not only for political stability, but also for reasons of common humanity.

Globalization can be considered in relation to its impact on various objectives. In the following section I shall analyse its impact on (1) growth and productivity, (2) employment and skills, (3) wages and inequality of income and wealth (both within and between countries), and (4) technological and institutional innovations.

Growth and Productivity

Different countries have different growth rates with respect to income, productivity and living standards. It is widely agreed that the rule of law and clearly defined property rights, large savings and investment in physical and human capital, good education, flexible labour markets, good macroeconomic policies aimed at labour-intensive growth, and high levels of technology, management and infrastructure have important roles to play. Some would add the need to redistribute productive assets (particularly land) in countries where they are very unequally distributed. In brief, certain legal and political institutions and certain policies are more conducive to growth than others. Whether the openness of an economy to trade and investment is a cause of high growth and good export performance, or a consequence of them, or both, is controversial, but these factors are clearly linked. Most economists say that openness is an important cause of growth.

Growing international competition is not solely the result of fewer barriers to trade. Another important cause is the accelerated pace of invention and innovation. As the ratio of GNP spent by high-income countries on R&D has risen from 2 per cent to 3 per cent and higher, social and technological change has accelerated in the last few decades. Today the time-lag between innovative ideas, inventions, engineering applications and commercial exploitation is much shorter than it used to be. The time lag between the invention of the steam engine and the railway age, and between the invention of the internal combustion engine and the economic, social and cultural (not to mention sexual) revolution wrought by the motor car was measured in generations; while that between the invention of television, the microchip, the jet engine and even the zip fastener and their engineering and commercial application, with all the intellectual and cultural transformations that came in their train, can be measured in years. The application of DNA to bioengineering took just ten years from the discovery of its structure. Faraday's law of electromagnetic induction was announced in the late nineteenth century, and gave birth to the first electric motor about forty years later. In contrast Bardeen and Brittain announced the laws governing semiconduction in the late 1940s, and transistor application followed just five years later. The lag in the application of laser technology was even shorter. As Gore Vidal (1992) wrote, 'Thanks to modern technology . . . history now comes equipped with a fast-forward button.'[6]

If the majority of economists are right, liberalization should lead to higher growth rates and more rapid improvements in living standards. Yet the evidence for this is slender if not absent. The annual per capita growth rate of GDP in East and South-East Asia was 6–8 per cent between 1986 and 1993; in Latin America and Sub-Saharan Africa in the same period it was only 0.36–0.37 per cent. Growth in these areas remained elusive. The exceptionally good performers were Chile and Costa Rica in Latin America, and Mauritius and Botswana in Africa. Comparing the annual growth rates of per capita GNP in the two periods 1965–80 and 1980–93, for all developing countries the rates were 4.6 per cent and 4 per cent and for the OECD countries 3.9 per cent and 1.6 per cent respectively (UNDP, 1995; World Bank, 1995a). Table 1.4 shows the growth rates enjoyed by a number of countries in the period 1972–81 and 1982–91 compared with the 1960–71 average.

Even if it were true that liberalization leads to higher growth, one would have to examine the policies in the preceding period that laid the basis for the subsequent success. All the successful liberalizers pursued selective trade and industrial policies, laying the foundations for their subsequent good performance.

There is, however, a puzzle. The introduction of information technology and the growth of new and more convenient services, particularly as a result of the computer revolution, have not shown up in correspondingly higher growth figures. If the figures are correct, they suggest growing inequality, as the benefits to the winners, some of them substantial, have been partly at the expense of the losers.

Table 1.4   Growth rate of per capita GDP compared with the 1960–71 average

	1972–81	1982–91
All countries (57)		
Decade ratio higher	18	10
Decade ratio lower	39	47
All non-oil exporting countries (48)		
Decade ratio higher	11	7
Decade ratio lower	37	41
OECD countries (20)		
Decade ratio higher	1	2
Decade ratio lower	19	18
Latin America (10)		
Decade ratio higher	4	1
Decade ratio lower	6	9
East and South-East Asia (7)		
Decade ratio higher	5	3
Decade ratio lower	2	4

Sources: Eatwell (1996); Felix (1995); World Bank, *World Tables*.

Many economists, including a panel of economists reporting to the US Congress,[7] have recently reminded us that the official figures overstate inflation and understate economic growth. Quality improvements (such as radial car tyres that are safer and last longer than the old ones), new products that did not exist 30 years ago (such as microwave ovens), new features of old products (such as colour TV with 50 channels and VCRs) and new services (such as the installation of more automatic teller machines in banks in outlying neighbourhoods) are not fully accounted for. Improvements in services are difficult to measure. Many non-market factors, for example a healthier environment, do not figure at all. Computers have contributed to an improved quality of life, greater convenience and higher consumption, but not to markedly higher productivity. If they do eventually lead to higher productivity, the time span is likely to be long: we shall have to wait and see whether the computer skills acquired by the children of today will show up in higher productivity when they join the workforce. Absorbing the innovations to which the computer gives rise will also require many changes in work practices and behaviour. Another explanation is that computers represent only 2 per cent of US capital stock, and less in other OECD countries, whereas railways in their heyday represented more than 12 per cent (Uchitelle, 1996).

Unemployment

Globalization requires firms to compete internationally, and international competition has reinforced globalization. Cost reductions, greater efficiency and higher incomes have been achieved at the expense of growing uncertainty, unemployment and inequality. Globalization has reduced the ability of national governments both to maintain full employment and to look after the victims of the competitive struggle.

Persistent high unemployment in most OECD countries has been a leading policy issue in the last two decades. At first it was thought that the oil price rises in the 1970s and the deflationary policies pursued in response to them were the cause of the deterioration in employment. But as these high unemployment levels persisted into the 1990s and as oil prices and other commodity prices have fallen since 1986, this explanation has had to give way to others. Overvaluation of some exchange rates has contributed to high unemployment. Some of the high unemployment has been attributed to globalization and to the new information and communication technologies. Kurt Vonnegut, in his novel *Player Piano*, describes a future nightmare society in which the divine right of machines, efficiency and organization has triumphed. The large underclass of unemployed are handed plenty of goodies by a small group of affluent managers, but they lack what John Rawls regards as 'perhaps the most important primary good' – self-respect. Vonnegut's unemployed eventually revolt.

The concern in the advanced countries has become jobless growth. In fact economic growth, whether measured in terms of overall productivity or productivity in manufacturing, has been considerably slower since 1981 than in the 1960s, when growth was not accompanied by unemployment. Since the growth of productivity has been less than the growth of demand, one would have expected jobs to be created rather than destroyed (Eatwell, 1995).

There has been a slowing down of productivity growth and a growth of unemployment. An increase in the output of goods accompanied by more leisure, is to be welcomed. It is what we mean by saying productivity for worker has increased. While some authors today regard employment as a basic need, Sidney Webb, cofounder of the Fabian Society and the London School of Economics, more properly regarded leisure as a basic need. Monotonous, dirty, hard or dangerous work is a burden, not a blessing. Increases in output per worker are to be welcomed. But this is only so as long as demand and/or output grow rapidly enough to absorb all those seeking work. There is no reason in theory why this should not be so. Although new technology displaces workers, it also lowers costs and therefore lowers prices or raises money wages or profits. In each case the demand for goods and services, and therefore for labour, is increased, though it will take time to retrain and relocate the labour.

Alternatively the productivity gain can take the form of leisure or other satisfying activities. The reduced work load can be spread evenly, with equally distributed rises in incomes. Various imaginative proposals have been made about flexible worktime, sabbaticals for workers, allocating time to high-tech self-provisioning, freeing time to do the things one really wants to do and so on. The main point is that the time- and labour-saving benefits of the new technologies should accrue to everyone, and not be maldistributed between an overworked group of workers and the unwanted unemployed.

These two conditions, or at least the first, were met in the Keynesian golden age after the Second World War. But if, as has been the case in the OECD countries in the last decade, output grows insufficiently fast to generate employment for the whole workforce, and if the workload is unevenly distributed, with part of the workforce working hard and long hours while the rest are unemployed, we find ourselves in a society in which John Kenneth Galbraith's private affluence amid public squalor is joined by private affluence amid private squalor. Anyone walking through the streets of New York or London can witness the homeless sleeping in the open. Whether growing unemployment is caused by the globalization of economic relations, inadequate growth of demand (due to government policy resulting from a fear of inflation and balance of payments crises), technological change that calls for new skills that are and perhaps will remain scarce, weaker trade unions, deregulation, or low-cost imports from developing countries, the unemployed underclass does not even benefit from Vonnegut's handouts. They lack both recognition and necessities. Doing 'more with less' (as a popular classic on reengineering puts it) is good for economic growth and for the economy as a whole, while people become superfluous. The market does not nurture the dignity of those who lose their jobs or live under the threat of losing them.

Jobless growth is not confined to the advanced countries. The Chinese economy has been enjoying spectacularly high growth rates, but unemployment, particularly urban unemployment, has become a major problem (Khan, 1996b). The pressures of globalization and foreign competition in the goods and labour markets have forced a cut in unit labour costs. Previously the state and collective firms practised a concealed system of unemployment insurance, a kind of in-house unemployment relief. All members of the labour force were guaranteed employment, which meant the gross overmanning of factories. When China began to integrate into the global economy it had to reduce its labour costs in order to become competitive and attract direct foreign investment. In 1986 a new regulation decreed that employment in state enterprises had to be based on fixed-term contracts of three to five years, and enterprises were granted the power to dismiss workers. In 1988 a State Bankruptcy Law was introduced that made it possible to liquidate or restructure state enterprises, with resulting reductions in employment. The decline in employment was sharpest in collective enterprises: 15.5 per cent between 1991 and 1994. In the absence of unemployment insurance and alternative ways of earning a living, unemployment has contributed to an increase not only in inequality but also in growing poverty in the midst of spectacular, unprecedentedly high growth rates. However China's high economic growth rate should ensure that most members of the workforce will be absorbed in due course.

Similar unemployment growth has occurred in many of the ex-socialist countries. Though official unemployment figures for Russia are low, there has been substantial withdrawal from the labour force and non-registration of many of those thrown out of employment.

Consumers' freedom to choose between different products has been rightly emphasized. But most people spend more time and have a greater stake in working and producing than consuming. Producer choice is therefore at least as important as consumer choice: the ability to choose between jobs and activities should be given at least the same weight as the ability to choose between different brands of detergent, different cars or different television channels. But general unemployment, combined with an inadequate number of vacancies, deprives workers of this choice, as well as of the means (earnings) with which to exercise consumer choice. In order for people to exercise free choice as producers, a situation of 'over-full' employment is necessary, that is, there must be more vacancies than job-seekers, so that free choice in jobs can be exercised. Of course full employment and over-full employment imply that the choices of the employers are reduced. This accounts for their opposition. But employers are fewer than workers. Full employment also means higher inflationary pressures, which accounts for the opposition of some electorates. And it is sometimes misinterpreted as the right to remain employed in any given job, which is a recipe for stagnation.

Basic human needs are not confined to food, water, health, sanitation, shelter, transport, education and protection from harm and injury, but also include job security. Job security is as important as food security, both in itself and as a means of ensuring food security. If job security is to be achieved in a progressive economy, it cannot mean tenure in a given job – for this will change with technical progress, changing demand and trade liberalization – but the option, if dismissed from one job, to enter a new job.

Justification for the existence and tolerance of widespread unemployment differs among industrial, ex-socialist and developing countries. In industrial countries it is fear of inflation and balance of payments difficulties that prevents the achievement of full employment. And inflation may severely hit the same groups of people who are hit by unemployment. The difficult and as yet largely unsolved task is to design a strategy that combines (1) full or over-full employment with (2) zero inflation and (3) free wage bargaining and democratic government. This happy triangle has so far been elusive. It seems that a reserve army of unemployed or a less metaphorical army of police and soldiers have so far been the only options for avoiding inflation.[8]

The efficiency wage literature points out several reasons why the quality of labour and the efforts of those employed are improved as a result of the existence of unemployment (and the threat of it for those who have jobs). This justification of unemployment is quite distinct from and additional to that of avoiding inflation. An important forerunner with respect to this literature was Karl Marx, who wrote of the need for a reserve army of unemployed to make capitalism work. The recent literature has put new clothes on Marx's analysis and discusses it in terms of the principal–agent relationship, and the inability to monitor properly the effort every worker puts into his or her work. Unless workers fear unemployment, they will slacken their efforts. Wages that are higher than the market-clearing level have the function of disciplining the workers.

Quite apart from the reduced opportunity to exercise free choice, unemployment also reduces the incentive for those with jobs to accept new, labour-saving innovations that are liable to cause them to lose their jobs. This effect seems to have been ignored by the efficiency wage literature. On the other hand, as the evidence from Eastern Europe shows, over-full employment can have a detrimental effect on product quality and variety, product and process innovation, and the discipline of workers and managers.

Another approach, that of the insider–outsider model, comes to similar conclusions. A small, élite mainly male, insider workforce coexists with poorly paid, not fully recognised outsiders. One group of workers – the insiders – are not perfect substitutes for others, who may be unemployed – the outsiders. They have more experience, are better motivated and more committed to the firm. Together with the capital and management of the firm they generate a rent, for part of which they bargain. Their higher wages, and their resistance to hiring outsiders, keep the outsiders out. Such polarization occurred in the United States until the second half of the 1980s. Since then there has been a shift towards a reduction of insiders and an expansion of outsiders in the service of 'flexibility'. Europe, in contrast, throughout the postwar period has shown greater job security, high wages and high social benefits, combined with a more rapid growth in unemployment.

A third approach, suggested by Robert Solow (1990), is to analyse the labour market as a social institution, and to attach the notion of fairness to a higher wage than that which would equate total demand for and supply of labour. The unemployed do not underbid this wage, in their self-interest, because at some later date they expect to benefit from it. Were they to offer themselves at lower wages, all workers would be thereafter worse off. Although it would be in the interest of any worker to underbid, irrespective of whether others do the same or not, this would lead to a prisoner's dilemma outcome, with everyone being worse off than if they had refrained from underbidding. Repeated 'games', however, lead to adherence to the norm that prevents such mutually destructive and ultimately self-destructive outcomes.

The answer to the employment problems created by globalization lies in the right combination or package of government policies. Simple Keynesian remedies, such as expanding effective demand, no longer work. Many unemployed are long-term unemployed. Expansion of demand would rapidly produce an excess demand for labour, since employers would reject the long-term unemployed as unsuitable. There would then be a rise in money wages and prices without a reduction in unemployment. Imports would grow (and jobs would be created abroad) without the ability to match them by exports. Among the additional measures usually mentioned are education and training programmes for workers (both to achieve higher productivity and to reduce unemployment), income support for low-paid workers, tax policies that create jobs and prevent environmental degradation, population controls, and social safety nets.

On the other hand there are those who say there is no need to fear inflation, that inflation is dead. Global competition and corporate restructuring will keep prices down while productivity gains will let growth flourish.

What about those whose 'disabilities' (lack of learning ability, self-confidence or self-discipline) in the light of globalization, the information and communication revolution, and rapid technological change render them unemployed and perhaps unemployable? This raises the set of problems that used to be discussed *apropos* structural unemployment, marginalization (mainly in Latin America) and social exclusion.[9]

The standard answers to the combination of skill shortages and surplus unskilled labour have been education, vocational training, adjustment assistance and flexibility (as well as, of course, raising the total level of demand). Experience has shown that these have worked for the bright and well-motivated; but for the not-so-bright and those not committed to the work ethic they have reinforced a sense of failure. As Ronald Dore (1996) has said, 'Vocational training is an area where Say's law does not operate; supply emphatically does not create its own demand'.[10] The new technologies in information and communication and their global spread have brought with them learning-ability-related inequality. The new underclass, consisting of the least educated, older workers and some women, should be our concern out of sympathy and social solidarity, and because of the threat that their condition may exacerbate social problems: crime, drug use and so on. The human costs of long-term unemployment go beyond the loss of income and production, and include lack of recognition, divorce, mental illness, violence in the home, suicide and other social costs.

There is also unemployment caused by low-cost imports from the low-income countries. Even though the percentage of these imports is small, they occur in the labour-intensive sectors, and firms often displace labour by capital in order to remain competitive.

To sum up, the causes of unemployment in the OECD countries are global competition in the form of imports from low-wage countries and the exportation of jobs, lack of skills in an age of sophisticated and rapidly advancing technology, slow growth of demand, immigrant workers and the entry of women into the workforce.

Even though few would maintain today that a higher level of effective demand (for example through public investment), even if buttressed with an incomes policy to keep inflation under control, is the whole answer to 'structural unemployment', it would surely make a contribution to reducing unemployment as part of a package. And it is not at all clear that our society cannot use plenty of health workers, nurses, child rearers, gardeners, plumbers, sweepers, protectors and restorers of the environment and other service workers who do not need the high and scarce skills demanded by modern technology and whose services cannot be replaced by either computers or imported low-cost goods from low-income countries (though imported low-cost labour from poor countries should be welcomed). Many of these jobs are, however, in the currently despised or neglected public sector and may call for even more despised higher taxation. They are also often ill-paid and not recognised as valuable. We need to change our valuation of such work and should guarantee minimum standards of reward for them.

In ex-socialist countries the reason for unemployment is the need to close down inefficient, overmanned public enterprises and those that produced for the military, and to relocate labour to more efficient activities and the production of goods in demand. The breakdown of institutions is largely responsible for the large amount of unemployment, which is often not registered as such.

In developing countries there are many causes of unemployment, mainly the following:

- The absence of factors such as capital, materials, management, infrastructure, and so on.
- The absence of institutions such as labour exchanges, credit banks, training schemes, security of land tenure, and systems of widespread land ownership.
- Employment aspirations or inhibitions that prevent some workers from accepting certain jobs, so that unemployment is accompanied by labour shortages.
- Barriers to work that result from low levels of living, such as inadequate nutrition, health and education.
- The low level of demand in industrial countries for the exports of developing countries, a result partly of slow growth, partly of technical progress and partly of trade barriers.
- Policies of developing countries that overprice labour, underprice capital and overvalue exchange rates. These policies stand in the way of full and efficient labour utilisation.[11]

Also prevalent in many low-income countries is the existence of conditions where higher wages enable workers to be better nourished and therefore to become more productive. Freedom from malnutrition increases their alertness and their physical strength, and reduces absenteeism due to illness. Individual firms are not in a position to decide to pay these higher wages, partly because they might not be able to hold on to their more productive workers (who may leave the firm for all sorts of reasons other than pay) and might only be financing the profits of others, and partly because they may not recognise the profit opportunities and the economy of high wages. When factory legislation was introduced in England in the nineteenth century, English industrialists predicted that the higher costs would ruin British industry. In fact it flourished.

Income Distribution

How does globalization affect income distribution within rich and poor countries and between them?

Theoretical arguments suggest that increased North–South trade in manufactured goods and services reduces inequality between skilled workers and semi-skilled workers (with primary and some secondary education) in the South, while increasing such inequality in the North (Wood, 1994). This is so because exporting more from the South raises the demand for and the wages of workers with basic education relative to those with higher skills in the South. (The exception to this is where the abandonment of minimum wage legislation and the weakening of trade unions and colonially inherited wage levels as a result of international competition lowers the wages of factory workers and public employees.) The reverse is true in the North, where skill differentials in wages can be expected to widen and semi-skilled workers to suffer a relative reduction in wages, and with sticky wages, unemployment among the semi-skilled can be expected to grow. The relatively abundant factor gains from opening up trade, the relatively scarce factor loses.

Empirical evidence confirms growing wage inequality in the North. Trade liberalization raises the wages of skilled workers in rich countries, where they are relatively abundant, and lowers those of unskilled workers. But the prediction does not seem to hold for the South. Changes similar to those observed in the North appear to have occurred in some developing countries. In Mexico, for example, the difference between a typical university-educated worker's pay and that of an unskilled worker rose by a third between 1987 and 1993. Similar differentials can be observed in Brazil, Argentina, Chile, Uruguay, Colombia, Costa Rica, Thailand and the Philippines (*The Economist*, 7 December 1996, p. 74; Robbins, 1996).

There are several possible explanations for this. First, factors other than trade liberalization have influenced wage differentials, among them economic growth, capital accumulation, new technologies, inflation, recession, inflows of foreign capital and so on. Second, the theory assumes that the same technological production functions exist in all countries and that there is an absence of capital mobility. In fact reduced trade barriers may bring in more new capital equipment and new technology, which tends to raise the demand for skilled workers. Third, some developing countries, particularly the more advanced ones, have much larger skilled workforces than others. The impact that trade liberalization has on them will therefore be similar to that on the rich countries of the North. With China and other large low-income countries entering world markets for labour-intensive products, the comparative advantage of the middle-income countries has shifted to goods requiring intermediate skills. Unfortunately, only a few countries collect figures on wage differentials so it is not possible to make these comparisons over a wide range.

The rise in demand for skilled labour in the North is only partly due to increased manufactured imports or the threat of this from foreign countries. Another important reason is technical progress, which saves semi-skilled labour. To some extent the two are interdependent. In order to meet foreign competition, firms have to introduce new technology that improves their ability to compete. But a large part of technical progress is independent of trade. Cheap energy and the first wave of automation eliminated a large proportion of manual jobs. Electronics is now eliminating routine white-collar jobs. But technical progress also saves some types of skilled, even highly skilled, labour, as 'Deep Blue', IBM's chess-playing super-computer demonstrates. It proved itself a fair match for Garry Kasparov. Activities that can be reduced to simple rules, even if these may give rise to apparently infinite possibilities, are targets for automation (Kolata, 1996).

The income differentials between semi-skilled and unskilled workers are expected to widen in the South, but unskilled workers are to be found mainly in agriculture, not in manufacturing, which requires a minimum of skills. Where unskilled workers are plentiful, the country does not export many manufactures. The situation in countries that export primary goods, often among the poorest, is different (Bourgignon and Morrisson, 1989, pp. 273–81, Wood, 1994, p. 244). Mineral exports tend to increase inequality because they require little unskilled labour and the ownership of minerals is usually highly concentrated. Reductions in inequality depend on the government capturing a large share of the rent of the mining companies and spending it on the poor. The effect of agricultural exports on distribution depends on the pattern of land ownership. Where exports are produced on plantations or by privately owned large farms, their expansion will tend to increase inequality unless the workers are organised into powerful trade unions. If the increased exports are produced on small farms that are worked by the owners and their families, inequality will tend to be reduced.

This analysis has several limitations. The Stolper–Samuelson theorem predicts that the absolute reward of the scarce factor will fall under free trade. In the present context the absolute real wages of unskilled and semi-skilled workers in the North would fall. But the areas in which the theorem is true are very restrictive. It may be more realistic to assume that relative wages fall. We are then concerned with inequality – which many would regard as an evil – rather than with absolute poverty, which the same people and many more would regard as a greater evil. In an expanding economy it would not be surprising to find that some groups move ahead of others; but this would not matter, indeed should be welcomed, as long as there is not an increase in absolute poverty, and as long as those left behind eventually catch up with or overtake those ahead. Development means a shift in the structure of production. Employment in industry and services increases, while that in agriculture drops both relatively and, beyond a certain point, absolutely. Wages in industry and services are higher than incomes in agriculture. The result is an increase in inequality, but most workers are better off and no one is worse off.

Another limitation of the analysis is that it is concerned only with different kinds of wages and not with other types of income, such as profits and rents (apart from a brief discussion of exporters of primary goods). There is much evidence that globalization has led to growing inequality between income gained from labour and that from capital.

So far we have considered the impact of globalization on domestic income distribution. One can approach international income distribution between countries by examining the impact of multinational corporations, whose role in the globalization process has enormously increased. Foreign capital, know-how, enterprise, management and marketing are highly mobile internationally and are combined with the plentiful but internationally much less mobile domestic semi-skilled labour. The supply of one set of factors (enterprise, management, knowledge and capital) is relatively *inelastic* in *total*, but if these factors are not dependent on local natural capital such as mines or plantations, they are easily moved around the world in response to small differential rewards. Their supply, therefore, is highly *elastic* to *any particular country*. The supply of the other factor, labour, is *highly elastic* domestically, but relatively *immobile* across frontiers. The situation is aggravated by the fact that if the workers produce manufactured goods that can be produced anywhere in the world, demand for their labour is also elastic, so that raising their wages would lead only to unemployment. The situation is equivalent to one in which the plentiful supply of semi-skilled labour, rather than the product of labour, is exported. The surplus of the product of labour over the wage, resulting from the cooperation of other, less elastic factors, accrues to foreigners. The differential international and internal elasticities of supply in response to differential rewards, and the monopoly rents entering the reward of these factors, have important implications for the international distribution of gains from investment.

Since the firms operate in oligopolistic and oligopsonistic markets, cost advantages are not necessarily passed on to consumers in lower prices or to workers in higher wages, and the profits then accrue to the parent firms. The operation of this type of international specialization depends upon the continuation of substantial wage differentials (hence trade unions must be weak in the host country so that low wage costs are maintained), continuing access to the markets of the parent companies (hence stronger political pressure from importing interests than from domestic producers displaced by the low-cost components and processes, including trade unions in the rich importing countries) and continuing permission by host countries to operate with minimum taxes, tariffs and bureaucratic regulation.

The packaged or complete nature of the contribution of the transnational enterprise, usually claimed as its characteristic blessing, is then the cause of the unequal international division of gains. If the package were to break or leak, some of the rents and monopoly rewards would spill over into the host country. But if it is secured tightly, only the least scarce and weakest factor in the host country derives a limited income from the operations of the transnational firm.

These tendencies can be and have been offset in some cases by several factors. The developing country can use its bargaining power to extract a share of these rents (though taxation of footloose transnationals suffers from the prisoner's dilemma discussed above) and apply them to social services or public works for the poor; or investment in human capital can create domestically some of the scarce factors and skim off some of the rents. Indeed, this has occurred in the more successful developing countries. Indeed, this is what development is about. As the developing country increases the domestic value-added in its exports, its growth rate rises. This is one of the forces that make for globalization. It also shows the limits of the conventional distinction between import substitution and export orientation. For increased domestic value-added is a form of import substitution, while at the same time increased exports represent export orientation.

Now assume that the package can be unbundled and that some of its components, such as high skills, can be transferred to the developing country. Consider a model in which two types of service have to be combined, one highly skilled, the other less skilled, such as air transport. The providers of the skilled service, say pilots, are in relatively scarce total supply, but highly mobile between countries in response to financial incentives. On a clear day an airline pilot can see the world, while the people who clean the ashtrays and remove rubbish from the aeroplanes on the ground are wholly earth-bound. Supply of the semi-skilled factor, ground personnel, is highly elastic locally but immobile between countries. Other examples are transnational advertising, hotel chains, tourist enclaves and so on. The result is that pilots earn large rents, while ground personnel get the bare minimum wage. Any country, even a very poor one, wishing to have an airline will have to pay its pilots not much less than the high international salaries or it will lose them. An egalitarian domestic incomes policy will be impossible if trained professional manpower is not to be lost. Both international and domestic inequalities will have to be large. Once again, partial international integration (that of skilled and professional people) leads to national disintegration. Increasingly there are First Worlds to be found within Third World countries: Belgiums within Indias, or Belindias as this situation has been called.

Technology and Institutions

Institutions are lagging behind technology. The revolutions in the technologies of transport, travel, communications and information have unified and shrunk the globe,[12] but our organization into nation states dates back to the Peace of Westphalia in 1648, to the American constitution and the French

Revolution in 1789, to the nineteenth century when Germany and Italy were unified, and to the break-up of empires into nation states after the First World War. And while technology marches on to organize the world into a single unit, nations are becoming more numerous and more acutely self-aware. Or to put it in Marxian terms, there is a contradiction between the forces of production, which have been globalized, and the relations of production, which reflect the nation states.

Biotechnology and materials technology offer considerable promise, but it is the microelectronic revolution in information and communication technology that is most relevant to globalization. Few manufacturing and service industries have remained untouched by the application of the microprocessor to new products and processes (Oman, 1996). Communication, information and the media have been transformed by it. Advances in telecommunications and information technology are expanding the boundaries of tradability in services – the fastest-growing component of trade and foreign direct investment.

When the nation states were founded, the city states and the feudalism that preceded them had become too small for the scale of operations required by the Industrial Revolution. The political institution therefore was adapted to the new industrial technology, to the roads, railways and canals. The nation state was then a progressive institution. But I am not a technological determinist. The adaptation of institutions to technology is not an inevitable process. By the Middle Ages, for example, the Roman technology behind roads, baths, aqueducts and amphitheatres had been lost and they were allowed to fall into disrepair. But now the nation state, with its insistence on full sovereignty, has become, at least in certain respects, an obstacle to further progress. It has landed us in several prisoners' dilemma situations: each nation acts in its own perceived rational self-interest, and the result is that every country is worse off. It pays each nation to pursue this mutually destructive course, whether others do likewise or not. Overcoming such destructive outcomes calls for a high degree of trust, moral motivation (even if, as in the case of the prisoners' dilemma, it is honour among thieves), cooperation or compulsion.

At the international level, prisoners' dilemma outcomes move the world economy away from a more to a less efficient allocation of resources. Therefore potential gains are to be had by moving back to more efficient allocations. According to Coase's theorem, in the absence of transaction costs and with full information, a legal framework and well-defined property rights, it pays each state to reach agreements with other states to avoid, by compensation payments, this damage, and make them all better off than they would have been in the outcome of the prisoners' dilemma.[13] For example the United States emits acid rain that falls on Canada. If the damage to Canada is greater than the benefits to the United States, Canada could offer compensation to the United States for relinquishing its right to emit sulphur dioxide, the chief component of acid rain, and still be better off than it would be in accepting the acid rain; or if the benefits are greater than the damage, the United States could offer compensation to Canada for accepting the acid rain and still be better off than it would have been if it had been prevented from inflicting the damage. But as we all know to our regret, we are far from the outcomes of Coase's theorem, although we are not always at the other end of the spectrum, the prisoners' dilemma. Coase's theorem remains useful, in spite of its unrealistic assumptions, in drawing our attention to the fact that there are unexploited mutual profit opportunities when prisoners' dilemma situations arise. I obviously do not wish to say that compensation always, or even often, ought to be paid. The losers, such as the English landlords after the repeal of the Corn Laws in 1846, may not deserve to be compensated; or even if they do deserve it, the administrative costs and the losses from imposing taxes to finance the compensation may be so large as to make the compensation uneconomic. But the fact that it *could* be paid draws our attention to potential unexploited gains.

Add to the prisoners' dilemma the free-rider problem, according to which each country relies on others to bear the costs of arrangements that benefit everybody. As a result public goods such as peace, an open trading system, common standards of weights and measures, freedom of the seas, well defined-property rights, international stability, a working monetary system or conservation of the global environment are undersupplied, while public bads such as wars, pollution and poverty are oversupplied. The situation has been described in parables and similes such as the tragedy of the commons, social traps, the isolation paradox and so on.

Under the present system there are apparent gains to uncoordinated action. It pays any one country to put up protectionist barriers, whether others do so or not; building up its arms supply promises security to any one country, whether others do so or not; any one country can, if it is to its advantage, pollute the air and the oceans, whether others do so or not; it pays any one country to attract capital from abroad by tax incentives, whether others do so or not, thereby eroding the tax bases of all countries. In the absence of self-restraint, these mutually damaging and ultimately self-damaging and possibly self-destructive actions can be avoided, only by a dominant world power imposing the restraints, or by cooperation or, most effectively of all, by delegating of some decisions to a supranational authority with the power to enforce restraint or contributions.

The ranking of preferences with respect to, say, contributing to a common public good by each country is the following:

1. My country does not contribute while others do (free rider, defection of one).
2. My country contributes together with others (cooperation).

3. No country contributes (prisoners' dilemma outcome).
4. My country contributes while no other country does (sucker).

Behaviour by each according to 1, or the fear of 4, leads to outcome 3. Although 2 is preferred to 3, we end up with the less preferred situation, 3, unless either rewards and penalties or autonomous cooperative motivations lead to 2. Incentives and expectations must be such as to rule out outcomes 4 and 1, so that if I (or you) contribute, I (or you) will not end up a sucker. In the absence of such motivations, such public goods as peace, monetary stability, absence of inflation, expansion of output and employment, an open world economy, environmental protection, debt relief, raw material conservation, poverty reduction and world development will be undersupplied.

It has been shown that iterative games of the prisoners' dilemma type lead to non-destructive outcomes (Axelrod, 1984). The partners learn and adopt mutually beneficial strategies. I have already said that we find ourselves in between the two extremes of prisoners' dilemmas and Coase's outcomes. For several reasons it is harder to reach cooperative agreements in international transactions than in transactions where mutual trust and a sense of duty play stronger parts. The world now has many states, nearly 200, and large numbers make agreements more difficult and defection more likely. We do not have a world government or a global police force that could enforce agreements. Change is rapid, which undermines the basis of stability on which agreements are based. The absence of a hegemonic power also removes the sanctions against breaking the agreement. All these factors prevent trust from being built up, and trust is an essential prerequisite for international agreements.

Examples of prisoners' dilemma on the global scale are ubiquitous. Above all there was the arms race, which, although a major nuclear war was avoided, has contributed to hundreds of minor wars, mostly in the Third World. Then there is competitive protectionism, through which each country casts its unemployment onto others; competitive exchange rate movements, by which unemployment or inflation are exported; investment wars in which countries forgo taxation to attract a limited amount of investment; research and development wars and the resulting technological nightmares; the denial of debt relief by banks and of guarantees by governments; environmental pollution; competitive interest rate increases; overfishing, the depletion of ocean reserves and the destruction of species. These are just some of the areas in which battles are now being fought.

This problem applies not only to government policies but also to those of firms. In the field of technology there is a tendency for firms (and countries) to move away from basic research with long-term results that are not easily appropriated and benefit other firms and other countries, to short-term, commercial research, the results of which show up quickly in profits to the firm. For example basic research into the new, high-yielding varieties of wheat and rice that gave rise to the Green Revolution in the 1960s was financed neither by private firms nor by national governments but had to rely on the philanthropic Ford and Rockefeller Foundations. Their resources are clearly inadequate to fund research into the modern high-technology problems that will drive globalization in the next century.

To avoid these traps, coordination, cooperation and enforcement of policies are needed. But coordination means that each country has to do things it does not want to do. The United States has to balance its budget in order to lower world interest rates; Germany has to grow faster, but it does not want to suck in guest workers from Turkey and Yugoslavia; many say Japan should import more, but it does not want to hurt its domestic industries. And so on.

The challenge is to replace the past international orders based on dominance and dependence, for example Pax Britannica and Pax Americana, or the disorders that showed fragmentation and lack of coordination, by a new pluralistic global order built on equality and fairness.

GOVERNMENT AND OPEN ECONOMIES

Most economists expect globalization to go hand in hand with a shrinkage of government – that is, the more open the economy, the smaller the government.[14] This is so for two reasons. First, liberal trade policies tend to reflect a preference for markets, and therefore less government. Second, globalization has made government monetary and fiscal policies less effective. This could be expected to lead to smaller government. Yet Rodrik (1996) has shown that the scope of government has been larger, not smaller, in economies that have taken greater advantage of world markets. There is a positive correlation between openness, as measured by the share of trade in GDP, and the scope of government, as measured by the share of government expenditure in GDP. Small, open economies such as Sweden, Austria, Switzerland, Belgium, Luxembourg and the Netherlands have large governments. Rodrik suggests that the explanation is to be found in the role of government as an insulator against external shocks, as a kind of insurance against external risk, a way of alleviating market dislocations. He proposes two measures of external risk: the volatility of the terms of trade and the concentration by products of exports (that is, the ratio of the value of one or two products to the total value of exports). According to the 'new' growth theory it could also be argued that, challenged by fiercer competition, governments spend more on public goods such as education, R&D and infrastructure.

Rodrik's hypothesis depends on three assumptions: (1) that increases in trade lead to greater external risk; (2) that increases in external risk lead to greater income volatility; and (3) that a larger share of government purchases in GDP reduces income volatility. The first assumption is subject to doubt. Diversified international trade (diversified by goods, services, countries of origin and countries of destination) can be a good way of insuring against risks. For example a country depending wholly on domestic food production is in great trouble if its domestic harvest fails; or one depending on domestic coal for energy is in great trouble if its miners go on strike. If coal mining is in the public sector, government ownership presents greater risks than a diversified policy of importing fuel. Self-reliance is sometimes confused with self-sufficiency, but the latter can be at the expense of the former. But it is true that certain shocks, such as that of the oil price increases in the 1970s, are the result of international trade.

Rodrik eliminates other possible explanations of the positive link between openness and government, for example that small countries are both more open and tend to have higher government expenditures, and that European countries have larger government sectors but are more open because of their membership of the European Union. His conclusion that globalization may well require big, not small, government is in line with my argument elsewhere that markets and pricism do not call for state minimalism, but for an active, interventionist state (see Streeten, 1993).

Views on globalization versus separatism and government versus non-intervention can be put into four rubrics:

	Separatism	*Globalization*
Government intervention (national and global)	Nationalistic dirigistes	This chapter's position
Laissez faire	Nationalistic (classical) liberals	Global (classical) liberals

THE CASE FOR A QUIETER LIFE

Sir John Hicks said that the best reward of a monopolist is often a quiet life. The effort to maximize profits by equating marginal returns is itself subject to diminishing marginal psychic returns. The free trade gospel, based on the doctrine of comparative advantage, bids us always to strive for higher incomes from the international division of labour. Information technology, it has been said, brings us nearer to the textbook model of economics: it provides more information, reduces transaction costs, and removes barriers to entry. 'Computers and advanced telecommunications help to make these assumptions [of perfect knowledge, zero transaction cost and absence of barriers to entry] less far-fetched' (Woodall, 1996, p. 46). But adjustments in response to changing comparative advantage are costly, and the need for these adjustments has been speeded up by the new technologies. In an international environment in which comparative advantage changes rapidly, trade policy can, as we have seen, become a policy for tramps: it imposes the imperative to move from one occupation to another, from one residence to another, not once or twice, but continually. The citizens of an already fairly rich country, or a like-minded group of such countries, may say: we already enjoy many earthly goods. We wish to forgo some extra income from international trade for the sake of a quieter life; for not having to learn a new trade, for not being uprooted from our community. There is nothing irrational or 'non-economic' in such a choice.[15]

It will of course depend upon how important international trade is in the economy of the country. It must avoid suffering reductions in income resulting from having opted out, even if only at the margin, of remaining internationally competitive. It will also depend on not permitting those who will benefit from the protection (including capitalists and managers, as well as workers) to become so powerful as to drive the economy beyond the point where forgone income from international specialization just balances the benefits of a somewhat less disruptive life. It is probably true that many countries have sought protection beyond this optimum point, and the real costs to the community of keeping workers employed in industries that really should be shrunk greatly exceeds the benefits that could be reaped by a redeployment of labour.

The qualification introduced above for countries heavily dependent on international trade will, in turn, have to be qualified if international cooperation is to be implemented at the optimum rate of technical progress, where such progress involves disruption. In most lines of advance we accept the application of some form of benefit/cost calculus, but where advances in knowledge and its technical and commercial application are concerned we do not ask questions about its social and human costs. When technological progress in synthetics knocks out the lines of raw material exports upon which a country is heavily dependent for foreign exchange, the costs of adjustment of the exporting country may greatly exceed the benefits to buyers in the importing countries, quite apart from the distributional impact. It would then be reasonable either to ask for some form of international agreement to slow down the pace of scientific and technological progress, or to contract out of the international competitive race. The issue here is not the forgoing of some income for the sake of a quiet life, but, by international cooperation, the avoidance of impoverishment that results from deteriorating terms of trade or growing unemployment.

There is a body of literature on the so-called 'non-economic' objectives of policy makers, such as the desire to maintain a large agricultural sector (or industrial sector) as an end in itself, and on how to modify free trade policy to accommodate them.[16] But my point is not to introduce non-economic objectives. Leisure is a conventional economic objective, as is avoiding the psychological and financial costs of disruption: the costs of resettlement, rehousing, retraining and so on. These benefits and costs are entirely within the domain normally surveyed by economists. In the context of international trade they have, however, been largely ignored. If taken into account, they modify the conclusions of the doctrine of free trade and justify some protection.

In the European Union, people's preferences include greater leisure, longer holidays, more generous social security provisions, higher minimum wages and greater worker participation in the management of firms. Insofar as these preferences do not interfere with the ability to maintain high rates of growth, free trade can be pursued. But in so far as they are bought at the cost of economic growth and therefore some reduction in income compared with free trade, some closing off and some management of trade relations is legitimate if such closing off can prevent or reduce the losses from and the continuing costs of free trade. Private benefits and private costs may diverge from social benefits and social costs; an example of excess social costs would be the relief of the unemployed, the destruction of whole communities or the harm done to the environment as a result of a shift in technology.

It could be that the social harmony and homogeneity achieved by maintaining similar values adds to efficiency and makes for higher economic growth. If so, trade interventions that lead to the formation of Orwellian trading blocs could lead to a *higher* volume of trade between the blocs. The ratio of trade to national income would be reduced, but as a result of higher incomes there would be *more* trade.

CONCLUSIONS

In this chapter I have tried to show that international integration can lead to national disintegration. National disintegration may manifest itself in growing unemployment, poverty, exclusion or marginalization.

The power of national governments and their ability to make national policies and pay for social services has been reduced without a corresponding increase in supranational government or effective international cooperation. Welfare expenditures on and subsidies for the poor have been cut or privatized, so that those who cannot afford to pay have to do without. The result of political institutions lagging behind globalizing technology, deregulation and liberalization is a deterioration of the capacity to govern. Karl Polanyi (1944) wrote that the national market is embedded in society and the state, but no such authority governs the international market.[17] The state promotes the public good of the market while combating the public ills that it entails. But we do not have the global equivalent; at the global level the market reigns supreme. There are few global regulations, policies, protection or safeguards. National governments are in retreat, reducing social services, tax bases and safety nets, though the rhetoric is ahead of actual actions.

Global forces reduce the power of people to influence policy democratically at the national level. At the same time, at the global level there are no democratic institutions to enable people to control or even influence their destiny.

These developments have implications for analysis and policy. The first task is to explore the ways in which different regions, countries, sectors and groups are affected by globalization, who gains and who loses (absolutely and relatively), and the manner in which ways to protect the weak, the poor and the excluded can be built into the globalization process from the beginning. Strategies should aim to select the positive impulses of globalization and encourage them, while minimizing the impact of negative impulses, or cushioning the losers against them. This cannot be done by combining globalization with *laissez faire*.

There is both an obligation and a prudent need (in order to avoid a protectionist backlash) to look after the victims of the competitive struggle and the groups that are hurt by it. How to reduce the heightened insecurity in people's lives that has resulted from a combination of unemployment, job insecurity, poverty, inequality, marginalization and exclusion; how to match economic globalization with social globalization; how to embed globalization in socially responsive institutions – all these imply two things. First, the speed of progress towards globalization has to be determined. A slower pace gives more scope for adjustment. Second, where globalization and the liberalization of trade and finance have caused unemployment, poverty, exclusion and marginalization, the state should provide various kinds of safety nets and social insurance, including public works programmes, education and retraining facilities, a programme for changing attitudes and motivation, and so on. The answer to the detrimental impact of globalization is not to stop the process but to take action against the harmful effects, ideally at the global level, but until then at the national level. Since globalization reduces available public resources global taxes should be considered.

At the level of policy and action there is the need for both transnational and global (or regional) – not just international – institutions as well as for local ones. I have argued that technology has moved ahead of institutions. Revolutions in transport, travel, communication and information have (partially) unified the world. But institutionally we are stuck with the nation state. The nation state has usurped too many functions, which it can no longer carry out efficiently or humanely. Some of these should be delegated upwards, others downwards. Upward delegation is necessary because technology and private enterprise have become global, while their supervision and regulation have remained national. A global antimonopoly, anticartel and antirestrictive-practices policy, for example, would bring international policies in line with national ones. As things are, American companies are prohibited from colluding and forming cartels in the home market but are encouraged by the Webb Pomerane Act to do so against foreign countries. Japanese companies' distribution networks are barriers to trade. Many Japanese firms rely exclusively on local component suppliers. The World Trade Organization should, in principle, be able to take on these issues. Now only price discrimination in international trade is ruled out by permitting antidumping duties to be imposed. But these are used by most governments as protectionist devices, not to promote competition but to thwart it. Clearly a competition policy is a task for a supranational institution, for national governments would be tempted to tailor them to the advantage of their national firms. At the same time, reduced monopoly power will reduce incentives and ability to conduct basic research, increasingly the most important engine of growth in our high-technology age. This may have to be taken over by supranational agencies or by international research consortia. Research is needed on whether this is necessary, and if so, how it should be done.

Finally, the interaction of policies and institutions at five levels should be explored: the micro-micro level (what goes on inside the firm, farm, household), the micro level, the meso level (the impact of policies and institutions on different groups and regions) the macro level and the macro-macro or global level; and the division of duties at each of these levels between private, public (national, international and global) and voluntary agencies.

Notes

1. I am grateful to Ajit Bhalla, Albert Berry, Louis Emmerij, Réal Lavergne and Hans Singer for helpful comments on earlier drafts.
2. It is the non-historical touting of the current trend towards globalization that has led the critics to call it globaloney.
3. This increase in the trade/GDP ratios occurred in spite of a general increase in tariff protection between 1870 and 1913. It was therefore not the result of trade liberalization. In the pre-1913 period of globalization the role of the state increased rather than declined (see Bairoch and Kozul-Wright, 1996, p. 113).
4. But see the section on government and open economies in which a positive relation between the size of government and public expenditure ratios is suggested. Also, social expenditure (on education, health and so on) has made a recovery in Latin America since 1993 (see IDB, 1996). This could be the result of pressure to compensate those adversely affected by globalization.
5. It should, however, be remembered that downsizing in companies such as AT&T, Nynex, Sears, Philip Morris and Delta Airlines cannot be attributed to

international competition. Businessmen like to blame global forces for actions for which they should bear responsibility.

6.   Ronald Dore (1996) has argued that technological change has been more important than globalization in promoting competition and changing the character of our societies.

7.   The Congressional Advisory Commission on the Consumer Price Index, whose chairman was Professor Michael Boskin.

8.   Hans Singer has pointed out that the Golden Age of the Keynesian consensus of the 1950s and 1960s proved that this happy triangle is in fact possible if the necessary mild controls of inflationary pressures are accepted. Critics would reply that it took two decades for the workers to see through the money illusion.

9.   Dore (1996) has written illuminatingly about these problems. See for example his comments on Lord Dahrendorf's lecture (mimeo).

10. Ibid.

11. Card and Krueger (1995) have found that for some fast food restaurants in New Jersey and neighbouring Pennsylvania (as a control group) higher minimum wages have led to *higher* employment. These findings led to considerable controversy.

12. This does not mean that people have necessarily benefited from this technological globalization. Economic and technical progress translates into human well being even less automatically at the global level than at the national level.

13. I am indebted to Michael Lipton's analysis of the relation between the prisoners' dilemma and Coase's theorem in a different context (see Lipton, 1985). Farrell (1987) has shown that the Coase theorem, according to which individuals can resolve problems of externalities and public goods as well as governments provided that property rights are assigned, is not correct (see pp. 113–29).

14. This section draws on Rodrik (1996). See also Garrett and Lange (1995) and Garrett (1995). I am grateful to James Robinson for having drawn my attention to these articles.

15. Another option would be to train a force of workers who must be ready to move to new places and learn new skills in response to the changing international scene. These 'commandos' would enjoy higher pay and better conditions. The life might appeal to young bachelors or people keen on frequent change. But as Dore (1996) has pointed out, with the reduced importance of unskilled and semi-skilled labour, and the growing importance of highly skilled people, retraining is difficult or impossible.

16. Among the contributors to this literature in the 1950s and 1960s were Jagdish Bhagwati, Max Corden, Harry Johnson and T.N. Srinivasan.

17. I owe this argument to Mohan Rao. See also Rao (1995). The expression 'embedded liberalism' for the postwar bargain between trade liberalization and social government policies is due to Ruggie (1995, pp. 507–26).

2 Information Technology, Globalization and Marginalization

Jeffrey James[1]

Globalization is an undeniably real phenomenon defined in terms of increased flows of trade and investment between countries regardless of however meaningful it may or may not be according to various other definitions. Over the ten-year period from 1985 to 1994, for example, the ratio of world trade to GDP rose more than three times more rapidly than during the ten previous years, while the ratio of foreign investment to GDP doubled (World Bank, 1996b). In this sense globalization is just as meaningful a notion from the standpoint of developing countries as it is for the world economy as a whole. For not only did the overall ratio of trade to GDP in those countries increase by 1.2 per cent per annum over the decade, but they also registered a rising share of total foreign investment (to more than one third) (ibid.)

When they are disaggregated, however, these data indicate that developing countries are not participating equally in the process of global integration. On the contrary, a recent World Bank study depicts a disturbingly unequal pattern of integration (ibid.) For example the wide variance around the average increase in the ratio of trade to GDP for the developing world as a whole is reflected in the fact that that ratio actually fell in 44 of 93 developing countries, while of the total direct foreign investment going to those countries some two-thirds was concentrated among only eight of them (ibid.) The purpose of this chapter is to examine the role played by the new information technologies in these divergent global integration patterns, which, as the following section demonstrates, point firmly to the marginalization of a large number of developing countries.

PATTERNS OF GLOBAL INTEGRATION

The main finding of the World Bank (ibid) on the economic prospects of developing countries is that their integration into the global economy in recent years has been a highly uneven process. Table 2.1 shows the extent of that unevenness. In particular it shows that some parts of the developing world – notably East Asia, South Asia and Latin America – have experienced substantial integration (as measured by the growth of exports and foreign direct investment), while other regions – the Middle East and Africa – are integrating much more slowly. Table 2.1 also reveals a clear correlation between degree of integration and rate of economic growth: that is, the regions that integrated most intensively grew the fastest, whereas the slowest integrating economies exhibited the least rapid rates of economic growth.

Other data from the World Bank report can be used to focus more closely on the process of global marginalization; that is, the process whereby some countries are experiencing a decline in the ratio of (1) trade and (2) foreign direct investment to GDP. With regard to the former ratio, the World Bank data indicate a decline in 44 of the 93 developing countries, 'representing more than one billion people, or 26 per cent of the sample population'(ibid., p. 21). The majority of those 44 countries are in the Middle East and Africa. Similarly, 'Over the past decade ratios of FDI to GDP fell in thirty-seven of the ninety-three countries studied' (ibid., p. 22). Of these, 20 were in Sub-Saharan Africa, nine were in Latin America and the Caribbean and seven were in the Middle East and North Africa.

Generally speaking, therefore, marginalization seems to be most pronounced on the African continent (see Chapter 6). Indeed the conclusion of one recent article on the subject is that 'Africa is currently more marginalized within the world economy than at any time in the past half century. Its shares of world trade, investment and output have declined to negligible proportions' (Collier, 1995, p. 556).

Table 2.1   Uneven integration of developing countries into the global economy (per cent)

Region	Real GDP growth per capita, 1991–95	Export growth per capita, 1991–95	FDI inflows as a share of GDP, 1993–95
East Asia	8.0	14.1	3.1
South Asia	2.2	8.4	0.3
Latin America and the Caribbean	1.1	7.2	1.1
Middle East and North Africa	−0.2	−0.4	−0.4
Sub-Saharan Africa	−1.5	−1.6	−0.9

Source: World Bank (1996b).

Alternative Explanations

There are undoubtedly many reasons for these divergent patterns of global integration, perhaps the most obvious of them being intercountry differences in macroeconomic, trade and industrial policies. It is often argued for example that the Asian newly industrializing economies have adopted far more outward-looking trade and industrial policies than other developing countries in general and those in Sub-Saharan Africa in particular. Another frequently heard explanation is that some regions are far more prone to political risk and uncertainty than others (with Africa again featuring prominently in the latter category). It is not our intention to minimise the importance of arguments such as these, rather that the influence of information technology has not yet received the attention it deserves in this context. There are, we will show, a variety of different mechanisms through which information technologies influence the process of globalization. And in each case the nature of this influence tends to correspond in a broad way to the patterns of globalization that have just been described. What will also become apparent is that these same influences also tend to *increase* the extent of globalization itself. Thus the relationship between information technology and globalization is one of mutual causation rather than unidirectionality.

THE INFLUENCE OF INFORMATION TECHNOLOGY ON PATTERNS OF GLOBAL INTEGRATION

Because we have defined globalization and marginalization in terms of foreign trade and investment flows, it is in relation to these same variables that the role played by the new information technologies needs to be examined. Let us therefore turn first to the foreign-trade-induced mechanisms of technological influence.

Trade-Induced Mechanisms of Technological Influence

Information technology influences not only the extent of international trade but also the degree to which different countries (and firms in those countries) benefit from the relationships thus induced. In turn these technological influences are exerted through two different mechanisms. One of them has to do with the adoption and diffusion of information technologies across countries and among firms in those countries. By reducing production or communication costs and improving product quality, these technologies tend to create new trade opportunities for adopting units;[2] non-adopters, however, may find themselves at a competitive disadvantage, which over time may result in their becoming increasingly marginalized. The second mechanism has more to do with the *production* than the *adoption* of information technology. In particular the rapid growth in demand for electronic products affords valuable export opportunities to firms and countries that can sell those products on international markets.

Let us consider each of these mechanisms in turn, although before so doing we should take note of a possibly important connection between them, namely that the user skills required for successful adoption of the new technologies may also be necessary for the skills needed to produce them. The underlying argument is that technological capabilities tend to be sequentially acquired, beginning with the capability to use imported machinery efficiently, a stage that is usually followed by repair and maintenance capabilities and ultimately by the ability to produce and export the machinery itself. Thus user and producer capabilities can not be separated from new technology in general or information technology in particular. Indeed 'The experience of OECD countries suggests that intensive users of information technology (IT) often become competitive suppliers of information systems in their own industries, such as banking and airline services' (Hanna and Dugonjic, 1995, p. 38).

The Adoption of Information Technology and International Trade

We begin this section with telecommunications not just because this form of information technology influences the extent to which certain new industrial technologies can be adopted (for example in the garments and textiles industries) (Mody and Dahlman, 1992), but also because many observers initially saw in electronic switching technology an especially favourable opportunity for developing countries to engage in technological leapfrogging, that is, to assimilate that technology even more rapidly than the industrialized countries. By expanding their main telephone lines and reducing their comparative transport and communication costs, developing countries would be able to compete more effectively in international markets for goods and services. (Electronic or digital switching involves the use of microelectronics to connect terminals and coordinate the entire telecommunications network as opposed to the use of electromechanical parts. The former type of switching tends to be cheaper than the latter and it also requires less maintenance because it involves no moving parts.)

The Adoption of Advanced Telecommunications Technology

The possibility of leapfrogging by means of electronic switching technology arises because (1) this technology is cheaper and less complex to install from scratch than when it has to be added to an existing electromechanical network, and (2) it is developed rather than developing countries that tend to have large existing networks of this kind. The latter countries 'thus had a remarkable opportunity to completely leapfrog the electromechanical technology, avoiding the expense of replacing obsolete (though young in age) capital stock and problems of technological cumulativity, and start their telecommunications infrastructure from scratch' (Antonelli, 1991, p. 71).

Not all developing countries, however, were well placed to take advantage of the opportunity thus presented, and while some were indeed able to assimilate the new switching technology more rapidly than the developed countries, others lagged far behind. Table 2.2 shows that most of the fastest adopting countries (as defined by the ratio of electronic lines to total switching capacity) were first- and second-tier newly industrializing countries in the Far East that enjoyed high rates of investment, technical skills and other attributes.

To the extent that these countries generally achieved more rapid rates of penetration than the developed countries, technological leapfrogging has indeed taken place (ibid.) On the other hand, many of the developing countries, especially but not only in Sub-Saharan Africa, that lack these features seem to have achieved very low or non-existent rates of adoption, a consideration that helps explain why the total number and quality of lines remains so low in that region compared with other parts of the developing world. 'For example, there are only 0.3 telephones per 100 people in Sub-Saharan Africa.

Table 2.2   Extent of adoption of electronic switching in developing countries, 1987

	Latin America	Asia	Africa
Leaders[1]		Singapore	Morocco
		Thailand	
		Malaysia	
		Hong Kong	
		Republic of Korea	
		Sri Lanka	
Fast followers[2]		Philippines	
	Chile		
	Colombia		
	Peru		

Notes:
1. Countries whose ratio of electronic lines to total switching capacity was greater than 50 per cent in 1987.
2. Countries whose ratio of electronic lines to total switching capacity was 35–50 per cent in 1987.
Source: Antonelli (1991), p. 50.

The figure is twice as great in Asia (excluding Japan), 16 times greater in Latin America, and 60 times higher in the industrialized countries of Europe' (Moussa and Schware, 1992, p. 1738). In addition,

> subscriber equipment is often out of service for long periods, in particular due to cable faults. Lines are noisy: new connections are limited, and long waiting lists exist: tariffs are high; new services are not readily provided, and what service is available is often limited to the larger urban areas. The international service is often better than the national service (Winsbury, 1995, pp. 233–4).[3]

Inasmuch as the differential rates of digital switching technology vary directly with per capita income levels, and because this technology has fostered additional trade and growth among the adopting countries, it seems to have exerted an inegalitarian influence on the global distribution of income. Moreover, according to some observers, the distributional impact may have been negative *within* the adopting countries themselves. For example in Table 2.2 the Philippines is listed as a 'fast follower' country, but the growth that took place there has apparently benefited foreign rather than locally-owned enterprises, urban rather than rural areas and those who make long-distance rather than local telephone calls (Sussman, 1991; see also O'Siochrú, 1993).

The Adoption of New Industrial Technology and International Trade

Although much more research needs to be done on the diffusion of new industrial technologies in developing countries (for example computer-aided design, CAD, and computer numerically controlled machine tools, CNCMTs), two broad tendencies are already apparent. One is that, because they are skill- and infrastructure-intensive and tend to be associated with sophisticated 'high-income' products, the new industrial technologies are being adopted primarily in the more industrialized of the developing countries (especially, but not exclusively, in Asia).[4] The second tendency is that, for similar reasons, these technologies tend to be adopted by relatively large-scale, export-oriented and often foreign-owned enterprises in the countries concerned.[5]

What is less clear, however, is how these differential patterns of adoption influence the competitive position of firms and countries *vis-à-vis* non-adopters. That is, to what extent is the competitive position of the latter being undermined – or marginalized – by the technological behaviour of the former? The problem in addressing this question is that within broad product categories, such as textiles and footwear, some goods are close substitutes for one another, while others are entirely non-competitive (as may be the case, for example, with products embodying essential and luxury characteristics in very different proportions). Technical change that affects one product (when, say, it is produced by CNCMT) will thus tend to have a very different impact on the other products in a given category, depending on the closeness of the substitutes they represent. Consider in this regard the situation portrayed in Figure 2.1, where three different products, A, B and C, embody two characteristics in different proportions.

In the initial situation (prior to technical change) we assume that the prices of the goods and available income are such that the efficiency frontier is represented by OPQ. Depending on their preferences, consumers will choose a particular point on this frontier. For example where preference is represented by IC^2, a point between O and P will be selected, whereas the consumer with the indifference curve IC^1 will be best off consuming good C. One can usefully conceive of these two indifference maps as representing two different markets, one with a distinct preference for one combination of characteristics and the other with an equally distinct preference for an entirely different combination of characteristics. Assume now that technical change endows good A with more of both characteristics than before, so that the new efficiency frontier becomes, say, O^1PQ (with a given income, that is, the consumer derives more characteristics from the same product). As one would expect, the technical change thus specified improves the competitive position of the producer of good A;[6] the effects on the producers of goods B

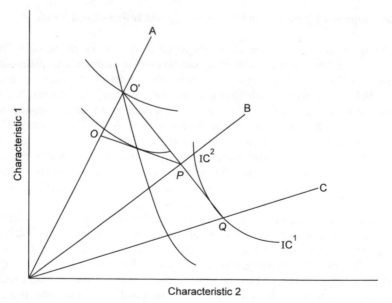

Figure 2.1   Adoption of new technology and product competitiveness

and C however are not at all the same, because while A and B are relatively close substitutes for one another, A and C are not. Thus in a market where A and B compete, the latter loses out to the former in the new situation because the consumer moves to point O^1. The consumer of good C, on the other hand, remains entirely unaffected by the technical change and remains in his or her initial position at Q (as might be the case in practice, for example, with the consumer of a highly standardized, price-sensitive item of clothing in the face of technical change at the more design-intensive end of the spectrum).

It follows from this analysis that the degree to which different developing countries are actually made worse off when new industrial technologies are adopted by developed and newly industrializing countries will need to be determined on a case-by-case basis using a considerable amount of highly disaggregated information about particular product categories. The current four-digit classification of trade data is far too aggregated to be useful in this regard.

The Adoption of Electronic Communication Technology and International Trade

In addition to the industrial technologies that have just been described, firms in developing countries may also adopt electronic communications technology such as the Internet and e-mail. These latter technologies may enhance the competitive standing of adopting firms by providing them, among other things, with information about prices and markets and by enabling them to place orders more rapidly. To the extent that installation and use of electronic communications technology is simpler and less expensive than the new industrial technologies, one could expect a more even diffusion of the former among firms of all sizes. As yet, however, there are no data that can be used to test this hypothesis.

The Production of New Technology and International Trade

As noted above, information technology affords developing countries the chance to become more actively involved in the international trading economy not only through the technology-adoption behaviour of firms, but also because of the opportunity to produce and export the new technologies. The latter is made all the more attractive by very rapid growth in the global demand for many of the products that together constitute the electronics sector.[7] Which developing countries, then, have best been able to meet this rapidly growing demand?

To the probably substantial extent that production and export capabilities presuppose the prior acquisition of user capabilities in information technology, one would expect that the successful developing-country exporters are also among its most intensive (per capita) users.

Table 2.3 tends to confirm this expectation for it shows that, over a range of different subsectors of the electronics industry, exports are concentrated among a narrow group of newly industrializing countries, mainly but not exclusively in the East Asia region. Indeed for a number of these countries, these exports account for a sizeable proportion of manufactured exports as a whole, for example, 45 per cent and 50 per cent for Singapore and Malaysia respectively (UNCTAD, 1995a). At the other extreme, one can also see from Table 2.3 that the Africa region has barely participated in the international market for electronics products. This region's share of the total market is in fact even less than its export share of manufactures as a whole,[8] suggesting that it is more difficult to compete in electronics than in manufacturing more generally.

To a large extent the export of electronics by developing countries has been generated by foreign direct investment, and hence one needs to look to the factors that determine the location of such investment in order to explain the

Table 2.3   Developing-country exports of selected electronics, 1993

Electronic micro-circuits		Diodes, transistors, etc.		ADP peripherals*		Digital computers	
Major exporters	*% of world market*	*Major exporters*	*% of world market*	*Major exporters*	*% of world market*	*Major exporters*	*% of world market*
Rep. of Korea	9.5	Malaysia	8.6	Singapore	27.2	Singapore	24.0
Singapore	7.6	Hong Kong	6.3	Rep. of Korea	6.1	Mexico	3.2
Malaysia	7.5	Singapore	6.0	Malaysia	2.6	Rep. of Korea	3.1
Hong Kong	4.3	Rep. of Korea	4.7	China	1.5	Hong Kong	0.6
Thailand	1.6	Mexico	2.6	Hong Kong	1.4	Malaysia	0.4
Philippines	0.9	Philippines	2.1	Mexico	0.7	China	0.3
Total	31.4		30.3		39.5		31.6
Exports from Africa	0.0	Exports from Africa	0.4	Exports from Africa	0.0	Exports from Africa	0.0
Exports from N. Africa	0.0	Exports from N. Africa	0.4	Exports from N. Africa	0.0	Exports from N. Africa	0.0
Exports from Latin American Integration Association	0.5	Exports from Latin American Integration Association	2.7	Exports from Latin American Integration Association	0.9	Exports from Latin American Integration Association	3.3

* ADP stands for automatic data processing.
Source: UN (1993).

patterns summarized in Table 2.3. In the 1960s and 1970s overseas investors in semiconductor production, for example, were attracted not only by the availability of cheap unskilled labour in East Asia, but also by the political stability, open financial systems and excellent telecommunication facilities that that region generally offered (Henderson, 1989). Subsequently, as the production of electronics products became more automated, those same firms were attracted instead by the availability of low-cost skilled and semi-skilled labour in first- and second-tier newly industrializing countries in East Asia. Regions such as Sub-Saharan Africa, in contrast, tend to lack the factors that have just been cited and consequently they have failed to attract foreign investment in the electronics industry. One exception in the African context, however, is Mauritius which has managed to enter the export market for electronics partly on the basis of foreign investment (Moyo, 1996). This can be attributed in large measure to the fact that Mauritius has the only success-ful export-processing zone in the region.

Foreign-Investment-Induced Mechanisms of Technological Influence

The trade-induced mechanisms described above have implications for foreign investment behaviour in developing countries, and hence for the differing degrees of global integration exhibited by those countries. The reason is that trade tends to promote economic growth (recall the correlation between these variables, as shown in Table 2.1) and rapidly growing economies generally attract more foreign investment than economies that are not growing or growing relatively slowly. Because of agglomeration economies (Wheeler and Mody, 1988), moreover, the additional foreign investment that thus accrues tends to attract further foreign capital and so on, in a cycle of cumulative causation. Inasmuch as it helps to determine the patterns of international trade that give rise to this cumulative outcome, information technology may thus be said to exert an indirect influence on foreign invest-ment behaviour. But there are also several *direct* mechanisms of technological influence, and it is to these that we now turn.

As it happens, these mechanisms exert two fundamentally opposing influ-ences on the transnational corporation: whereas one of them induces the corporation to disperse its activities ever more widely across developing countries, the other has just the opposite effect of inducing a geographical concentration of foreign investment in a relatively narrow group of countries (OECD, 1993). The first of these tendencies is driven mainly by traditional supply or cost considerations, while the second has more to do with demand-side factors, especially those that are related to the so-called 'new competi-tion' (see below). In both cases, though, it seems that once again the more advanced developing countries stand to benefit, rather than – or at the expense of – the least developed.

Dispersion

In so far as they reduce the costs of intrafirm communication, coordination and control,[9] the new technologies make it feasible and potentially attractive for the multinational corporation to engage in a more geographically dispersed pattern of economic activity. As applied to production, this 'distance shrinking' effect of information technology affords firms the opportunity to reduce costs in a number of different industries, especially those where production is based on distinct components and operations that can be physically separated (ibid.) In the clothing industry, for example,

> One vital contribution a [computer-aided design] CAD system interfaced with a modern telecommunications network can make is its ability to separate human capital-intensive activities from the locations where the purely labour-intensive production activities can take place, without sacrificing necessary information linkages.... Given that the labour-intensive core of the clothing manufacturing process has remained widely unaffected by the introduction of microelectronics, a microelectronic/telecommunications revolution can accelerate a migration of clothing industries to low labour cost areas by reducing natural (that is, communication) barriers to trade (Spinanger, 1992, p. 99).

Computer software is another industry where spatial production possibilities are being altered by information technology in a direction that favours certain developing countries. Already apparent, for example, is a tendency for routine data-processing activities to be relocated from the United States to the Caribbean, as advanced telecommunications facilities and a plentiful supply of skilled operators can be found at a relatively low cost in countries such as Barbados and Jamaica.[10]

When applied to research and development (R&D), information technology permits multinational corporations to undertake 'self-contained divisible activities that can take place in geographically separate locations, to be subsequently integrated, and they also allow, where needed, R&D activities that are undertaken on an integrated, on-line manner across borders' (UN, 1995, p.151). Texas Instruments, for example,

> has been able to perform geographically dispersed, but globally integrated, R&D activities because of information and communication technologies that allow the exchange of detailed integrated chip designs and scientific simulations across the world without a time delay. Texas Instruments (India) has the latest HP and Sun workstations and a variety of computers that are interconnected by a Local Area Network, which in turn is connected to Texas Instruments' worldwide data communications network.

Texas Instruments (India) is connected to it on a 'real-time' basis through a dedicated 128 KB link, enabling the company to send and receive the latest support information, design technology and applications information for its products and services (ibid., p. 153).

Although it is difficult to assess the extent to which individual developing countries are currently involved in examples of this kind, early data for the period 1982–89 (Table 2.4) indicate that the increased R&D spending by US transnational corporations in the Third World is concentrated mainly in Asia, and especially in India and Hong Kong. Thus whereas R&D in direct product design and development tends to favour the first-tier newly industializing countries (NICs), which have a sophisticated technology base (accompanied by a relatively limited science base), R&D into generic and disembodied technology favours 'advanced' developing countries that are strong in science relative to technology (Reddy and Sigurdson, 1994). India in particular has become a prominent recipient of this type of R&D, offering as it does an especially large pool of skilled research personnel.

Although the degree to which it is taking place is as yet limited (ibid.), the emerging pattern of R&D dispersion across the developing world represents a fundamental departure from the traditional product cycle model of international investment behaviour. It will be recalled that, in the traditional model, foreign R&D activities are undertaken only when a new product or process has matured to the point where production is located abroad. Such overseas

Table 2.4   Research and development expenditure of US majority-owned affiliates as a percentage of sales, by developing regions and countries

Developing region/country	1982	1989
Latin America	0.20	0.20
Argentina	0.40	0.25
Brazil	0.40	0.30
Mexico	0.30	0.20
Africa	0.01	0.02
Asia and the Pacific	0.04	0.20
Hong Kong	n.a	0.10
India	0.50	0.60
Indonesia	0.02	0.03
Republic of Korea	n.a	0.30
Malaysia	n.a	0.10
Singapore	n.a	0.30
Thailand	0.03	0.02
Taiwan	0.30	0.40

Note: n.a = data not available.
Source: UN (1992).

R&D is 'mainly concerned with adapting the products (for example, to account for differences in consumer tastes) and the production processes (for example, to account for differences in the labour market) to suit the local market conditions' (Patel, 1995, p. 172). Inasmuch as it gives rise to products and processes that benefit the majority of the population, this adaptive type of research can be described as appropriate to developing-country circumstances.

The newly emerging forms of R&D, on the other hand, tend to be driven by very different considerations, with possibly important consequences for the nature of the resulting innovations and the distribution of the benefits of those innovations between and within countries. For one thing it is supply rather than demand-side factors that now dominate the location decision of transnational corporations.

> Thus firms are now assumed to assess a wide range of different geographic locations purely in terms of the strength of their science and technology base and the availability of adequately qualified scientists and engineers. In such a scenario the home country of the firm is assessed on the same basis as all other potential locations (ibid., p. 153).

A related distinction is that foreign R&D is now designed not so much to produce locally-oriented products and processes as to generate technologies that can be used internationally throughout the transnational corporation. In the previously cited case of the Texas Instruments Corporation, for example, all the innovations developed by the Indian affiliate are exported by satellite to the US parent firm for distribution throughout the corporation as a whole (UNCTAD, 1995a). By the same token, the Indian affiliate benefits from the information that flows from other R&D centres within the corporate communication network. 'In this respect', writes Cantwell (1995, p.172), 'innovation in the leading transnationals (TNCs) is now more genuinely international or, in the terminology used here, it has become *"globalised"*.

However R&D is not the only mechanism through which the new information technologies are promoting the globalization of activities conducted by transnational corporations. On the contrary, an important line of recent research has revealed a wide variety of additional mechanisms such as joint research ventures, technological exchanges and unidirectional technology flows that are collectively referred to as international strategic technology alliances (Hagedoorn and Schakenraad, 1993). Indeed the growth of those alliances 'is considered by many observers as one of the major characteristics of economic globalisation' (Freeman and Hagedoorn, 1995, p. 41), and most of that growth, as shown in Table 2.5, has been concentrated in the new information technologies themselves.

As can also be seen from Table 2.5, however, apart from the NICs, developing countries have been almost entirely excluded from such arrangements,

Table 2.5   International distribution of strategic technology alliances in information technology, 1980–9

	No. of alliances	% for developed economies	% for triad	% for triad/ NICs	% for triad/ LDCs	Other
Computers	199	98.0	96.0	1.5	0.5	–
Industrial automation	281	96.1	95.0	2.1	1.8	–
Microelectronics	387	95.9	95.1	3.6	–	0.5
Software	346	99.1	96.2	0.6	0.3	–
Telecommunications	368	97.5	92.1	1.6	0.3	0.5
Misc. IT	148	93.3	92.6	5.4	0.7	0.7
Heavy electronics	141	96.5	92.2	1.4	2.1	–

Source: Freeman and Hagedoorn (1995), p. 44.

which are overwhelmingly concluded between firms from the 'Triad' region (Europe, Japan and the United States). When it is combined with the evidence shown in Table 2.4 concerning the emerging distribution of global R&D investment, this pattern of technological relationship only seems to underline what some authors rightly refer to as a 'divergence of technological development on a world scale' (ibid., p. 55).

Concentration

Whereas the supply-side mechanisms described in the previous section facilitate the dispersion of economic activities by transnational corporations, the demand-side aspects of information technology give rise to just the opposite tendency. That is, when they are broadly defined to include organizational changes, those technologies offer firms the opportunity to engage in what Best (1990 p. 144) refers to as 'the new competition'. By this he means that a new competitive paradigm is emerging that 'is not about maximizing profits for a given material, product, process, and organizational method, but about seeking a competitive advantage by continuously upgrading product, process and organization'.

In this emerging competitive process, success depends not on being the lowest-cost producer (as in the supply-side type of situation described in the previous section), but rather 'upon the minimization of product development and product changeover times' (ibid., p.14).

A key element of this 'new competition' is the use of new organizational practices – often in combination with information technology – that are variously referred to as 'post-Fordist', 'lean' or 'flexible' production systems. By means of techniques such as 'just-in-time production' and 'quality circles', firms that adopt the new organizational practices tend to be better able to compete successfully in the 'new competition', mainly because they can usually respond more flexibly than non-adopting firms to changes in demand. The spatial implication of the new technology in this case, however, is concentration rather than dispersion. In particular, transnational firms that are engaged in this form of non-price competition on the basis of flexible production systems are likely to concentrate their investment activities in developing (and developed) countries that are physically close to their major markets. Such proximity matters

> because one of the keys to the competitive strength of post-Fordist production is its flexibility and continuous innovation, which depend heavily on close 'synergistic' relations between firms and their suppliers, and the just-in-time system. Proximity to customers is also important for establishing the continuous two-way information flows that allow producers to adapt quickly to changing market demands and consumer preferences.... The importance of proximity, for a given production unit, in turn militates against global sourcing, that is, against the use of suppliers scattered around the globe.... It militates in favour of the constitution of production networks in each of the world's major markets: Europe, North America, and Pacific Asia (Oman, 1994, p. 90).

Textiles and cars are two sectors that are especially subject to the 'new competition', and for the reasons just mentioned one does indeed find that foreign investment tends to be concentrated near the largest markets for those products (UNCTAD, 1995a). In the case of the United States for example, Mexico and the Caribbean are major recipients of foreign investment in cars and textiles respectively, while the recent decision by General Motors to establish a full-scale assembly plant in Thailand or the Philippines attests to the growing importance of the Asian market for cars (*The International Herald Tribune*, 29 May 1996).

Summary of the Technological Influences on Patterns of Globalization

It is useful at this point to summarize the numerous trade and foreign investment-induced mechanisms of technological influence as they involve different forms of information technology and benefit different groups of developing countries (Table 2.6). In fact, our analysis has identified four separate groups of developing countries that benefit from at least one of the mechanisms shown in Table 2.6, namely the first-tier NICs (such as Korea and Taiwan), the second-tier NICs (such as Malaysia and the Philippines), large developing countries with an advanced scientific or technological base (such as India and Brazil) and countries in close proximity to major markets, which by virtue of their particular competencies are able to participate in the 'new competition'. Some of these country groups, particularly the first-tier

NICs, tend to benefit from almost all the mechanisms while other groups benefit from only a few of them. If one looks at the country groups least likely to benefit from the mechanisms described in Table 2.6, Sub-Saharan Africa is the obvious choice because the necessary technological capabilities are conspicuously absent. Indeed the absence of such capabilities means that African countries may even have become worse off as a result of the adoption elsewhere of information technologies in the manner described earlier in relation to Figure 2.1 (see also 'Implications for Research and Policy Formulation' below).

Our conclusion is thus that the unequal patterns of global integration shown in Table 2.1 – and especially the extreme experiences of East Asia on the one hand and Sub-Saharan Africa on the other – are to some extent an outcome of the influence exerted by information technology.[11] Some of the entries in Table 2.6, moreover, suggest that a parallel type of influence may be at work *within* countries, where the gainers tend to be large-scale, foreign-owned, urban-based firms, rather than – or at the expense of – small-scale rural enterprises. In this respect information technology may also have contributed to income inequality within the developing countries themselves. One should note, however, that the relationship between *firms* is only one component of the total effect that technical change has on inequality within a country. What also needs to be considered is the question of how new technology influences the dispersion of wages within that country. This question mainly relates to the skill intensity of technical change, and in particular whether that change primarily concerns skilled or unskilled labour. If, as is widely believed, information technology tends to increase the relative demand for skilled labour, then the wages of this group will rise relative to those of workers in the unskilled category. Indeed one comprehensive study of wage dispersion trends in the United States 'points toward skill-biased technical change as the major driving force behind rising wage inequality' (Davis and Haltiwanger, 1991, p. 174).

This particular feature of information technology may also help explain the sharp rise in wage inequality in certain Latin American countries, for example Mexico and Chile (World Bank, 1995a), though reliable empirical evidence of this has yet to be gathered. Research is also lacking on yet another way in which information technology may affect inequality within a developing country. Apart from its influence on firms and workers, this technology also affects those consumers who are able to benefit from product improvements (with regard to say durability) and price reductions. What one needs to know in this regard is whether the beneficiaries are based in rural or urban areas and whether they have relatively high or low incomes.

So far our conclusions have been based on a consideration of each of the separate mechanisms shown in Table 2.6. These conclusions are reinforced if one also looks at the relations *between* the mechanisms rather than just at

Table 2.6   Summary of trade and foreign-investment-induced mechanisms of technological influence on globalization

Form of information technology	Mechanism of influence	Developing countries and firms most likely to benefit	Developing countries and firms least likely to benefit (or to be made worse off)
Telecommunications	Technological leapfrogging via digital switching	Countries with high rates of investment, skills and transnationals located in urban areas (e.g. Asian NICs)	Countries with low rates of investment, inadequate skills and small-scale firms in rural areas
Industrial technologies (e.g. CAD, CNCMTs)	Adoption enhances competitive advantage of adopting firms and countries at expense of non-adopters	Countries with large-scale firms competing in 'high-income' markets (e.g. more industrialized LDCs)	Countries with small-scale firms competing in price-sensitive markets
Electronics (e.g. diodes, peripherals, computers)	Exports of electronics to world markets	Countries and firms with advanced production capabilities (e.g. Asian NICs)	Countries and firms lacking advanced production capabilities
Communications technology (telecommunications and computers)	Information technology promotes global dispersion of production and R&D by transnationals	Countries with an abundance of low-cost skilled labour (e.g. Caribbean region for data processing). Countries / regions with advanced base of science or technology (e.g. India, Hong Kong)	Countries lacking skilled labour or with relatively high labour costs. Countries lacking either an advanced science or technology base
Organizational technology combined with information technology	Promotes concentration of investment by transnationals near major markets	Countries near major markets that are able to participate in "post-Fordist" production systems (e.g. Mexico)	Countries far from major markets
Information technology in general	International strategic alliances in information technology promote globalization (e.g. NICs)	Countries with innovation capabilities in information technology or advanced research capabilities in those technologies (e.g. NICs)	Countries lacking innovation capabilities or advanced research capabilities in information technology

each individual mechanism on its own. The reason is that there is considerable degree of *cumulativeness* in the technological processes that underlie the integration of developing countries into the global economy. This is partly a question of the synergy between the various information technologies themselves, as is the case for example with the integration of computers, telecommunications and office automation into an integrated services digital network (ISDN). But it also has a great deal to do with the Myrdalian notion of cumulative causation, which envisages a widening rather than a narrowing of the initial gap between competitors of unequal strength. We have already suggested, for example, that foreign investment is more likely to accrue to rapidly growing than to slowly growing economies, and it is also more likely to flow in the direction of those developing countries whose initial conditions include a well-developed telecommunications infrastructure. Or again, those countries or firms that at a given point in time are capable of using information technology effectively are also more likely to benefit from the production and export opportunities afforded by such technology.

IMPLICATIONS FOR RESEARCH AND POLICY FORMULATION

The implications for further research revolve around the mechanisms of technological influence on recent patterns of globalization that have formed the main part of this chapter and were presented in summary form in Table 2.6. First of all, we feel that there is a need for a better understanding of some of those mechanisms. For example we have suggested that the manner in which information technology influences the pattern of gains and losses is more complex than is usually thought. In particular we have argued that the effect that the adoption of certain information technologies has on non-adopting firms and countries depends crucially on the characteristics of the products made by the competing units. These demand-side relationships need to be examined empirically on the basis of far more disaggregated data than is now available in international trade statistics. Some of the other mechanisms require further research because they have only begun to emerge relatively recently. We are referring here especially to the way in which information technology is enabling transnational corporations to disperse their economic activities more widely than has hitherto been possible. Among the issues that need to be researched in connection with this emerging phenomenon, is the question of how it will alter the nature of innovations generated by transnationals in developing countries. For whereas at least part of that investment used to be undertaken for the purpose of adapting products and processes to host-country conditions, the R&D that is now being undertaken in developing countries on the basis of advanced information technologies appears to be directed towards more 'global' products that can be used throughout the corporation, rather than towards local adaptations. To the extent that this switch in the focus of R&D does occur, it raises the disturbing possibility that the technical changes arising out of direct foreign investment will be even less appropriate to the needs of the majority of those living in the Third World than is currently the case. This possibility deserves to be investigated theoretically as well as empirically, and the research could perhaps best be set in the broader context of finding alternatives to the product cycle as a model of foreign investment in the era of information technology.[12]

The second main area where further research is needed has to do with the role of government policy in the process by which information technology causes some developing countries to become increasingly marginalized over time. For while it is true that these technologies possess characteristics – such as skill intensity and a tendency to be associated with sophisticated high-income products – that make them more accessible to relatively advanced developing countries, it is also true that accessibility is influenced to an important extent by government policy. We know, for example, that OECD countries have used a variety of national policies to maximize the diffusion of information technology and it is more than likely that those policies have improved the ability of OECD countries to compete effectively on world markets.[13] We also know a good deal about the policies towards information technology that have been pursued in the NICs and in large industrially advanced developing countries such as India, Brazil and China.[14] We know very much less, however, about policies in those countries that have integrated least successfully into the global economy in the past decade. It is therefore difficult to assess the extent to which that lack of integration can be ascribed to the governments of those countries, important though this issue obviously is.

Then there is the closely related normative question of how the marginalized countries (located mainly but not exclusively in Sub-Saharan Africa), could make better use of information technology in their relations with other countries. What seems most crucial in this regard is the formulation of a national information technology strategy

> to address the systemic constraints to the effective use and wide diffusion of IT. This involves organizational adjustments and coordinated actions at the firm, industry and national levels, with investments in management skills and restructuring. A long-term perspective and a coherent framework are needed to identify economy-wide information and communication needs, to target large-scale application areas for strategic impact and demonstration effects, and to create the funding mechanisms, policy environment and common services necessary to support a combination of top-down/bottom-up initiatives and pilot projects, accelerate learning and meet the needs of smaller organizations (Hanna and Dugonjic, 1995, p. 36).

Such a framework seems particularly necessary for small and low-income countries (for example in Sub-Saharan Africa) that depend heavily on foreign donors for information technology. The problem is that these interventions are frequently uncoordinated and are made in response to events rather than conforming to a coherent policy framework.

By no means the least important purpose of a national information technology strategy is the setting of certain policy priorities, since it is unrealistic to conceive of progress being made simultaneously along all the technological dimensions that influence a country's degree of integration into the global economy (unfortunately much of the policy advice that is given to developing countries in this as in other areas fails to recognize this need). What probably warrants particular attention in this regard is the telecommunications infrastructure because, among other reasons, of the powerful influence this variable exerts on not just one, but on several of the other mechanisms that are summarized in Table 2.6 above. Not only does it affect trade-induced mechanisms of technological influence (via, for example, an enhanced capability to adopt industrial information technologies), but also the mechanisms that operate through foreign investment (through, for example, an enhanced capacity to attract dispersed data-processing activities).

Two types of electronic communication systems appear especially promising in the context of Sub-Saharan Africa and other marginalized regions of the Third World. One of them, called 'FidoNet',

is a low-cost method of linking together computer bulletin board systems through ordinary phone lines. Its virtue – and its usefulness in developing countries – lies in its ability to overcome the limitations of inadequate phone systems. FidoNet systems automatically contact each other at night – when phone rates are low – to exchange conference postings and electronic mail messages. They keep dialing until they make a connection, and do not stop transmitting until assured by the machine at the other end that all messages have been received free of errors. Regular connections, called gateways, between FidoNet computers and other systems such as the Internet and the Association for Progressive Communications (APC) networks, allow FidoNet users to communicate with virtually anyone with an electronic mail address, with most messages reaching their destination within 24 hours (Young, 1993, p. 33).

FidoNet computers are able to operate even without a telephone system by means of so-called 'packet radio' sets, which are small devices attached to computers in much the same way as a modem and allow e-mail and other data to be exchanged automatically.

The second type of communications system that seems especially well suited to African conditions makes use of (relatively inexpensive) low-Earth-orbit satellite technology rather than the telephone network. While in orbit the satellite passes every point on Earth at least twice a day and during each 'pass' data can be up- or downloaded to other parts of the world using packet radio technology. One low-Earth satellite already forms the basis of an important medical network in Africa. It serves thousands of physicians and health-care workers by enabling them to communicate with colleagues elsewhere in the world and by providing them with recent medical information in electronic form (*The New York Times*, 22 January, 1996).

Notes

1. I am indebted to Ajit Bhalla, Paul Streeten and the IDRC for comments on an earlier draft of this chapter.
2. For a detailed description of these changes see James (1985).
3. Winsbury (1995, p. 234) reports that 'low income countries still have less than a 5 per cent share of global telephone main lines although they have 55 per cent of the world's population'.
4. According to Watanabe (1995, p. 345), for example, 'The use of microelectronic industrial machinery in the Third World is heavily concentrated in a small number of economies. Most of them have already been classified as "high income economies" by the World Bank (Singapore and Hong Kong), or are preparing to join the "rich men's club" (The Republic of Korea and Taiwan Province of China). Apart from these,... the diffusion of the new technology is marginal.'
5. Bhalla (1996) provides some evidence in support of this assertion.
6. Evidence that the adoption of information technology enhances international competitiveness takes different forms. On the one hand there are econometric estimates of the relationship between country export performance and rates of technological diffusion. Antonelli *et al.* (1992), for example, find that international competitiveness in the market for cotton fabrics is 'strongly and positively influenced' by the rate of adoption of shuttleless looms. On the other hand there is case study evidence based on surveys of individual firms. See, for example the series of country case studies conducted by the International Labour Office (ILO) referred to in James (1994).
7. The value of world trade in electronic microcircuits, for example, grew by almost 7 per cent between 1989 and 1993. Diodes and transistors recorded a similar rate of growth over this period (see UN, 1993). The rapid growth in world demand for electronics and the central role played in that growth by the East Asian NICs is emphasized by Freeman *et al.* (1995).
8. Africa's share of world manufactured exports during the period from 1970–90 was 0.4 per cent (see UNCTAD, 1995b).
9. UN (1992) notes that 'recent developments in information technologies tend to increase the internationalisation advantages of Transnational Corporations'.
10. For details see Howland (1995) and Schware and Hume (1995).
11. A similar conclusion was reached by Castells and Tyson (1988) for the period before the 1980s and 1990s.

12. Recent literature on the changing relevance of the product cycle model includes Patel (1995) and Cantwell (1995).
13. See, for example, Hanna *et al.* (1995).
14. See the studies on these countries reviewed in James (1994) and the various chapters in Brundenius and Goransson (1993).

3 The Impact of Globalization and the Information Revolution on Latin America

Albert Berry

Two of the outstanding phenomena of the last couple of decades are 'globalization' and the 'information revolution' upon which the so-called 'information highway' has been built. The current information revolution, like its predecessor, has created many jobs while destroying many others, thus leading to change and uncertainty in both the labour market and society. The same may be said of globalization. It remains to be seen what their longer-term impact on average incomes, income distribution, poverty and marginalization will be; and until this becomes clearer it is natural that many fears and uncertainties will accompany the hopes and expectations these phenomena create. Given the turbulent economic trends in Latin America over the last two decades, it is natural that such mixed feelings are common in that region.

DEFINITIONS, APPROACHES AND BACKGROUND

Concern about globalization is partly based on the idea that the gains in national income it may produce are closely connected to cost cutting via employment reductions ('downsizing'), streamlining government in order not to hamstring firms by high taxation, vigorous pressure to raise worker productivity, and pushing down wages or slowing their increase. Such fears are heightened by the doubts that developing countries often harbour about their ability to compete in open markets, in which case they worry that the pain will yield little gain. Ironically and unfortunately, the focus on national competitiveness via productivity and cost cutting (each of which does or can bring benefits of its own) is somewhat misguided. In implicitly rejecting the theory of comparative advantage it reflects a basic misunderstanding of how a country benefits from international trade (Berry, 1997c).

An important aspect of the background to these issues in Latin America is the high level of inequality, currently closely related to the unequal distribution of education or more generally of human capital, and historically to the concentration of land. These and other determinants of inequality and hence of poverty must be borne in mind, both when assessing the mechanisms linking globalization and information technology (IT) to poverty (whether positively or negatively) and when considering how policy may improve those effects.

Globalization and the information revolution are linked in various ways, as discussed by Streeten in Chapter 1. The focus of this chapter is the way in which these two phenomena, separately and together, are affecting and will affect the social and economic evolution of the countries of Latin America, in particular the levels of poverty and marginalization in that part of the world.[1] Much of the extensive literature on marginalization in Latin America has pointed to economic processes that bring benefits to some groups but leave others behind. In varying degrees the concept can refer to countries, regions, occupational categories and individuals.

Exports

In Latin America and the Caribbean the ratio of exports to GDP (measured in constant 1980 prices) averaged around 14 per cent in the 1970s; since then it has shown a continuous upward drift to over 23 per cent in 1994 (Table 3.1). In current price terms,[2] however, the story is quite different. World Bank (1996a, p. 213) figures indicate that the ratio fell from 16 per cent in 1980 to 15 per cent in 1994. The difference between these two patterns reflects the large negative terms of trade effect estimated by UNECLAC (1995a), equal to 5.7 per cent of GDP in 1994 (*vis-à-vis* 1980) or about 30 per cent of the value of imports in that year. The ratio of imports to GDP (again using constant 1980 prices) averaged around 14 per cent during the 1970s, peaked at around 16 per cent in 1980–81, and fell to a low of less than 11 per cent in 1984–85, since which time it has risen systematically. Because, by the early 1990s, the terms of trade effect had grown to a large negative number of around 6 per cent of GDP, it was only in 1992 that the constant price import ratio surpassed that of 1980–81.

Between 1980 and 1994 the share of manufactures in the region's merchandise exports rose from 17.4 per cent to about 50 per cent (Table 3.2), partly, it should be noted, as a result of the falling prices of primary exports. The share of manufactures in total exports rose for all groups of trading partners (Table 3.3), and most notably for the industrialized countries, where the figure was still low in 1980 (7.7 per cent) but then rose sharply to nearly 27 per cent by 1991 and has presumably risen further since then.

Capital Inflows

The net inflow of capital, which was low throughout the 1980s except for 1980–81 (it peaked at $40.1 billion in 1981), rose sharply in 1991–92 and exceeded $60 billion in 1992 and 1993 (Table 3.4). As a result the net resource transfer (which also includes the net current payments to factors of production),

Table 3.1 Relative shares of the components of GDP and gross national income: Latin America and the Caribbean (at market prices[1], GDP = 100)

	Total final consumption expenditure[2]	Gross fixed capital formation	Domestic demand	Exports of goods and services	Imports of goods and services	Terms-of-trade effect	Net factor payments to rest of world	Real gross national income
1980	78.2	23.5	101.7	14.1	15.8	–	2.6	97.6
1981	77.9	23.3	101.2	15.0	16.2	-0.8	3.7	95.7
1982	77.2	20.7	97.9	15.5	13.3	-2.4	5.1	92.7
1983	76.2	17.2	93.4	17.1	10.5	-2.7	4.9	92.6
1984	76.3	16.6	92.9	17.9	10.8	-2.3	5.2	92.8
1985	76.3	16.6	93.0	17.6	10.6	-3.0	4.9	92.5
1986	76.9	17.2	94.1	16.8	11.0	-4.1	4.5	91.8
1987	76.4	17.2	93.6	17.5	11.2	-4.2	3.9	92.3
1988	76.2	17.0	93.2	18.9	12.1	-4.4	4.1	91.9
1989	76.1	16.3	92.4	19.8	12.2	-4.7	4.3	91.5
1990	76.6	15.9	92.5	20.7	13.2	-5.0	3.7	92.0
1991	77.4	16.4	93.8	20.9	14.7	-5.5	3.4	91.9
1992	78.0	17.5	95.5	21.6	17.1	-5.6	3.1	92.2
1993	77.6	18.1	95.7	22.4	18.1	-6.0	3.2	91.5
1994[3]	77.2	19.0	96.1	23.2	19.3	-5.7	3.1	92.1

Notes:
1. Official figures converted into dollars at constant 1980 prices. Nineteen countries.
2. Includes variation in stocks.
3. Preliminary figures.
Source: UNECLAC (1995b, p. 62).

Table 3.2 Exports of manufactured products from Latin America, by country (percentages)

	1970	1980	1985	1990	1991	1992	1993	1994
Argentina	13.9	23.1	20.8	29.1	28.2	26.3	31.9	32.7
Barbados	25.3	52.5	83.8	43.3	58.7	54.7	61.7	n.a.
Belize	n.a.	17.6	24.9	15.4	n.a.	18.2	20.6	17.0
Bolivia	3.2	2.9	0.4	4.7	3.8	12.5	17.0	22.2
Brazil	13.4	37.1	43.7	51.9	54.8	56.9	58.8	54.8
Chile	4.8	11.3	6.7	10.9	12.7	13.2	16.1	16.4
Colombia	9.0	19.7	16.9	25.1	33.3	31.8	39.9	36.9
Costa Rica	18.7	29.8	22.3	27.4	24.5	25.6	n.a.	n.a.
Ecuador	1.8	3.0	0.8	2.3	2.4	4.0	7.1	7.4
El Salvador	28.7	35.4	25.7	35.5	40.6	47.8	46.1	44.7
Guatemala	28.1	24.4	20.2	24.5	27.9	29.9	30.7	31.3
Honduras	8.2	12.8	4.0	9.5	11.6	12.9	12.8	15.0
Mexico	33.3	12.1	20.6	43.3[1]	50.8[1]	71.1[2]	74.6[2]	77.4[2]
Nicaragua	17.8	18.1	8.9	8.2	9.1	7.0	9.4	13.1
Panama	3.5[3]	8.9	12.8	17.0	20.8	16.7	16.4	17.7
Paraguay	9.0	11.8	5.5	9.9	11.3	15.2	16.7	21.3
Peru	1.8	16.9	11.8	18.4	22.6	16.7[1]	15.8	13.9
Trinidad & Tobago	12.8	5.0	18.2	26.7	28.5	29.9	34.2	42.5
Uruguay	17.6	38.2	35.0	38.5	40.1	40.8	42.2	42.9
Venezuela	1.0	1.5	10.0	10.9	9.6	11.0	13.3	13.8
Regional Total	10.8[4]	17.4	23.4	32.8	36.4[4]	45.8	50.1[5]	50.0[6]

Notes:
1. Preliminary figure.
2. Includes goods for processing (*maquila*).
3. Does not include the canal zone.
4. Does not include Belize.
5. Does not include Costa Rica.
6. Does not include Barbados and Costa Rica.
Source: UNECLAC (1995a), p.111.

which had been negative over the period 1982–90, became positive and was around 20 per cent of the value of exports in 1992 and 1993, around the level of 1980–81. This transfer was, however, small again in 1994 (Table 3.2). Foreign direct investment (FDI) also jumped in the early 1990s, from $6–7 billion a year in 1989–90 to an estimated $18 billion in 1994 (Table 3.5).

Information Technology

The impact of the information technology revolution and of increased integration into the world economy began to be felt in Latin America at a time

Table 3.3   Direction and composition of trade of Latin American countries

	World	Developed[1]	Developing	Latin America[2]	Other developing
Absolute values in $ billion:					
1970	17.5	14.1	3.4	3.0	0.4
1980	107.9	79.0	28.9	23.0	5.9
1991	136.6	103.7	32.9	23.1	9.8
Percentages:					
1970	1.86	1.04	0.82	0.76	0.06
1980	15.86	7.68	8.18	6.98	1.20
1991	42.63	26.94	15.69	11.60	4.09

Notes:
1. Including the countries of Eastern Europe and the communist countries of Asia (the latter of which do very little trade with Latin America).
2. Includes exports from each country of Latin America to the other countries of the region.
Source: UNCTAD (1993).

when most of these countries were in the throes of, or just emerging from, the macroeconomic downturn of the 1980s, brought on by the debt crisis. In the wake of that crisis most countries adopted a market-friendly set of policies that represented a marked change from the past, and they have now integrated or are integrating rapidly into the world economy. The absolute levels of trade, capital flows and foreign direct investment have all increased sharply over the last decade, the combined result of recovery from the depths of the recession induced by the debt crisis, of policy liberalization and of the more general process of globalization, with the associated decline in transport and communications costs, the formation of trade blocs and the reduction of tariffs via the Uruguay round of the GATT negotiations.

The extent of diffusion and use of IT in Latin America is harder to assess quantitatively. The telecommunications networks in this region have lost ground relative to many parts of the world over the last couple of decades due to the slow economic growth associated with the debt crisis. In countries such as Argentina and Venezuela extremely inefficient public sector enterprises have also accounted for part of the lag. Mexico, Brazil and Argentina participate as exporters of electronics items, with Mexico in particular showing dynamism during the 1990s, largely through the *maquiladores*, one presumes. Independent technological capacity has been limited by the fact that the region's expenditure on R&D as a share of GDP has remained low, having fallen further behind the LDC average since 1970, when the two figures were about equal at 0.3 (see Chapter 7, Table 7.9).

Table 3.4 Net capital inflows and resource transfers: Latin America and the Caribbean ($ billions and percentages)[1]

	Effective net inflow of capital[2] (1)	Unregistered transactions[3] (2)	Net inflow of capital (1 + 2) (3)	2/1 (4)	Net payments of profits and interest (5)	Resource transfers (1 − 5) (6)	(3 − 5) (7)	Export of goods and services (8)	6/8 (9)	7/8 (10)
	($ billions)	($ billions)	($ billions)	(%)		($ billions)			(%)	(%)
1980	33.6	−2.3	31.3	−6.8	18.8	14.8	12.5	101.6	14.6	12.3
1981	51.8	−11.7	40.1	−22.6	28.9	22.9	11.2	109.6	20.9	10.2
1982	32.7	−13.1	19.6	−40.1	38.8	−6.1	−19.2	99.6	−6.1	−19.3
1983	6.8	−4.1	2.7	−60.3	34.8	−28.0	−32.1	99.5	−28.1	−32.2
1984	13.6	−3.1	10.5	−22.8	37.5	−23.9	−27.0	110.8	−21.6	−24.4
1985	8.5	−4.9	3.6	−57.0	35.7	−27.2	−32.1	105.6	−25.8	−30.4
1986	11.0	−1.3	9.7	−11.8	32.4	−21.4	−22.7	91.3	−23.4	−24.9
1987	13.6	1.6	15.2	11.8	31.1	−17.5	−15.9	104.1	−16.8	−15.3
1988	7.9	−2.0	5.9	−25.3	34.3	−26.4	−28.4	119.4	−22.1	−23.8
1989	7.6	4.5	12.1	60.0	38.3	−30.7	−26.2	132.7	−23.1	−19.7
1990	17.8	0.1	17.9	0.6	33.8	−16.0	−15.9	146.0	−11.0	–
1991	37.0	0.4	37.4	1.1	31.0	6.0	6.4	146.0	4.1	4.4
1992	59.8	1.5	61.3	2.5	30.9	28.9	30.4	154.5	18.7	19.7
1993	66.5	0.2	66.7	0.3	33.0	33.5	33.7	164.9	20.3	20.4
1994[4]	43.3	–	–	–	34.2	9.1	–	189.2	4.8	–

Notes:
1. Covers 16 Spanish-speaking countries (Cuba and Panama are not included), plus Brazil and Haiti.
2. Equal to net inflow of capital minus unregistered transactions.
3. Corresponds to the errors and omissions entry on the balance of payments.
4. Preliminary estimates.
Source: UNECLAC (1995b), p. 106.

Table 3.5   Sources of external financing: Latin America and the Caribbean
($ million)

	1989	1990	1991	1992	1993	1994[1]
Debt:						
Bonds[2]	833	2 760	7 242	14 018	24 404	19 866
Banks[3]	−6 497	5 559	6 800	10 943	1 636	3 200
Commercial paper	127	–	1 212	840	315	400
Certificates of deposit	–	–	670	1 100	65	–
Investment:						
Direct[4]	6 134	6 728	10 830	12 727	13 805	18 057
ADR/GDR[5]	–	98	4 120	4 063	5 726	4 689
External funds[6]	416	575	727	293	10	565[7]

Notes:
1. Preliminary estimates.
2. Gross value.
3. Net, short- and medium-term.
4. Includes reinvestment of profits.
5. ADR – American depository receipts; GDR = global depository receipts.
6. Close-ended funds; initial capital.
7. First six months.
Source: UNECLAC(1995b), p. 104.

The overall impact of globalization and IT on marginalization/poverty can be thought of as a combination of their impact on growth and on distribution,[3] in particular the income share of the group in or near the poverty category (at present most studies suggest that about a third of the population of the region is in poverty). In the case of the poorer countries, growth is especially important as a major contributing factor to poverty alleviation. If its impact on material poverty is positive enough, it could offset any effects from an increase in inequality. From a policy perspective, it is not so much the overall impact of globalization and IT on poverty that matters as (1) the effect that policy has on the advance of these phenomena, and (2) how, given the extent of globalization and dissemination of IT, which is either desirable or inevitable, policy can affect its impact on poverty. The main policies that affect the rate and pattern of globalization are those that affect trade flows, direct foreign investment and the flows of financial capital. The main influences on the evolution of IT, while harder to identify with any confidence, clearly include the country's R&D policy as well as the pace and pattern of human capital formation.

For neither globalization nor IT can the impact on Latin American society be more than crudely guessed at this time. The attempt to identify those effects is at an early stage. But both phenomena warrant an increasing effort in that direction because *the effects could be large, they could go in either direction, and it is possible that policy could affect them significantly.*

The next section looks at the nature of the processes of globalization and technology change in the information area and their possible effects. A second point of departure, the focus of another section, is a review of a number of outcomes in the region – rates of growth, levels of employment/unemployment, and income distribution. These outcomes provide another test of any predictions made, and allow one to try to 'work back' from the outcomes to identify the mechanisms that are most likely to have been responsible for them. The distribution of income became more concentrated in most Latin American countries at around the time the economic reforms were introduced, one of which was a reduction in trade barriers, leading to more open economies and higher trading ratios. It is possible that the technological changes have had an impact in this direction as well.

All of the standard arguments in support of the view that international integration and new technologies will bring benefits are potentially valid (see Streeten, Chapter 1), but there are serious grounds for concern that expectations may have been overblown. Thus far the empirical record is ambiguous, but the post-crisis, post-reform outcomes in the Latin American region are worrisome on both the growth and the distribution front.

THE EFFECTS OF GLOBALIZATION AND INFORMATION TECHNOLOGY

As noted above, both technological change (of which the new information-related technologies are the most prominent component) and integration into international markets are likely to affect the region's growth and distribution performance in significant ways.

The 'Dependency' Critique of Latin America's Earlier Experience of International Integration: its Relations to Marginalization

During the early postwar decades much concern was expressed about the dependency of the Latin American economies on the industrial powers. Frank (1969) presented a classic Marxist interpretation. Sunkel's non-Marxist views constituted one of several strands of postwar thinking on the need to intervene in markets, following a pattern of thought set in motion by Prebisch (1950) and his fears that primary goods exporters such as Latin America would fare badly over time due to a secular decline in the terms of trade for such goods. Sunkel (1973) argued that Latin America ran the risk of being trapped into continuing dependence, and that income and productivity gaps might widen as backwash effects outweighed the spread effects of economic growth in the Centre countries. He associated this outcome with the increased difficulty of gaining access to the elements of the 'development package', because such access was becoming increasingly dependent on purchasing the complete package at a high price from transnationals (TNCs), which were taking advantage of the protection of the local market under import-substituting industrialization (ISI) to get good returns on their investments while centralizing all the R&D in their own countries and keeping their technical knowledge close to their chests. Very high estimates by Vaitsos (1974) of the returns achieved – through transfer pricing, among other mechanisms – by foreign pharmaceutical companies in Colombia underlined such worries. Meanwhile the literature on marginality debated the extent to which the blame for the mushrooming urban squatter settlements (and poverty more generally) lay with the process of capitalist accumulation and growth in these dependent economies.[4]

Neither subsequent events nor the accumulation of research have confirmed the more pessimistic views expressed on the effects of dependency and on the trends in marginality, unless one interprets the economic crisis of the 1980s as a natural outcome of the mechanisms described by these authors rather than as a mainly chance historical event afflicting the region. Although growth varied markedly across countries, it was generally good until the crisis arrived in the early 1980s, averaging 5.5 per cent per year for the region from 1950–80, a 'performance not significantly surpassed by any other group of countries, either developed or developing' (Teitel, 1992, p. 356). Some countries did especially well, including Brazil and Mexico. Manufacturing exports expanded significantly, albeit from a fairly small base. There was no systematic evidence of a technological 'slipping behind' of the sort that exercised the dependency theorists.[5] For most countries of the region income distribution did not change markedly over this period; to the extent that there was some worsening (for example Brazil in the 1960s) it was not large enough to significantly offset the positive effects of growth. Employment generation occurred at a pace sufficient to raise the share of the labour force in the modern sector, with its relatively high labour productivity, and to bring about a continuous decrease (for the region as a whole) in the share of the population living in conditions of poverty. In other words, the decades leading up to 1980 saw a quite important degree of 'trickle down'. With the region's per capita income rising by about 3 per cent per year from 1950–80, the incidence of poverty – using Altimir's poverty line (Altimir, 1982) – fell quickly from around 65 per cent in 1950, 38 per cent in 1970 to about 25 per cent in 1980 (Berry, 1997a).

All too soon, however, the worries of the *dependistas* with respect to the region's inability to control its own fate and break out of the older modes of interaction with the industrialized countries were replaced by the trauma of the debt crisis, during which an excessive presence of TNCs or FDI was the least of region's worries. Foreign capital withdrew rather than knocking on the door. Serious recessions hit all the major countries except Colombia, unemployment rose and most countries suffered serious bouts of inflation. Meanwhile the policy preference switched to 'outward orientation', with its strongest proponents arguing that the import-substituting industrialization (ISI) strategy was misguided and had contributed both to slow growth and to unnecessarily high income concentration (Corbo, 1988). The new view, like the *dependista* one, needs to be viewed with caution; the creditable growth performance and the essentially stable income distribution during the ISI phase seem to contradict them both (Berry *et al.*, 1997). Now that the region is reentering world markets and capital is again flowing in, the roles of foreign trade, foreign capital and the TNCs need to be reassessed.

Though the worst fears of earlier times were exaggerated, up to a point some of the concerns were no doubt justified – for example the long-standing contention that technological change was a key factor underlying the inability of Latin America's growth to generate the desired amount of employment and hence reduce the concentration of income. Pinto (1965) argued that technology developed in the industrialized countries was not suited to the factor proportions of the region, and that it was usually transferred with little attempt at adaptation. Tokman (1989) concurred, noting that studies of elasticities of substitution (for example ILO–PREALC, 1980) have usually found these to be low, and suggesting that the prevalence of foreign techno-logy has played a role in the falling real wages of unskilled workers in a number of Latin American countries. As discussed below, the 'appropriate technology' question is an especially tricky one for the Latin American region. Since it is less labour abundant than the Asian countries, the idea that its comparative advantage lies in labour is less obvious.

An Optimistic View of Globalization

The current optimistic view of globalization and freer trade anticipates growth benefits arising from allocative gains, gains in X-efficiency (because freer trade means more competition, which promotes efficiency), capital inflow raising the total capital stock and hence output, greater technological transfer through TNCs, greater imports of capital goods, a greater flow of ideas resulting from greater overall contact, and other positive mechanisms. All of this helps to make plausible the 'convergence theory', that income gaps between countries and between regions of countries are narrowing. Mean-while the optimistic view of the distributional implications of freer trade comes from the belief that the demand for less-skilled labour will increase and that the prospects of agriculture, which as a whole tends to be penalized by import substitution, will be improved. Optimists also believe that the scaling down of public-sector activity and the introduction of more market principles into that which remains will greatly increase the sector's efficiency in the provision of public goods and services, including poverty redressal services.

The Effects of Freer Trade

Because Latin America's experience under globalization and freer trade has not thus far led to a clearly better or worse performance than the previous ISI model, it is useful to draw on the more general developing-country experience, even though it too remains surprisingly ambiguous in a number of respects. A vast array of empirical cross-country studies show that export growth and overall economic growth have tended to go together. But there remain questions with respect to how systematic the link is across groups of countries and periods of time, to what extent it is due to 'reverse causality' from output growth to export growth,[6] and to what extent it is due to joint causation.[7] Despite the absence of overwhelming confirmation of the positive role of exports in growth at the country level, few students of development doubt that it is true for individual countries and in a variety of contexts.

Two other major qualifications have been made. First, the elasticity of world demand for developing-country exports may be too low for the benefits from exporting to be generalized. Second, though trade may often be quite beneficial, this does not necessarily make the virtual absence of trade barriers the optimal policy choice. To so assume is to deny the potential validity of the infant-industry argument for protection.[8] This qualification is also of possible importance in Latin America. However mixed the signals provided by the empirical analysis on the mechanisms connecting levels of trade and growth, researchers have barely attempted (with cross-section or time-series analysis) the more refined task of analysing the effects that degree and type of barriers to trade have on growth. The historical record in East Asia provides evidence that ISI policies have been the normal prelude to and have complemented strong export performances. Persuasive arguments can be made that the region's successes (beginning with that of Japan) owed much to the effective management of trade in the context of organized industrial policies (Wade, 1990). The cross-country evidence (see especially Helleiner, 1994) that the exchange rate is the key variable determining export and growth success is consistent with the proposition that trade liberalization is not necessarily or generally the best way to achieve potential benefits from trade.

The Effects of Capital Inflows

Much less analysis has been undertaken on the effects of capital flows into developing countries. As with trade, the main debate concentrates on whether there should be any significant restrictions on capital inflows, beyond such obvious rationales as environmental protection. Along with considerable microeconomic evidence that important benefits can be reaped by hosting FDI, there is concern that such capital may seek out high-profit activities in the host economy and, helped by a process in which developing countries bid against each other to attract it, succeed in appropriating nearly all of the rents it generates.

Short-term capital flows clearly have negative effects as well as providing benefits. They have led to macroeconomic instability in some Latin countries and discouraged export production, hence slowing the rate of growth (as in Mexico and Argentina). Much of international trade and FDI is undertaken by TNCs, most of them large and in possession of considerable oligopolistic power. Although FDI by TNCs has trade-creating effects, it tends to assign to countries a specific type of commercial specialization in the international division of labour, and often to lock the country into that role. In the case of primary products, countries are vulnerable to replacement of their exports by synthetic substitutes. In that of export platform manufactures, they are vulnerable to TNC strategies. For these and other reasons, Japan and later Korea chose to develop without extensive use of FDI. Not being locked in is of special importance to middle-income countries such as those of Latin America.

The technological and managerial advances of the last 15 years, along with deregulation and liberalization, have strengthened the position of large international firms. The power of FDI-led intraregional, intraindustry and intrafirm trade is exemplified by the rapid increase in commerce between Mexico and the United States. In the second half of the 1980s Mexico accounted for two thirds of all employment in LDCs via affiliates of US TNCs (Chesnais, 1995, p. 20). These affiliates increased their share of Mexican exports to the United States fourfold to more than 25 per cent, and their share of Mexican imports from the United States to more than 40 per cent. The LDC worker, however, depends more on whether smaller firms can form an important part of the industrial structure. Some but not all TNCs have the capacity to draw smaller, more labour-intensive firms into the international circuit through subcontracting and other contractual arrangements.

One possibly damaging constraint of globalization as it is presently unfolding in Latin America is the pressure it puts on countries to bring inflation to very low levels, by historical standards. In the 'pro-investment macroeconomic environment' maintained by the East Asian countries as part of their development process, there have been long periods of large fiscal and current account deficits, financial repression and inflationary pressures (UNCTAD, 1996, p. 128). These countries generally tried hard to boost investor confidence in other ways, for example, by avoiding extreme policy shifts. The deployment of some pro-investment incentives may have an inflationary impact, and some degree of inflation can facilitate changes in relative prices (for example movements in real wages). A rigidly low inflation policy could have significant costs. The long-term experience of Brazil, with its high-growth/high-inflation combination, is consistent with this hypothesis.

Perhaps the greatest fear of globalization involves its impact on income distribution; that fear has its greatest empirical basis in Latin America, where the switch to a more open and market-oriented strategy has been accompanied by a sharp increase in inequality in the majority of the countries (Berry, 1997a; Bulmer-Thomas, 1996). The expectation that freer trade would raise wages has been the exception rather than the rule. One factor probably at work is the domination of international trade by large firms – a combination of TNCs and large national firms, whose high labour productivity limits employment creation.

Possible Impacts of the Information Technology

There is a rather widespread expectation that the information revolution will have a positive productivity/growth effect, but that this will be associated with a negative distributional effect. The impact of the information revolution, like that of any other technological advance, depends on who adopts the new techniques and how well they fit the factor proportions of the adopting countries. With the industrial countries adopting first, what remains to be seen is how quickly they spread to other countries, the resulting impact on the roles of transnational firms, larger national companies and smaller firms, and the overall impact on the demand for different types of labour. The effect on national income depends on how much IT raises total factor productivity (TFP). The effect on distribution depends on the factor proportions of the technology adopted and on who adopts it; as a first approximation, it is more negative the greater the unskilled labour-saving bias and the more adoption differentially favours larger firms. The medium- and longer-term impact of technology on distribution also reflects any effect it may have on the country's factor stocks; some new technologies lead to major bursts of investment or to changes in education/training levels and hence influence factor proportions.

The evolution of IT in Latin America appears to include the following scenarios. First, in spite of its being revolutionary in some senses, IT is best thought of as another wave of technological advance, not qualitatively different from earlier ones in the mechanisms and speed of dissemination or in the character of its impact. Latin America borrowed technology at a considerable rate over most of the postwar period (that is, up to the debt crisis of the 1980s), overall growth was relatively fast and the region did not suffer any major worsening of income distribution (Berry, 1997a). So a continuation of these trends would be relatively satisfactory. Though most countries invested at least modestly in science and technology, and some (especially Brazil) mounted serious efforts in this direction, these were curtailed by the debt crisis and in any case were not of the intensity envisaged by those authors emphasizing the importance of this area for Latin America's future economic progress (Perez, 1992; Teitel, 1992).

Second, the region might continue to borrow as successfully as in the past without mounting an extensive R&D operation, but only if the rate of human capital formation is increased enough to permit efficient borrowing, dissemination and use of the new technologies. In this scenario, effective incorporation of the new technologies will require more and different skills than in the past.

Third, the above options might be either unfeasible or, inferior to a more aggressive technology policy. Such a policy could range from an attempt to keep technologically up-to-date by whatever means best achieves that goal (for example licensing, reverse engineering and so on), to one aimed at effective adaptation, including the 'blending' of new IT with traditional technologies, to one aimed at leapfrogging over some of the previous technologies to the newest ones.

Finally, the worst situation would be one in which it would be very hard not to lose ground in the technology race and hence lose income-earning capacity. This is more likely if the overall rate of technological change is faster than before (reflected in the term 'revolution'), if the information is more closely held (if strategic alliances among TNCs delay dissemination) or if the factor intensity of the technology that does disseminate fairly readily is more damaging than before. In this scenario IT, and technological change more generally, could be damaging to the region. On the question of potentially 'inappropriate' technology, optimists point to the fact that factor proportions do have an effect on the direction of R&D (Hayami and Ruttan, 1971; Binswanger and Ruttan, 1978). Though induced innovation does exist – in that the effective demand for new technologies affects the broad directions of research and of the resulting technological change – this effective demand reflects the economic weight behind it and the resources available to complement it. It explains why such a high share of research takes place in industrialized countries; why it is so concentrated on products that will benefit groups with high purchasing power; why so little is directed to producers of less important crops, to small and medium enterprises (SMEs), and to the least developed countries; and, finally, the labour-saving bias of most innovation. At the other end of the spectrum from the 'induced innovation' point of view is the description by Fransman (1991, p. 2, as cited by James, 1993, p. 406), whereby the pace and direction of R&D reflects not factor scarcities but various 'technological trajectories and momenta that are relatively uninfluenced by economic considerations'.[9]

The interface between globalization and IT is important in the sense that the former raises the stakes associated with country policy choices in the latter area. With an inward-looking strategy the costs of a wrong decision with respect to a new technology are simply the lost benefits from its local application. In the global economy an error can cost the country the large rents to be had from having the right products at the right time. In Latin America, perhaps more than in any other major area of the Third World, the appropriate degree of scientific/technological capacity is an important and vexing question, as evidenced by the widely contrasting views expressed in the literature. In East Asia the requisite capacity is in place in several countries, especially Korea; in Africa it is not likely to be in place in the immediate future. Latin America is able to step to a higher level of technological capability; the question is whether this would be a good use of resources.

With such risks in mind it is important, as James (1993) emphasizes, to know a lot about the appropriability of the new technologies. TNC alliances are cause for concern on this front. But it may be that the technologies that really matter to Latin countries (on both the consumption and the production side) are not these frontier ones, but rather those whose prices tend to fall quickly as new breakthroughs appear and competition does its job. For example, CD-ROM enables the storage of vast amounts of medical and bibliographic information, benefiting agricultural research, health information and medical research and library development (Mody and Dahlman, 1992, p. 1714). Desktop publishing lowers the fixed costs of small-batch publications. With the declining cost of hardware, demonstration projects have become more feasible. Licensing of proprietary microelectronics technology from small firms in industrial countries might be more accessible to certain developing countries (Evans and Tigre, 1989). Unlike large firms these firms are more willing to share the technology. The diffusion of some automation techniques may depend on whether the equipment suppliers want to send service personnel to marginal markets, so the evolution of this market is important (James, 1993, p. 420).

Together with the factor proportions characterizing the new technologies, the way governments and other institutions respond to IT may be a key factor in determining whether its distributional impact will be negative or positive. James (ibid., p. 413) refers to the area of biotechnology, where a number of ILO case studies show clearly that the existing capabilities in the Third World are generally not being applied in ways that will alleviate mass poverty, in spite of the important potential that many of the new techniques have in this respect. Thus, micropropagation techniques are being applied mainly to commercial crops to meet the needs of the large-scale, commercial agricultural sector. Public policy (including the regulations set for private-sector participants in the R&D area) is based on the fact that private actors focus on what will benefit those who are able to afford to pay for the research. Any benefits ultimately accruing to the poor are 'trickle-down' in nature, and although they may be substantial, nothing is guaranteed.

In the case of the new IT, much attention has been given to its presumed effect of raising the productivity and wages of those with skills in information use, and on the special value of mental flexibility to allow new learning and retooling in line with changing demands for skills.[10] It is well recognized, in Latin America as elsewhere, that the educational/training process should be modified to take account of the pay-off to information-related skills, but translating that recognition into effective action is very difficult, especially in the context of tight budgets and typically inefficient ministries of education and labour. As higher skills become more valuable in the market it is important that the variance of skills between people – currently extremely wide in countries such as Brazil – be shrunk; otherwise there is a serious risk that the information revolution will increase inequality, poverty and marginalization. It may be equally important for the system to facilitate the entry of workers displaced by IT into other activities.[11] Optimists point out that none of the earlier technological revolutions has led to a permanently more skewed distribution of income, as far as can be ascertained.

Information technology could accentuate inequality by improving the relative situation either of the more skilled workers or of larger firms. At the moment large organizations use more IT – both computing services and telecommunications – than do small ones. It remains to be seen how this gap will change over time. Mody *et al.* (1992, p. 1813) conclude that in a period of rapid technological change, significant productivity differences can emerge among competing firms and that these 'can be magnified if the past accumulated learning creates an advantage in the adoption of new innovations'. The fact that such initial differentials favour larger firms curtails the demand for labour. Such differentials could also have a regional dimension; income gaps related to productivity tend to be magnified by weaker demand effects and externalities in the poorer areas. The chronic persistence of the income gap between the north-east of Brazil and the southern region suggests that such income-equalizing mechanisms as the high rate of migration from the former are only moderately strong.

The overall importance of IT in Latin America and elsewhere will depend on how it affects the region's trade. Thus far, although there is no evidence of a boom on the scale experienced by East Asia, there are some indications of real potential. There is no doubt that, IT is becoming essential to serious contenders in many markets. The benefits are viewed by some as 'strategic', that is, non-price. An important determinant of the employment effects of trade increases resulting from the spread of IT will be the degree to which it facilitates the relocation of routine parts of production to lower-wage countries or regions.[12]

It is clear that many elements of IT are being transferred to Latin America, but as yet many of them are not at all widespread. If those elements that have mainly beneficial effects are non-frontier, have falling prices and can be disseminated widely (for example to smaller firms), then the net impact could be quite positive. In the opposite scenario it could be negative.

TNCs, IT and Globalization

TNCs play a big role in R&D that undermines developing-country exports of primary products and light manufactures. Conversely information technology reduces the costs of intrafirm communication and thereby encourages firms to engage in more geographically dispersed patterns of activity (see Chapter 2). This has helped to keep the location of labour-intensive activities such as in clothing relatively unaffected, in spite of the introduction of some modern technology and the need for short turnaround times. It accounts for the relocation of computer software activities involving routine data processing from the United States to the Caribbean (Barbados, Jamaica), where advanced telecommunications facilities exist and a plentiful supply of skilled labour is to be found. Such potential is of special interest to Latin America, because of the proximity of part of it to the United States, its reasonably advanced telecommunications system and the expanding supply of skilled operators.

One issue is thus the way in which evolving IT will affect the decision of TNCs to locate their production activities in regions such as Latin America. Another is the implications of TNC locations for the desirability of R&D and significant technology development within the region. Patel (1995, p. 151) concludes that there is no systematic evidence to suggest the widespread decentralization of TNCs' R&D activities in the 1980s. An overwhelming majority of technological activities are still located close to the home base. This, however, does not preclude the possibility that what does occur in developing countries is quite important to them (for example microelectronics and biotechnology R&D in India, biotechnology in Mexico and other countries). To the extent that it is more directed at producing internationally relevant products than was the case under the product cycle model (when its main purpose was to adapt products or processes to local tastes and production conditions), the positive effects on the host country may be reduced (see Chapter 2).

At this point, then, the international activities of TNCs do not provide a reason for Latin America to downgrade the importance of developing its own capability in the technology area. Pack and Westphal (1986, p. 111) argue that 'pecuniary externalities related to investments in technology – in acquiring technological capability and in undertaking technological effort – are ubiquitous in industrialization'. James (1993, p. 411) notes that the importance of these activities is heightened by convergence among the major new technologies: microelectronics and communications technologies are converging, and the former is also interacting extensively with biotechnology (for example automated bioprocess control, automatic DNA synthesizers). What remains to be done, however, is to assess the separate roles of activities that are complementary to international research, that is, those that facilitate domestic purchase, adaptation and dissemination, compared with those that are more competitive with, or at any rate not simply derived from the activities of international agents. The general view is that the former function is quite important and requires considerable effort and expenditure in the technology area. As for the latter, which is vigorously pursued only by a modest number of countries, a judgment in the Latin context is more difficult. In their comparison of the super-mini industry in Korea and Brazil, Evans and Tigre (1989, p. 1752) note that the Korean state exhibits a degree of cohesiveness that far exceeds what Brazil can achieve, allowing it to focus and coordinate various organizations and instruments in a policy area like this. Chesnais's (1995, p. 28) summing up is worthy of note:

> The future of countries in the international trading system now depends essentially on their capacity to build domestically (or within close regional cooperation and protection) the skills and interactive mechanisms on which technological accumulation and capital formation both depend. While the possession of these attributes will in due course make them attractive to MNEs, the current priorities of the latter and the basis on which international investment decisions are taking place mean that it is preferable that countries do not lay undue expectations on FDI.

SOME EMPIRICAL EVIDENCE

As noted above, IT and globalization arrived in Latin America at about the same time. In many other parts of the world, including the industrial countries and the rapidly growing East Asian economies, the advance of IT has been part of the process of investment and technological change for a longer period. In Latin America, however, investment rates were low during the 1980s (Table 3.1) so embodied technological advance was slow. As the recovery came, accompanied by trade liberalization and rising trade and foreign investment ratios, the backlog began to be made up. As a result of this simultaneity, it is especially hard to identify from the aggregate record of growth, distribution and poverty, what may be due to trade and other policy change, what to IT and other aspects of technical change, and what to other factors, including the process of recovery from the crisis.

The Impact of Globalization on Growth

The 1990s, while obviously better for Latin America than the disastrous 1980s, have been disappointing in that the region has not been able to recover the sustained growth of the pre-1980 period (Table 3.6). Nor has overall unemployment declined from the high levels suffered in most countries during the mid-1980s; instead the levels in most countries and the regional average have risen during the 1990s, putting the latter at 7.7 per cent in 1996 (Table 3.7). Per capita output in 1995 was still a bit below that of 1980 and per capita income nearly 10 per cent below; the regional growth rate through 1996 was close to 3 per cent, hardly dramatic but enough to edge per capita incomes up by about 6 per cent since 1990 (UNECLAC, 1996a, p. 14) and to contribute to a return of optimism about the region's economic future. Much of that optimism is based on the widespread belief that the currently more market-friendly economic policies are a change for the better *vis-à-vis* those of the precrisis period.

How well-founded is this optimism? On the growth front, there are several causes for concern. First, the performance of Chile, while stellar in many respects, is that of a small, mineral-rich country that was able to disregard popular dissatisfaction while putting its reforms in place and ultimately managed to get much of its microeconomic policy right from a growth perspective. It would be expecting too much to presume that the region as a whole could do this well. Second, those countries that have opted for uncontrolled exchange markets may continue to suffer the exchange rate instability and periodic overvaluation that is interfering with their attempt to induce healthy export growth. Third, there remains the possibility that protection, as previously implemented in the major countries of the region, rather than impeding the considerable economic success achieved during the ISI era

Table 3.6   GDP growth rates for Latin American countries (per cent per year)

	1970–80	1980–90	1990–94	1995
Argentina	2.5	−0.3	7.6	−4.6
Bolivia	4.5	−0.4	3.8	3.7
Brazil	8.1	2.7	2.2	3.9
Chile	1.8	4.1	7.5	8.2
Colombia	5.4	3.7	4.3	5.7
Costa Rica	5.7	3.0	5.6	2.3
Dominican Republic	6.5	2.7	4.2	4.7
Ecuador	9.5	2.0	3.5	2.7
Mexico	6.3	1.0	2.5	−6.6
Peru	3.5	−0.2	4.2	7.7
Uruguay	3.1	0.4	4.4	−2.8
Venezuela	3.5	1.1	3.2	2.3
Latin America	5.4	1.7	3.6	0.3

Sources: World Bank (1995a, 1996a); UNECLAC (1996a).

Table 3.7   Urban unemployment rates for Latin America, by country
(average annual rate)

	1980	1985	1990	1991	1992	1993	1994	1995	1996[1]
Latin America & the Caribbean	6.2	7.3	5.8	5.8	6.3	6.3	6.4	7.3	7.7
Regional average:									
Argentina (total urban rate)	2.6	6.1	7.5	6.5	7.0	9.6	11.5	17.5	17.2
Bolivia (department capitals)	–	5.8	7.3	5.8	5.4	5.8	3.1	3.6	3.5
Brazil (six metropolitan areas)	6.3	5.3	4.3	4.8	5.8	5.4	5.1	4.6	5.7[2]
Chile[3] (metropolitan region)	11.7	17.2	6.5	9.3	7.0	6.2	8.3	7.4	7.2[4]
Colombia[5] (seven metropolitan areas)	10.0	13.9	10.5	10.2	10.2	8.6	8.9	8.9	11.4[6]
Costa Rica (total urban rate)	6.0	6.7	5.4	6.0	4.3	4.0	4.3	5.7	–
Ecuador[5] (total urban rate)	5.7	10.4	6.1	8.5	8.9	8.9	7.8	7.7	–
El Salvador (total urban rate)	–	–	10.0	7.9	8.2	8.1	7.0	7.0	7.5[7]
Guatemala (nationwide total)	2.2	12.1	6.5	6.4	5.7	5.5	5.2	4.3	–
Honduras (total urban rate)	8.8	11.7	7.8	7.4	6.0	7.1	4.0	6.0	6.3
Mexico (total urban rate)	4.5	4.4	2.7	2.7	2.8	3.4	3.7	6.3	5.7[2]
Nicaragua (nationwide total)	–	3.2	11.1	14.2	17.8	21.8	20.7	18.2	16.1
Panama[5] (Metropolitan region)	9.9	15.6	20.0	19.3	17.5	15.6	16.0	16.2	16.4
Paraguay[8] (Asuncion metropolitan area)	4.1	5.2	6.6	5.1	5.3	5.1	4.4	5.3	–
Peru[6] (Lima metropolitan area)	7.1	10.1	8.3	5.9	9.4	9.9	8.8	8.8	8.7
Uruguay (Montevideo)	7.4	13.1	9.2	8.9	9.0	8.4	9.2	10.8	12.6[4]
Venezuela (total urban rate)	6.6	14.3	11.0	10.1	8.1	6.8	8.9	10.9	11.9[7]

Notes:
1. Preliminary figures.
2. January – October.
3. From 1991 on the data have been drawn from a new sample.
4. January – September.
5. Includes hidden unemployment.
6. Average for the rates in March, June and October.
7. First half of the year.
8. From 1994 onwards the figures shown correspond to the total urban rate.
9. The data for 1995 and 1996 have been taken from a new survey and refer to the first half of
   each year.
Source: UNECLAC (1996b, p. 40).

contributed to it. This may be because, as hinted by Khan in Chapter 4, it provided a level of certainty about the future that encouraged high levels of investment, perhaps by facilitating learning by doing, or perhaps through other mechanisms. If such was the case, it may be hard to match those earlier performances. MERCOSUR and its ilk may be the answer to the need for some protection from industrial-country competition, at least for some of the countries. Fourth, to the extent that high levels of investment in human capital, especially broadly based ones, are a key element of growth, as is currently so widely alleged, it remains to be seen how many countries will satisfy this requirement in these days of fiscal constraint, especially those starting from a modest base. Finally, as has been widely noted of late, increasing inequality constitutes a direct impediment to continued stable growth. While strong regional growth in the future is far from a foregone conclusion (the 1990–96 average has been just 3 per cent), it is nonetheless reasonable to expect growth in the 4–5 per cent per year range. Given that population growth has decelerated substantially from its peak, and now runs at well under 2 per cent per year, this could produce a decent rate of increase of per capita income and lower the incidence of poverty, unless the level of inequality increases.

The Impact of Globalization on Income Distribution

On the distribution front, unfortunately the news is nearly uniformly bad. The economic reforms – trade liberalization, labour market reforms and so on have coincided rather systematically with a severe accentuation of (primary) income inequality; the 'normal' observed increase in inequality accompanying reforms is 5–10 percentage points, as measured by the Gini coefficient of primary income; among those Latin American countries for which the statistical evidence is adequate to reach conclusions on this issue, the only probable exceptions to this generalization seem to be Costa Rica, Jamaica and Peru (Berry, 1997a). Available data are insufficient to judge whether the distribution of secondary income (after allowing for taxes, transfers and the public provision of goods) has moved differently from that of primary distribution. Effective targeting has made a positive impact in some cases, but the reduction of government activity and changes in tax systems towards the greater use of indirect taxes may have had a regressive effect.

It seems likely that the observed increases in inequality are typically the result of a jump in the share of the top decile, with most of this accruing to the top 5 per cent or even the top 1 per cent (as in the case of Colombian and Ecuadorian households), and most of the bottom deciles losing ground. At a moderate per capita GDP growth rate of 2 per cent per year, it would require nearly 10 years of distribution-neutral growth for the bottom decile in urban Colombia to recover the ground lost as its income share fell. In urban

Ecuador where the percentage decline for the bottom decile was sharper (from 2.2 per cent to 1.5 per cent), nearly 20 years of such growth would be needed.

Too little research has thus far been done to establish causality between the increases in income concentration and the specific reforms or other changes (such as rapid technological change) that have accompanied them. The economic cycle appears to have played a role, but it cannot in any obvious way be held accountable for the large, lasting (at least to date) shift towards inequality.[13] Other possible factors include technological change and the elements of globalization (more open trade regimes and increasing foreign investment,[14] together with the associated market-friendly reforms), the dismantling of labour institutions and the 'socialization' of debts (whereby the state makes itself responsible for certain private debts that might otherwise threaten macroeconomic or financial stability).

Trade and labour market reforms have been consistent elements of the reform packages instituted in those Latin American countries where distribution has worsened significantly. The prediction that more and freer trade would raise wages at the expense of capital has not been fulfilled; instead wage inequality seems to have widened in a number of countries (including Chile, Costa Rica, Colombia and Ecuador) as trade increased or was liberalized.[15] Among the alternative theories put forward to explain the correlation between the removal of trade distortions and increasing inequality, several authors (for example Wood, 1994) assume that the labour involved in producing exports is relatively skilled, with the result that increased trade widens earnings differentials in accordance with level of education. Other theories involve 'skill-enhancing trade' (Robbins, 1995a): the increased imports of capital goods that result from trade liberalization can increase the returns on skilled labour, which is complementary to capital goods (Hamermesh, 1993; Stokey, 1994). It has also been widely noted that globalization tends to favour the 'large-scale sector' of the economy – large firms, large cities, the more developed regions of the economy and so on.

The dominance of large firms in the production of manufactured exports implies less employment creation than would otherwise be expected (Berry, 1992). Since earnings differences associated with firm size (including those across the formal – informal sector divide) and with region are often large in developing countries, an accentuation of this tendency constitutes a real risk. A third inequality-increasing mechanism related to international trade involves the fact that import liberalization appears to shift the price vector in favour of better-off families. Although optimists have argued that the opening up of trade should be expected to raise the relative incomes of agricultural workers, the evidence *on this point* is not encouraging. A significant feature of the 1984–89 period in Mexico was a widening gap between urban and rural incomes and of the sharp decline in income from agriculture and livestock as a share of rural income both of which contributed to the overall increase in inequality (Alarcon, 1993, pp. 139, 148). In Colombia an unprecedented increase in the gap between urban and rural incomes in the early 1990s, coincided with the process of liberalization. In such countries it appears that a significant part of the agricultural sector cannot compete easily with an onslaught of imports and that its labour resources cannot easily shift to other sectors. Paraguay provides a longer-run test of the implications of outward orientation for agriculture, since it is unique among Latin American countries in having pursued such a strategy more or less systematically since the 1950s (Weisskoff, 1992, p. 1531). Some exports (for example cotton) are produced by small peasant farmers, soybeans and wheat are grown on medium-sized farms with machinery and international technology, while cattle are the domain of the *latifundia*. Although all groups have participated in it, Weisskoff concludes that export-led growth has worsened the structural inequities of the economy. The three-country study by Carter *et al.* (1996) suggests that Paraguay's experience with export-oriented agricultural growth is probably among the most negative in terms of its distributional consequences. It provides few grounds for optimism that the rural–agricultural side of the outward-orientation picture will be positive enough to alter greatly the negative conclusions reached mainly on the basis of urban data.

Some policies that countries have chosen as complements to liberalization (of trade and foreign investment) may also be contributing to increased inequality; three such are privatization, financial reform and labour market reform.

Although privatization is not inevitably associated with trade and investment liberalization, the international financial institutions have strongly encouraged it as an accompaniment to liberalization packages. Thus significant privatization steps have been taken in Latin American countries as part of liberalization. The World Bank (1996c, p. 53) cautions that 'poorly managed privatization, even if it delivers short-term revenue or performance gains, may be seen as corrupt or highly inequitable, concentrating economic and political power in the hands of a domestic elite or foreign investors'. Privatization in Chile clearly contributed to wealth and income concentration; 'the sales led to an acute concentration of ownership and to the formation of large conglomerates' that continue to dominate the economy (Meller, 1992, p. 27).

Meanwhile the 'socialization' of international and other debts in order to save teetering financial and non-financial enterprises has doubtless had a significantly negative impact on distribution as well, as detailed most clearly for the case of Chile by Meller (ibid.) This was in part a crisis-response policy. But such liberalization contributed to financial crises during the 1970s, the 1980s (Diaz-Alejandro, 1985) and more recently. Mexico once again provides the most dramatic example. Both Argentina and Mexico have recently engaged in official bailouts to contain banking crises. Solid evidence is yet to appear on the distributional effects of financial liberalization, apart from those occurring via financial crises *cum* bailouts, but there are reasons to suspect that these too could be negative.

Labour market reforms that decrease job protection and labour's bargaining power appear to open the way for wider wage and salary differentials among individuals. The record in Latin America, together with evidence from developed countries, which implicates them as a factor in increased wage inequality, suggests that such reforms and labour market functioning more generally need to be carefully assessed as possible contributors to inequality.

Identifiable Effects of IT

Latin America, like other countries introducing the new IT technologies, awaits the outcome as far as growth is concerned. In industrialized countries it has been widely commented that no significant positive impact on growth of output or on total factor productivity (TFP) has yet been identified (see Chapter 7, Table 7.9 for estimates of TFP over time), a fact that seems strange to some observers given the consensus that this is a technological revolution. But students of earlier bursts of technological change note that it takes a long time for the changes to work their way through the system, with the main productivity effects showing up only after dissemination has reached a rather high level; so it is not surprising that no obvious positive output effects can be identified in the aggregate national accounts figures for Latin America.

On the distribution front, the difficulty of identifying the sources of the widespread increase in inequality has been noted above; however IT and technological change more generally are obvious candidates at this point. Evidence from other countries provides some help in this respect. The consensus for the industrial countries seems to be that new technology, and increased imports of labour-intensive goods are the main suspects for the widespread tendency towards increasing inequality during the last 15 years. As we note in Chapter 7, the experience of East Asian countries shows that such a tendency is clearly avoidable.

POLICY ISSUES AND RECOMMENDATIONS

It is assumed here that the outward-oriented strategy of most Latin American countries will continue for some time, although the precise mix between the unilateral freeing of trade and investment, maintenance of some restrictions and participation in trade blocs remains to be seen. Thus much of the policy concern, including that in the technology area, will be aimed at complementing a relatively free-trade strategy in a globalizing world. Though external pressures from the industrial world leave countries much less policy space than before, there are important decisions to be made on how to design and implement an economic policy in this new context. Greater emphasis on exports now must affect the thinking on most of the policy areas discussed here.

The IT area is also characterized by limited policy space. In terms of adoption or non-adoption of some of the new technologies, it is possible that policy may have at most a modest impact. It may certainly influence the speed and extent of their dissemination, and that may be important to their overall effect. Here, as with trade, the main decisions revolve around (1) which types of IT would be beneficial to the country, if properly complemented by policy in other areas; (2) whether policy tools exist to guide adoption in the desirable directions and away from the undesirable ones; (3) the details of policy in the areas of complementary infrastructure, education and training; and (4) special support for the adoption of IT by small and medium-size enterprise.

There are three striking similarities about policy making in the context of globalization and information technology. First, there is no assurance that the broad effects of either globalization or IT will be positive in Latin America, even though many policy makers have embraced greater openness as desirable and accepted IT as largely inevitable. Second, it is widely believed that the effects of both phenomena will be large. If such effects are both large (the general expectation) and unpredictable (my view, as argued above), it is clearly important that decision makers continue to monitor the effects as closely as possible in order either to backtrack or to redesign policy.[16] Third, positive output (efficiency) effects appear likely in each case but the distributional effects are worrisome. So the policies surrounding both phenomena should give greatest attention to guarding against and alleviating those effects. In the case of Latin America, with its legendary high levels of inequality to start with, it more generally puts a greater onus on governments to design good antipoverty and inequality policies.

In the case of IT especially, decisions have to be made about whether significant support should be given to improving local capacity. It appears that some types of benefit will not be forthcoming in the absence of such an effort, but whether it should be made is unclear since the effects of IT in general remain ambiguous.

Policies on Globalization

An optimal set of policies to help Latin America to respond to and take maximum advantage of the process of globalization includes some that will affect the rate and extent of integration into the international economy, some that are related to the accompanying policy package. Others that are not directly related to globalization or to IT but affect poverty are increasingly important owing to the risks associated with those two phenomena.

First, there should be *astute management of the new system of freer trade, investment and capital flows* so that it does not lead to instability or premature loss of productive capacity, especially in those activities and firms that create many of the lower-paid jobs. In part this involves further development of the instruments now in widespread use in industrial countries to defend against dumping and other unfair practices, import surges and so on. The small and medium sectors, which create large numbers of jobs, can be vulnerable to import surges.

Second, great care is needed in the *management of the capital account* to avoid overvaluation and instability of the real exchange rate, since both of these tend to discourage exports, reduce growth and increase unemployment. The two countries with the most successful growth performances in recent years, Chile and Colombia, both impose controls in this market.

Third, *policies designed to assure a healthy demand for labour* should give due attention to what are likely to be the major sources of productive employment over the next decade or so: the rural and the SME sector. A strong rural sector has been a hallmark of the most successful development experiences around the world, including those of Costa Rica, Indonesia, Japan, Taiwan and others; and it has been the normal precursor to healthy overall development. Most countries of Latin America have been strikingly deficient in this area, for reasons that relate to the highly unequal distribution of land. But there are enough positive experiences in the region, albeit mostly on a small scale thus far, to give some grounds for optimism.

Fourth, *general support is required for small and medium enterprises* (including microenterprises) in the form of improved credit institutions, marketing assistance (fairs, for example) and technological and training assistance. Special support should be provided to enterprises with export potential as otherwise there is a risk that the export basket, being dominated by large enterprises, will not create much employment. The experience of many countries, including Japan and some of its Asian neighbours, illustrates the potential importance of linkages between efficient modern industry and smaller firms. Though the evidence from Latin America is scant, it suggests that such mutually beneficial synergies are significantly less common than in Asia. The contribution of effective linkages of this sort is likely to be more important in open economies than in closed ones. Where it is larger firms that do most of the exporting (as in Brazil for example, see Silber, 1987), export success may bring little productive employment in its wake unless smaller subcontractors are hooked into the process.

Finally, complementary to fostering a healthy demand for labour is *strengthening the human capital* at the lower end of the earnings profile through improved coverage and quality of primary education, better and more applicable vocational education, and support for on-the-job training for lower-skilled persons. In addition, reform of the labour institutions appears to be important in some countries since malfunction there can be prejudicial to a country's success in the world market. Some of the onus of protection against unemployment should be shifted from the firm to an unemployment insurance system; and a number of Latin countries have already moved in this direction. Perhaps most of all, labour institutions need to be considered with the needs of small and medium enterprises in mind, together with those of the workers. This includes responding to the possible use of 'labour standards' as a weapon of high-wage countries as opposed to lower-wage ones. If SMEs are extensively involved in trade, as they will have to be in some countries for employment generation to proceed satisfactorily, these issues may become especially contentious.

Policies on IT: Capacity Building and the Capital Goods Industry

There is fairly general agreement that a strong capacity to foster the right sort of technological change is important in most developing countries; the disagreement revolves around what sort of change (for example does it matter greatly whether it is labour saving or not?) and what sort of institutional capacity is needed to produce the requisite change.[17] As Lall (1992, p. 171) notes, healthy industrial development requires a continuous process of technological learning, adaptation and improvement, a process that still lacks adequate inducement mechanisms.

For the countries of Latin America it is helpful to consider *three policy levels or domains*. The first level involves policies that will contribute to the effective introduction and dissemination of those desirable components of IT that will come by transfer. The second envisages an important role for domestic capabilities in complementing the process of transfer in additional ways and in developing locally relevant technologies, where much of the progress is based on local capacities and less on borrowed knowledge (within this category one might or might not see a role for leapfrogging). The third level refers to a non-local role for the country or region, whereby it develops its capabilities in line with exports that draw significantly on that domestic capability. These might include direct exports of technology or exports of products that incorporate domestically developed technology. At the first two levels the main task of local science and technology capacity is to determine which technologies are borrowed, adapted and adopted locally, and improve the capacity to adapt so that the undesirable elements of foreign technologies can be bred out of them before being used locally. Exponents of the latter are mainly worried about inappropriate technology being introduced when there is too little local capacity.

In his argument for a strong-support strategy Teitel (1992, p. 366) notes the long-term trend towards the capability to export manufactures beyond the region – even in product lines involving fairly advanced stages of value added, skills and technology. While the region's recent export performance testifies to the competitive potential of industries fostered under the old policy regime, Teitel (ibid., p. 374) notes that a substantial technological discontinuity seems to have occurred in Latin America around 1975–80. For the industrial applications required in the new fields, the learning embodied in the stock of human capital acquired during ISI is of limited use. He feels that to boost the region out of its current stagnation an enhanced role on the part of the public sector may be needed.

Perez (1985) has been a strong proponent of this view. Her view that Latin America should be trying to 'get in early at the ground floor' in the present information technology revolution is based on the conclusion that this is both feasible and desirable for a region with its current factor endowments. The implicitly or explicitly interventionist views of such authors as Perez and Teitel contrast with the neoliberal view that the process of technical change is best left to the market, especially when it involves high technology.

The optimal levels of activity in and support for technological development and capacity building vary widely among the countries of Latin America. Only a few have the potential to operate at the third level discussed above – Brazil and perhaps Mexico and Argentina. Still, the recipe for taking maximum advantage of IT may be qualitatively similar. Newness of the technology, its riskiness and the very imperfect information about it among many economic agents would imply that education and training must focus on skills complementary to the IT. Moreover, public support to improve information about IT and assistance to economic agents to bear risk, and so on may be essential for getting the IT into application in the full range of places where it would be advantageous.

Widespread application is necessary if increasing technological dichotomy among firms (correlated to their size) is to be avoided, but since rapid adoption implies a high level of labour displacement it is important for the economy to be growing rapidly so that additional job opportunities can be created, whether in the sectors most affected by it or in others. This recipe seems to have been achieved in several of the East Asian countries. Distribution appears not to have worsened significantly during the rapid increase of IT in the four tigers. In Korea it actually declined, perhaps in part due to the great expansion of subcontracting there – an expansion that linked the SME sector to international trade in a major way. Such success stories notwithstanding, *there is much uncertainty about the magnitude and timing of the impact of IT in Latin America.* The risk of attempting the recipe but failing lies in the fact that if labour displacement occurs and this is not balanced by rapid growth, the main impact of the whole process might be damage to the distribution front. In Latin America, going 'all-out' on a high-tech path is riskier than in East Asia because of the likelihood and the costs of leaving people behind. This likelihood is greater since there is no reason to suppose that economic growth will be rapid, and the costs will be greater because of the currently high level of inequality. But the costs of not pushing ahead are also large. There is the danger of losing international competitiveness, if indeed these technologies are becoming increasingly central to such competitiveness. In addition, losing out on certain technologies that are successfully applicable at low scales of production and hence are SME-friendly, would deprive SMEs of the opportunity to raise their relative productivity.

Even the lower ranges of technological capacity, to which Latin countries should be aspiring, involve sometimes challenging levels of infrastructural and human capital development. An efficient telecommunications infrastructure is an essential condition for the conduct of everyday business and hence for export success. It is also 'the basis for a rapidly expanding network of new services which can be traded internationally and can greatly enhance the efficiency of many other services, especially education and health' (Freeman *et al.*, 1995, p. 592). The frequent claim (for example Kaplinsky, 1990) that the new technologies make it possible to produce at a smaller scale than with the earlier technologies remains controversial. James (1993, p. 432) observes that thus far there is virtually no empirical evidence to support this claim, while Alcorta (1992) has suggested that the impact at the firm level may be scaling-up rather than the opposite. It is important to sort out how much of the earlier adoption of IT by larger firms was due to economies of scale and how much was due to information asymmetries and different lags in the implementation of such technologies. Also relevant in this connection is the extent to which the increasing use of IT in banks and other financial institutions enhances their capacity to serve the needs of SMEs by lowering transactions costs. Improved performance in credit verification, a typical information-intensive area, might improve their outreach to SMEs. Certainly one of the main tasks of local technology efforts in Latin American countries should be aimed at reaching small and medium firms, which are often found in outlying regions, and improving their technological options. This can be done by making new technologies available to them, adapting these technologies, blending new with traditional technologies and so on. While the objective is obvious, it is less clear how far it might succeed, and what policies are most likely to make it successful. Several points can be made in this respect.

First, infrastructure development in the smaller urban and rural areas of many Latin countries, which is often desirable irrespective of the new IT, may be more so in the presence of those options. One of the striking aspects of the successful development of some East Asian countries (especially Taiwan) is the role of rural electrification, plus the rural industrialization and the general non-agricultural dynamism that went with it. Might rural communication improvements have a similar effect? They would be especially important in tying smaller firms to international markets; FAX machines are now *de rigueur* for many small exporters and constitute a major improvement in their information and communications capacity (Levy *et al.*, 1994).

Second, 'blending' should be given serious attention. As Bhalla (1996, p. 13) notes, 'A proper integration of new technologies into traditional modes of production offers much better prospects of learning-by-doing, of local experiments in adaptation and capacity development, than an indiscriminate use of new technologies in the advanced sectors of economic activity.'

Unfortunately few resources have been directed towards either blending or other approaches to the advance of appropriate technology in Latin America. Total spending on R&D has been small and the SME-directed component much smaller still. Information about the various activities that do contribute in this direction is quite unorganized.

The Capital Goods Industry

Bruton (1985, p. 81) argues that 'technological advance must occur in response to the conditions within the country's economic and social system rather than be imposed or simply made available from outside sources'. He argues that the first condition for the establishment of an indigenous capability lies on the demand side, that is, when the users are searching for new knowledge that begins the process of their production over broad areas of the economy.[18] For there to be an adequate supply response, a domestic capital goods industry is essential.[19] A related issue is assistance in the importation and refurbishment of used equipment. This is important both to widen the scope of available technologies (usually in the direction of more appropriate ones) and to facilitate the creation and survival of small firms, which are the locus of labour-intensive production in most countries.[20]

The Role of Government

The successful spread of IT depends on an active support policy, according to authors such as Mody and Dahlman (1992, p. 1703). They conclude that 'effective planning and organizational capabilities are essential to successful adoption of the new (information) technologies'. Though TNCs are an important vehicle for the transfer of technical knowledge, they are unlikely by themselves to satisfy the needs of the host country due to some combination of inappropriate technology being transferred, transfer that is unhelpful because of its focus on products rather than processes,[21] and more generally a failure to contribute to the domestic knowledge-accumulation process[22] and the associated indigenous technological capacity. 'Indeed, it is easy to find evidence that they may well harm any effort to do so' (Bruton, 1985, p. 101). Lall (1992, p. 198) notes that, despite its size and capital goods base, Brazil has retained a high dependence on foreign technology in the form of foreign direct investment. Its dynamic indigenous private sector is 'wedged between' TNC dominance in some industries and that of public-sector enterprises in others. Though it has had some major successes, the Brazilian strategy has thus far proved ineffective in improving the dynamism and competitiveness of large areas of industry. Mexico has not adopted the Brazilian style of intervention to develop specific technologies.

Notes

1. The term 'marginalization' is used in this chapter to refer to a situation or a process in which segments of a population do not share the fruits of economic growth and social change, or in more extreme cases, are isolated and made worse off by it. The main operational measures are low levels of income, education, health/nutrition and housing – the standard indicators of material poverty. Losses so measured often go hand in hand with social and political marginalization.

2. The current price trends are different from those in constant prices because the relative price of capital goods changes in individual countries, and also because the relative price of the currencies changes so that their weights in the regional totals change.

3. Since poverty is determined by private purchasing power and by what governments provide, a further relevant distinction is between private income and spending and public-sector income and spending. Globalization may affect the public-sector share, as well as the way in which the benefits of public spending are divided among people.

4. A prominent statement was that of Nun (1969). An interesting critique came from Perlman (1976).

5. Of course technological advance is harder to gauge than most of the other variables under discussion. Microeconomic evidence contradicting the theory has come from studies such as that of Fairchild (1979, p. 135). His comparison between national firms and joint ventures in the city of Monterrey found no evidence of greater technical innovation in the joint ventures, though the Mexican firms relied much more on the founders or other local people for technical information than did the joint ventures. Aggregate data, while subject to quality constraints, have likewise not suggested a low rate of technological change in Latin American manufacturing.

6. For example if a country tends to export what domestic demand does not absorb. The main tests of direction of causation have been intracountry (for example Sharma and Dhakal, 1995); though they clearly suffer from a range of methodological limitations and deficiencies of their own, they have detracted from the strong hypothesis cited above.

7. Most studies reporting the positive correlation in question have been consistency checks for the reference hypothesis rather than serious attempts to confront it with the more obvious alternatives – various other variables, including imports. Fishlow (1994) criticizes the World Bank's (1991) statement of the merits of openness on this count.

8. Such denial might be either on the ground that the 'learning by doing' on which the argument is based is quantitatively insignificant (a very hard position

to sustain in these days of emphasis on the importance of learning through this and other routes), or on the ground that governments do not have the skill to implement such protection competently. The second view seems more plausible.

9. In his survey of developments in the economics of R&D, Stiglitz (1987, p. 75) notes that in this area 'Adam Smith's invisible hand is not only not visible, but there is considerable evidence that it is not even there'.

10. Freeman *et al.* (1995, p. 600) predict that the bias that has appeared in the last 10–15 years against the use of unskilled workers, or those whose skills are wrongly suited to evolving needs and who are not easily retrainable, is likely to become much more pronounced in the rest of the decade.

11. Freeman and Soete (1994) note the potential value of job-creation programmes for these workers in community and personal services, which have a high growth potential partly because the imperatives of international competition will not exert the same degree of force there as on tradables.

12. This process may explain why countries such as China, Indonesia, Thailand and the Philippines have shown very rapid growth in trade in information and communication (ICT) products.

13. In Argentina, Chile and Mexico, for example, the increases in inequality occurred mainly during economic downturn or crisis but in Colombia and Ecuador they did not. Even in the former cases post-crisis inequality, while sometimes less than the peak level sustained during crisis, in general has been markedly higher than the pre-reform level.

14. The latter has also been proposed as a source of worsening in Mexico (Feenstra and Hanson, 1995).

15. Regarding the Latin American experience, see Berry (1997a) and Robbins (1995a, 1995b). Increases in inequality also coincided with the liberalization in Hong Kong and Taiwan in the 1980s, although not in Korea or Singapore, where the relative supply of more educated workers increased strongly (Wood, 1995).

16. James (1993, p. 425) refers to the striking absence of general equilibrium macro modelling of the impacts of microelectronics and biotechnologies in developing countries, even though these are becoming sufficiently widely adopted to be able to gauge their detectable effects.

17. The case for local technological capacity has been made in great detail by Lall (1993, 1995a) and Bruton (1985) in the context of Third World countries in general, and by Perez (1985) and Teitel (1992) in the Latin American context.

18. Bruton cites Freeman's (1973) study of the success and failure of innovations in the UK, which showed that the single measure most correlated with success was 'user need understood'; the innovation was designed to meet a need of the potential user.

19. A question that arises in these days of trade liberalization (and also of trade blocs) is whether the latter can improve the scope for fulfilment of this need.

20. The role of equipment specialists who imported, repaired, installed and guaranteed machinery used by small and medium firms in Colombia is discussed in Cortes *et al.* (1987) and Escandon (1981).

21. TNCs depend very heavily on the home market to develop their new products, and often bring to the LDC a new product (often a luxury) with little linkage to the domestic economy. Process technologies – for example, layout, testing procedures, properties of materials and so on – are more likely to be useful in developing countries than new products, since they may have wider application and be free from the undesirable features just noted.

22.   One manifestation is the infrequency of the common phenomenon in rich countries of engineers or other skilled personnel leaving the parent company to create their own businesses (Bruton, 1985, p. 100). It might be expected to be less common in the case of TNCs since a higher proportion are foreign and a higher proportion are likely to see their future as solidly linked to the firm. It is noteworthy that national firms often have considerable spin-offs of this sort. Cortes *et al.* (1987) emphasize the frequency and importance of new firms created in this way in the agricultural machinery industry and furniture industry in Colombia. In the former, such spin-offs were an integral part of the process of quality improvements and price reduction, as they increased competition and provided a challenge for the application of good ideas that were bottled up in the parent firm.

4 The Impact of Globalization on South Asia

Azizur Rahman Khan

The purpose of this chapter is to analyse the impact that the increasing globalization of the world economy is having on South Asia. The analysis focuses on five major countries – Bangladesh, India, Nepal, Pakistan and Sri Lanka – which account for an overwhelming proportion of the population of South Asia.[1] In 1994, these five countries together had a population of 1.2 billion, 21 per cent of world population and 38 per cent of the population of the low-income countries, a category to which they all belong.[2] By any absolute standard of poverty these five South Asian countries account for close to half of the world's poor.[3]

In this chapter, the term globalization refers to the trend reduction in barriers to the international movement of goods, services, capital and technology. The world economy has gradually been moving in this direction for a long time, but the process accelerated during the 1980s. Two events that provided a qualitative boost to this trend were (1) the gradual rejection of trade restrictions nurtured by the strategy of import-substituting industrialization (ISI) that an overwhelming majority of less developed countries (LDCs) had adopted in the post-Second World-War period, and (2) the demise of the socialist system that had insulated its members, now classified as LDCs, from the world economy, and indeed from each other. The first of these phenomena spread in the wake of the debt crisis and the subsequent adjustments that the developing countries adopted, often at the behest of the multilateral development agencies, from the beginning of the 1980s. The second phenomenon began at about the same time, with the launching of post-Mao reforms in China, but came to encompass the entire socialist world in the late 1980s. While the earlier trend towards the liberalization of world trade was led by the advanced industrial countries, the major impetus towards the globalization of the world economy in its current phase thus derived from the actions of the developing countries.

The principal elements of the process need to be clearly identified. First, there is an increased flow of goods and services among nations due to a reduction of protection of all forms: quantitative trade restrictions, tariff and non-tariff barriers. Second, there is an increased international mobility of capital due to a lowering of obstacles to its movement. It should be noted,

103

however, that there has not been a corresponding increase in the mobility of labour, especially of the unskilled variety with which the LDCs are relatively abundantly endowed. A third element of globalization consists of the flow of technology. Increased trade and capital flows have, by and large, meant an increased flow of technology among nations, although not all aspects of globalization have been unambiguously favourable to it. Under the rules of globalization, individual nations have been committed to a greater respect for intellectual property rights, which may have increased the cost of technology for many LDCs. Finally, the era of globalization has coincided with the revolution in information technology (IT), which has sharply reduced the cost of international information flow and thus facilitated trade and capital flows. This has also vastly improved the ease of cultural exchange among nations, with far-reaching social and political consequences.

Individual countries or groups of countries have the option of becoming integrated into the globalizing world economy or remaining insulated from it. But they do not have the option of stopping the process of globalization itself in so far as much of the world has become part of it. Individual countries must now compete more fiercely than in the past for a share of the widening world market in goods and services because many more countries have abandoned the inward-looking ISI strategy of the past. Similarly they must compete more vigorously than in the past for a share of international capital flows because many more countries have drastically reduced obstacles to capital movement. In this sense, individual LDCs do not have the choice of ignoring the process of globalization. They must find a way of coping with it.

Of course individual developing countries can opt not to integrate into the globalizing world economy by perpetuating some variant of the ISI regime and/or by maintaining obstacles to capital flows. It is easy to imagine that large social groups in many countries nurtured in an environment of comparative autarky in the past, would suffer adverse consequences, at least during the transition from the existing production structure to the more efficient production structure that would emerge after successful integration. Whether or not these countries wish to become integrated depends on their relative valuation of the possible loss due to the disruption of the existing structure of production and the potential gain to be derived from integration.

Once a country decides to become integrated into the global economy, success is not guaranteed. It must embark on a programme of economic reform that will make integration possible, that is, increase its external trade as a proportion of GDP and gain access to increased inflows of foreign capital and technology. Furthermore, successful integration into the global economy, according to the above indicators, does not guarantee the achievement of the economic and social goals that provide the impetus for integration. It is possible that the original estimates of potential gains and losses of integration will turn out to be false. Even if the original estimates prove to be valid, the accelerated growth in overall GDP may result in a distribution of incremental output that is inconsistent with the country's social goals.

The following section briefly surveys the reform programmes implemented by the South Asian countries to facilitate their integration into the global economy and analyzes their success in attaining this objective. The next section considers the growth and distributional consequences of the process of integration. The final section summarizes the main findings concerning the successes and failures of South Asia's quest for greater integration into the globalizing world economy.

SOUTH ASIA'S INTEGRATION INTO THE GLOBAL ECONOMY

The countries of South Asia followed similar strategies of development in the post-colonial era, adhering to an ISI strategy that varied among countries, not in terms of essence, but in the extent of successful industrialization. India achieved ISI on the broadest front, followed by Pakistan and Sri Lanka, with Bangladesh and Nepal lagging considerably behind. In terms of growth in GDP, only Pakistan exceeded an average annual rate of 5 per cent during the 1965–80 period. Sri Lanka and India averaged growth rates of 4 per cent or just under, while Bangladesh and Nepal averaged less than 2.5 per cent.[4]

Unlike much of the rest of the developing world, South Asia was not, however, severely hit by the debt crisis in the beginning of the 1980s. Bangladesh was the only country to have a debt–service ratio (DSR) of more than 25 per cent, with Pakistan coming second at 18 per cent. The other three countries had a very manageable burden of external debt service.

However it became clear that these countries' growth rates were far lower than what was needed to address their urgent problem of poverty reduction and social development. Some countries began to realize the limitations of the inward-looking development as fostered by the ISI strategy during the 1970s. But it was during the 1980s that *all* the South Asian countries gradually came to espouse a more outward-looking development strategy, emphasizing export growth, openness to foreign capital and technology and generally greater integration into the global economy.[5]

Policies for Greater Openness

To bring about the desired reorientation of development strategy, extensive policy and institutional changes were made in these countries. The first, and obviously the most important, area of reform was the trade regime. All these countries gradually moved away from an overvalued exchange rate regime towards a more market-determined, external valuation of their currencies. This was combined with a sharp reduction in quantitative restrictions on imports and a reduction in the tariff rates. There was also a move towards reduction of the variable tariffs on different kinds of imports. The general effect was to reduce discrimination against exports and to open up domestic industries to greater competition with producers abroad.

These countries also adopted extensive measures to attract foreign direct investment. Restrictions in the form of minimum domestic equity participation were eased, provisions for profit repatriation and tax concessions were made more generous, and export-processing zones were created. Domestic stock markets were opened up to foreign investors at the same time that measures were adopted for the expansion of these markets.

Industrial regulations were greatly reduced. There was a drastic reduction in the number of industries earmarked as public monopolies, and regulations were eased on the foreign exchange needed for the acquisition of raw materials, equipment and spares. In varying degrees these countries encouraged the privatization of nationalized industries and widened the area of operation of private enterprises, both domestic and foreign.

Deregulation also extended to the factor market. Market forces were allowed a greater role in the determination of prices and the allocation of credit. Attempts were also made to increase the flexibility of the labour market, although this had generally limited success.

Since the economies pursued greater openness within the broader objective of transition to a more market-oriented system, the above reforms were complemented with extensive price, distribution and macroeconomic policy reforms. Subsidies on agricultural inputs and utilities were reduced or abolished. Public procurement and distribution of food and other goods were drastically curtailed. There was a general emphasis on macroeconomic stabilization through reduction of the fiscal deficit and control of monetary expansion, with varying degrees of success.

The reforms did not progress at the same rate in all the countries. Nor did they proceed at a steady rate everywhere. But the system of controls and incentives were fundamentally altered everywhere between the late 1970s and the early 1990s with the following features: (1) the domestic currencies of these countries very nearly achieved current account convertibility; (2) quantitative restrictions on imports were drastically reduced in comparison with the past and the rate of tariff protection was brought down sharply, thereby substantially opening up the domestic market to imports from the rest of the world; (3) incentives (disincentives) to exports were improved (reduced) very substantially; and (4) it became possible for private foreign investors to operate in much wider area of these economies under more attractive terms than before.[6]

It is difficult to carry out a rigorous analysis of the effectiveness of the outward-looking reforms undertaken in the individual countries due to the difficulty of precisely dating their implementation. Sri Lanka and Bangladesh started in the late 1970s. In Pakistan reforms were begun in the early 1980s but intensified in 1987–88. The Indian reforms got under way in the early 1980s but were greatly intensified in 1991. Nepal began its reforms in the mid 1980s. It is likely that the reforms started to produce results some time in the second half of the 1980s, with more clearly discernible results coming later in India's case. As Tables 4.1, 4.2 and 4.3 show, the South Asian countries have achieved considerable success according to several indicators of integration, but they have not performed particularly well against other indicators.

Export Growth

All the South Asian countries were substantially more export-oriented in 1994 than in 1980. The growth rate of exports was particularly rapid during the early 1990s. Not only did exports rise as a proportion of GDP and as a proportion of world exports, the composition of exports also changed sharply in favour of manufactured goods and away from primary goods (Table 4.1).

The improved trade performance of the South Asian countries during the period of globalization should, however, be put in perspective. First, it should be noted that the weighted export/GDP ratio of these countries in 1994 (13.4 per cent) was well below the export/GDP ratio of the 51 low-income LDCs (19 per cent).[7] These countries have indeed increased their share of world exports during the era of globalization, but their combined exports only increased from 0.66 per cent of world exports in 1980 to 0.89 per cent in 1994.[8]

Second, the hope that increased diversification into manufactured exports would protect these countries from a decline in the terms of trade was not borne out in many cases: with the exception of India, all these countries have

Table 4.1   Indicators of export growth of South Asian countries

	Exports as % of GDP		Growth rate of exports (% per year)			Manufactured exports as % of total exports	
	1980	1994	1970–80	1980–90	1990–94	1986	1993
Bangladesh	6	12	3.8	7.5	12.7	73	81
India	7	12	4.3	6.3	7.0	62	75
Nepal	12	24	10.9	7.8	22.1	68	84
Pakistan	12	16	0.7	9.5	8.8	68	85
Sri Lanka	32	34	2.0	6.3	17.0	41	71

Note: The first two columns refer to exports of goods and non-factor services. All other columns refer to merchandise exports.
Sources: World Bank (1988, 1993a, 1995a, 1996a).

experienced a significant deterioration of their terms of trade during the period of globalization.[9]

Third, there has been little increase in trade *among* the South Asian countries. It is paradoxical that these countries, because of the large-scale, actual and potential complementarities that exist among their economies, should undertake an export-led development strategy while remaining virtually autarkic with respect to each other. As Table 4.2 shows, trade among these countries is extremely low. In recent years, shares of exports to other South Asian countries have fallen for Bangladesh, Pakistan and Sri Lanka and increased marginally for Nepal. Only India has registered a significant increase in exports to its South Asian neighbours; but nonetheless the share remains pitifully low. The time period covered by Table 4.2 is admittedly short, but information about the share of intraregional trade for the region as a whole is available over a longer period and it does not indicate a pattern of dynamic growth. Together the five South Asian countries sent 3.3 per cent of their aggregate exports to other South Asian countries in 1980. In 1994 the proportion rose to 4.1 per cent. Admittedly there is an unquantified flow of illegal trade between Bangladesh and India, between Pakistan and India, and between India and Nepal, but the very fact that trade among these countries has been partly driven underground is a testimony to the hostility

Table 4.2   Trade among South Asian countries (per cent of total exports of countries of origin)

	Destination					Total South Asia
	Bangladesh	India	Nepal	Pakistan	Sri Lanka	
Origin:						
Bangladesh						
1990	–	1.3	0.7	1.3	0.1	3.4
1993	–	0.4	0.2	1.3	0.6	2.5
India						
1990	1.7	–	0.3	0.2	0.7	2.9
1994	2.5	–	0.5	0.2	1.4	4.6
Nepal						
1990	1.6	12.2	–	–	–	13.8
1993	0.3	9.9	–	0.2	4.5	14.9
Pakistan						
1990	1.8	0.9	–	–	1.2	3.9
1994	1.6	0.6	–	–	0.9	3.1
Sri Lanka						
1990	0.5	1.1	0.1	1.7	–	3.4
1994	0.2	0.7	–	1.3	–	2.2

Source: United Nations (1995).

of public policy to integration among them, which is ironic in view of their membership of the South Asian Association for Regional Cooperation (SAARC).

Capital Flows

Table 4.3 shows the trend in private capital flows – foreign direct investment (FDI) and net portfolio equity investment (PEI) – in South Asia during the era of globalization.[10] Both these types of foreign capital, especially PEI, have increased in absolute magnitude in recent years. But South Asia's share of aggregate FDI flows into LDCs – the most dynamic component of foreign resources – representing a combination of capital, technology, management and international marketing – has actually declined over time. In recent years there has been a sharp rise in PEI due largely to the privatization programmes under which parts or all of the equity of state-owned enterprises were offered for sale, often to non-resident nationals.

Information Technology

Although little is known precisely about the development of information technology (IT) in South Asia during the period of globalization, two distinct aspects are apparent. The first of these is the development of the industry for domestic use and export. The importance of this lies in the fact that the world demand for this industry's products is rising faster than for most other products. A share in this rapidly expanding market provides assurance of rapid export growth. There are instances of LDCs setting up industries in microelectronics, semiconductors and software by attracting FDI and investing in physical and human capital. Korea, Taiwan and Singapore

Table 4.3   Private foreign investment in South Asia (value is in US$ billion, share represents percentage of total for all LDCs)

| | Foreign direct investment | | Portfolio equity investment | |
	Value	*Share*	*Value*	*Share*
1980	0.2	3.6	0.0	n.a.
1985	0.3	2.3	0.0	n.a.
1990	0.5	1.9	0.1	2.7
1991	0.5	1.3	0.0	n.a.
1992	0.6	1.3	0.4	2.8
1993	0.8	1.2	2.0	4.4
1994	1.2	1.6	6.2	17.8

Source: World Bank (1996c), pp. 134–6.

have already emerged as major IT traders, after the United States, Japan, the European Union, and Canada. Malaysia, Indonesia, Thailand and China are rapidly emerging as second-tier international IT traders.[11]

Quantitative knowledge about the extent to which the South Asian countries have succeeded in this kind of enterprise is virtually non-existent. It is, however, well known that India has made a successful venture into software, for which the prospects look bright. Until recently Western companies recruited large numbers of computer programmers from Bangalore at low wages (by Western standards), but many of those programmers have returned to Bangalore to launch their own software firms and have emerged as significant exporters to the industrial countries.[12] This clearly indicates that India (and some of the other South Asian countries) has the distinct possibility of becoming a significant producer and exporter of certain components of IT technology once the remuneration paid to trained personnel, in which the region is well endowed, is adequate and sufficient investment is forthcoming.

The second aspect of the development of IT is the improvement of IT infrastructure in order to improve the efficiency and productivity of the industrial and service sectors. It has been argued that an improved IT infrastructure reduces the cost of communications and increases productivity, especially of scarce skilled labour. Furthermore it has been suggested that IT improves the relative advantage of small-scale enterprises because of the relative efficiency with which it can be used even when the scale of operation is small.[13] Once again information on the spread of IT infrastructure is very limited, although it is known that several South Asian countries, notably India, have made significant strides in promoting IT at the firm level.

Table 4.4 shows South Asia's endowment in some of the more traditional components of IT. The region clearly lags far behind the average developing countries, although the better endowed of the South Asian countries are on a

Table 4.4 Indicators of communications technology in South Asia (per thousand persons in the early 1990s)

	Telephone	Radio	Television
Bangladesh	2	44	5
India	7	80	37
Nepal	3	34	2
Pakistan	9	91	18
Sri Lanka	7	200	49
LDC average	23	176	56
China	7	182	31

Source: UNDP (1996).

par with China, a country that has achieved unprecedented growth by taking advantage of the globalization process.

GROWTH AND POVERTY

The argument that integration into the globalizing world economy enhances growth, improves the distribution of income and helps reduce poverty is based on the standard theory of trade. Integration leads to an allocation of resources that is consistent with comparative advantage, which represents greater efficiency and higher output. The end of ISI means that industries are no longer insulated from international competition or condemned to the limited scale dictated by the domestic market. These changes enhance efficiency and ensure higher productivity. A greater inflow of foreign capital and technology further contributes to growth. Adherence to comparative advantage leads to a concentration of labour-intensive industries, the abundant factor of production in the LDCs. This leads to a faster increase in employment and wages, which improves the distribution of income and reduces poverty. To what extent have these expectations been realized in South Asia in the decade of increased integration into the world economy?

Globalization and Economic Growth

Table 4.5 shows the South Asian countries' rates of growth from 1970–95. Most of these countries achieved higher growth during the 1980s than during the 1970s. Several of them, however, failed to maintain this higher growth in the early 1990s. It is difficult to determine how much of the acceleration of the growth rate in the 1980s compared with the 1970s was due to greater integration into the world economy because in most cases this took place during the

Table 4.5   GDP growth rates for South Asian countries
(per cent per year)

	1970–80	1980–90	1990–94	1995
Bangladesh	2.4*	4.3	4.2	4.4
India	3.4	5.8	3.8	6.2
Nepal	2.0	4.6	4.9	5.8
Pakistan	4.9	6.3	4.6	5.3
Sri Lanka	4.1	4.2	5.4	5.5

* 4.2 per cent between 1975 and 1980.
Sources: World Bank (1995a, 1996a); Bangladesh Bureau of Statistics (1996); International Monetary Fund (1996).

decade itself, and generally quite late. A country by country analysis of periodic changes in the rate of growth illustrates the dilemma more clearly.

In Bangladesh, the annual average growth rate during the 1970s was biased downwards due to the dislocations of the war of independence. If the first few years of dislocation after independence are excluded, there has been no change in the periodic growth rates since 1975. Extensive reform of economic policies and institutions, leading to a far greater external orientation than in the past, has not led to any perceptible acceleration of growth in GDP.

In Pakistan, economic growth appears to have been a matter of political cycles.[14] Indeed the highest rate of growth was achieved during the 1960s (6.8 per cent per year) using an ISI strategy, supported by large capital inflow and under an authoritarian regime. Under the democratically elected regime the growth rate fell to 4.8 per cent per year between 1970 and 1977. Between 1977 and 1988, again under an authoritarian regime, the growth rate accelerated to 6.7 per cent per year. Economic reforms began with deregulation and privatization during this period, when a spectacular rise in remittances by migrants provided a major impetus to growth. From 1988, after the restoration of democracy and the acceleration of reforms aimed at greater integration into the world economy, the rate of growth fell below 5 per cent per year, on average.

In India, the rate of growth accelerated significantly during the 1980s and it has been claimed that this was, at least partly, due to the beginning of reforms in the early to mid 1980s. The strongly externally oriented and accelerated reforms from 1991, however, were accompanied by a fall in the growth rate, which was at least partly attributable to a weather-induced slowdown in agricultural growth in the early 1990s. In India the impact of globalization has been far weaker than in, say, China, where the sharp slowdown of agriculture after the mid 1980s was easily outweighed by the extraordinary surge of the non-agricultural economy under China's rapid integration policy.

In Nepal, the higher growth rate in the 1980s predated the beginning of reforms by at least half a decade. Sri Lanka's reform began in the late 1970s, but periodic interruptions to the reform programme and the serious ethnic conflict make it very difficult to judge its effects on growth, which was about the same in the 1980s as in the 1970s. Growth accelerated in the early 1990s and credit for this has been attributed to the country's increased commitment to reforms since 1989.

The growth performance of South Asia during the era of globalization has thus been mixed. Either there is no evidence of a rise in the trend rate of growth (Bangladesh and Pakistan), or the rise clearly predates the beginning of global integration (Nepal) or the increase in growth has been relatively modest (India and Sri Lanka) and not robust enough to prevent periodic lapses into low growth (India). The point is not that increased integration into the global economy has not resulted in further growth, but rather that the added impulse has not been strong enough to outweigh structural and cyclical shocks to the economy (for example bad weather and political cycles).

One popular explanation of the weakness of the growth impulse that should result from globalization is that the economic reform programme has not gone far enough. This view, which is dominant among the multilateral development agencies, is unconvincing though extremely difficult to refute. It is difficult to refute because it is always possible to show that the incentive system contains substantial irrationalities. However, it is obvious that the reforms have radically transformed the incentive systems of the South Asian countries. While it is difficult to compare levels of reform and incentive systems across countries, it could be argued that reform of the trade regime and the incentive system in general has been more extensive in South Asia than in China. The success of reforms has clearly been enormously greater in China than in South Asia (notably India).

The alternative explanation of the inadequate growth performance in post-reform South Asia is that successful integration into the world economy requires more measures than just reform of the trade regime and other incentives for greater allocative efficiency. Without additional measures the growth impulse is weakened or even rendered ineffective. The additional measures required vary from one country to another and their identification is too big a task to be tackled in the present study. There are, however, three common missing elements that stand out in the case of the countries of South Asia.

The first relates to the inadequate political structure within which South Asia has been pursuing its development goals. This has two distinct dimensions: regional and national. Regionally, South Asia consists of a group of countries with serious bilateral hostilities and tensions that are an impediment to their development. Quite apart from the commitment of intolerably large volumes of resources to defence, these hostilities and tensions have prevented the growth of trade among these countries, a phenomenon that was discussed in the previous section. Elsewhere – for example East Asia (see Chapter 5) – opening up to the world economy began with a sharp increase in trade with regional neighbours. When trade with neighbours is blocked by artificial barriers, much of the potential incremental effect on exports is lost. There are additional costs of such 'regional autarky', for example FDI would have been far greater had the state of autarky not existed among the SAARC neighbours.

Another political dimension inhibiting growth benefits from integration is that all the South Asian countries have had serious problems of governance. In Sri Lanka this has taken the form of open ethnic warfare. In Bangladesh and Pakistan there has been an endless quest for a non-dictatorial regime that is able to govern effectively. In India there has been a gradual erosion of the authority of the central government and a failure to create a system of governance that takes account of the great regional diversity of the country.

The second element is lack of an incentive system to compensate for the abolition of the incentive system under ISI. Whatever its inefficiencies, the ISI strategy provided a strong incentive to invest. Once the system was scrapped, an alternative incentive system should have been created to maintain the incentive to invest. This is especially important in view of the 'generalized infancy' suffered by industries in South Asia due to inadequate infrastructure and skills, as well as administrative overheads and institutional preconditions. It is well documented that a crucial element of success in East Asian development was targeted public support of potentially worthwhile industries.[15] That dismantling an ISI regime without creating an alternative incentive system can adversely affect the incentive to invest is most graphically demonstrated by Bangladesh, where the rate of investment fell from its peak of 16 per cent of GDP in 1980–81 to less than 12 per cent in the early 1990s.[16] This prolonged decline in the rate of investment is the central explanation of Bangladesh's stagnant growth rate. Similarly, in Bangladesh and elsewhere, agricultural production was adversely affected by the market reforms: the reduction or abolition of input subsidies and other forms of support were not compensated for by alternative incentives to produce. Without targeted support it is hard to see how these countries could establish industries such as IT even if they do have potential comparative advantage in them.

The third element is related to the issue just discussed. Compared with successful developing countries in East Asia, South Asia's infrastructure and human capital are relatively underdeveloped (Sri Lanka being an exception in the case of the latter).

Table 4.6 shows some of the readily available indicators for South Asia, developing East Asia and South-East Asia and the Pacific. South Asia's disadvantage relative to the rest of developing Asia is all-embracing but is particularly acute in basic human capital and the human capital endowment of women (reflected in the very low index for gender-related development). As human capital is a principal determinant of labour productivity, South Asia's international competitiveness in the globalizing world economy is seriously handicapped.

What about the argument that the gains from globalization will be greater in the future as a result of the reforms agreed during the Uruguay Round of GATT? OECD tariff and non-tariff barriers often constitute greater protection against exports from LDCs – particularly the South Asian countries – than from the industrialized countries.[17] Once the OECD countries fully implement the Uruguay Round reforms – including the tariff reduction for manufactured products, tariffication of non-tariff barriers in agriculture,

Table 4.6   Indicators of human development and infrastructure
(reference year 1993)

	South Asia	East Asia	South-East Asia & Pacific
Life expectancy (years)	60.3	68.8	63.7
Adult literacy (per cent)	48.8	81.0	86.0
Combined enrolment rate at all levels of education	52	58	59
Human Development Index	0.444	0.633	0.646
Gender-Related Development Index	0.410	0.610	0.621
Radios per thousand persons	87	212	153
Televisions per thousand persons	33	38	60
Commercial energy per capita (kg of oil equivalent)	267	711	380

Source: UNDP (1996), which explains both concept and measurement of the human development index and the gender-related development index.

reduction of export and production subsidies in agriculture, and elimination of the Multifibre Arrangement – there should be substantial gains for the LDCs, including the South Asian countries. Detailed numerical exercises have been carried out to estimate these gains. The model with the most detailed regional estimates shows that the total direct (that is, short-term) gains for South Asia from all these reforms will amount to 1 per cent of its GDP, and that when all indirect benefits are accounted for these gains will amount to 2 per cent of GDP.[18] Two points need to be noted. First, these gains, though significant, are not very high. Indeed South Asia will appropriate less than 4 per cent of the global benefits of Uruguay Round liberalization according to the model just cited. Second, these numerical estimates are based on continuation of the market shares of the individual countries concerned. There is nothing immutable about these market shares in a globalizing world economy. Rather the actual outcome will be determined by the international competitiveness of countries and regions.

Poverty Trends during the Era of Globalization

Reasonably good estimates of long-term trends in the incidence of absolute poverty – per cent of population below a defined, constant, real per capita income or expenditure, usually anchored to a minimum level of nutrition in a benchmark year with allowance for minimum non-food expenditure, and updated by increases in the cost of living – are available for Bangladesh, India and Pakistan. Some rudimentary estimates are available for Nepal, but estimates of poverty trends in Sri Lanka are not available.

Poverty Trends in Bangladesh

According to available estimates the incidence of absolute poverty in Bangladesh declined significantly between the mid 1970s and the mid 1980s, but since then the incidence of poverty appears to have increased. Evidence for this is available from several sources.[19]

Estimates of the incidence of poverty have been made by using data from the Household Expenditure Surveys (HES) of the Bangladesh Bureau of Statistics (BBS) for different years. According to the BBS estimates, the proportion of the population in extreme poverty, those with a per capita food energy consumption of less than 1805 kilocalories per day, increased from 22 per cent in 1985–86 to 28 per cent in 1991–92 (quoted in World Bank, 1995c). Alternative estimates of poverty have been made by Ravallion and Sen (1994) by applying a constant real income poverty threshold to the HES data. All three indices of poverty – the headcount ratio, the poverty gap index and the squared poverty gap index – used by Ravallion and Sen reveal a steady rise between 1985–86 and 1991–92.[20]

Unfortunately HES data are not available after 1991–92. Conflicting evidence from several alternative sources, each documenting change over short periods on the basis of relatively small samples of data, are often cited in support of divergent claims about trends in the incidence of poverty since 1991–92. The next HES data (for the year 1995–96) have not yet been released, so we shall take the trend in real wages of agricultural workers as an indicator of the living standard of the masses. In the past this index moved consistently with the trend in the incidence of poverty estimated from the HES. It is highly implausible that the living standard of the masses in Bangladesh's overwhelmingly dominant rural society would improve (deteriorate) while the index of real wages fell (rose) significantly. After rising steadily during the first half of the 1980s the real wages of agricultural workers declined by as much as 20.1 per cent – that is, 2.5 per cent per year – between 1985–86 and 1994–95.[21] It is true that wages are just one source of rural income, accounting for about two fifths of the income of poor rural households. It is, however, highly unlikely that the kind of decline in the supply price of agricultural labourers indicated by the above trend in real wages would be consistent with a non-diminishing real income of the households supplying agricultural workers. It, therefore, seems highly likely that in the early 1990s there was a further increase in the incidence of poverty in rural Bangladesh, the overwhelmingly dominant part of the country.

Another strong indicator of a fall in the real income of the poor is the decline in the real price of basic food (grain and rice) in spite of a fall in the per capita consumption of rice and cereals over the last two decades (this issue is dealt with in detail in Khan, 1990). More recently, between 1989–90 and 1995–96 there was a 7 per cent decline in the per capita consumption of cereals but a steady rise in per capita income. That this happened without a rise in the real price of rice – indeed the price fell – points to a negative income elasticity of demand for cereals, which is highly implausible given the low average level of food energy consumption in Bangladesh. The only way to make sense of the evidence is to assume that there has been a fall in the real income of the poorer population groups, who have a higher income elasticity for cereals than do the richer groups of people, so that the weighted average income elasticity of demand turned out to be negative.[22]

The rate of growth in per capita income was higher in the decade after 1985 than in the previous decade due to a decline in the rate of population growth. And yet the incidence of poverty declined significantly in the decade before 1985 while it appears to have increased in the subsequent decade. This asymmetrical performance needs careful analysis. Two possible reasons for the increase in poverty since the mid 1980s suggest themselves. The first is the decline in the growth of agriculture in this period, especially since the late 1980s, which must have been the main reason for the decline in real wages in agriculture. It has been alleged that the decline in agricultural growth was at least partly due to the withdrawal of subsidies on inputs, which was an integral part of the overall reform programme aimed at integration into the global economy. The second possible explanation is the gradual elimination of consumer subsidies and special programmes, which might have increased the cost of living and reduced the real incomes of the poorer segments of the population relative to others. This too was a part of the reforms to promote global economic integration.

Poverty Trends in India[23]

Headcount indices of poverty for selected years for India are shown in Table 4.7. Between 1969–70 and 1989–90 ten observations of poverty incidence are available (the intermediate ones have not been shown in the table) and they reveal a steady decline in the incidence of poverty, with only very minor exceptions. The first major break in trend occurred in the early 1990s with the intensification of outward-looking reform, when the incidence of poverty increased. By 1993–94 the incidence of poverty in rural India had once again begun to decline; but even so the incidence of poverty in rural India, where most people live, was higher than in the period before the accelerated reforms.[24]

The time series in the post-reform period is too short and erratic to permit unambiguous conclusions. It is, however, clear that during the period of accelerated reforms aimed at integration into the global economy, India experienced some of its nastiest poverty shocks in recent times and the steady trend of declining poverty over the preceding two decades was broken. The most obvious explanation of the rise in the incidence of poverty in the early

Table 4.7   Percentage of population in poverty in India

	Rural	Urban
1969–70	41.7	48.1
1989–90	19.8	32.3
1990–91	20.1	32.4
1992	28.7	33.9
1993	25.6	38.9
1993–94	21.1	31.0

Source: Tendulkar *et al.* (1996). Of the two sets of estimates made by the authors, the one pertaining to the lower poverty threshold (that is, showing lower incidence of poverty) has been quoted in the table.

1990s was the rise in the relative price of food, due largely to liberalization of the trade regime which reduced the wedge between the domestic and external prices of food that obtained in the years before reform. As the majority of the poor in India are net buyers of food, this rise in the relative price of food damaged the welfare of the poor.[25] This effect might have been mitigated if increased globalization had led to higher growth in per capita income. As already noted, the rate of growth in output actually declined in the early 1990s. The period of globalization also witnessed a sharp reduction in the rate of employment growth in India, an issue that is discussed below.

Poverty Trends in Pakistan[26]

Table 4.8 summarizes the trend in poverty incidence in Pakistan during recent decades. There was a steady decline in the incidence of poverty during the two decades leading up to 1987–88, when the reforms aimed at opening up the economy began. Thereafter Pakistan experienced an increase in the incidence of poverty.

Table 4.8   Percentage of population in poverty in Pakistan

	Rural	Urban
1969–70	49.1	38.8
1984–85	25.9	21.2
1987–88	18.3	15.0
1990–91	23.6	18.6
1992–93	23.4	15.5

Source: Amjad and Kemal (1996).

Amjad and Kemal (1996) identify a number of explanations for the rise in the incidence of poverty after the acceleration of outward-looking reforms. Some of these explanations are directly linked to the reforms, others are structural. The rate of growth of the economy, as noted before, fell while inequality in the distribution of income increased (as documented by the falling share of income of the poorest quarter of the population). Increased inequality was due partly to the reform process itself, for example a reform of the tax structure made it more regressive, and there was a reduction of the subsidies and public expenditure that had benefited the poor. The reduction in agricultural subsidies adversely affected the poor in two distinct ways: the productivity of subsistence farmers fell due to the partial withdrawal of modern inputs; and a large proportion of the poor, who were net buyers of food, were hurt by the rise in the price of food that resulted from the compensatory policy of increasing agricultural purchase prices. Growth in employment declined sharply from 2.5 per cent per year in the period preceding 1987–88 to just 1 per cent per year in the period after 1987–88. This was partly due to the fall in public employment that occurred as a result of the reform programme's emphasis on reducing public expenditure. Remittances from migrants – which in the past had helped the poor both directly by augmenting their incomes and by expanding employment through the increased investment that it financed – fell sharply. There was also increased concentration of agricultural landholdings among fewer hands.

Poverty Trends in Nepal

The evidence for Nepal, although far less convincing than the evidence for the countries discussed above, also suggests a rise in the incidence of poverty between 1985 and and 1992.[27] This change is not easy to explain in view of the steady rise in per capita income over the period and the absence of convincing documentation that the distribution of income sharply deteriorated. One adverse change for the poor was the rise in the relative price of food. This was due to the reform of the trade regime, food being a net import. Most of the poor being net buyers of food, the rise in the relative price of food contributed to an increase in the incidence of poverty.

To summarize, South Asia's steady progress towards a reduction of the incidence of absolute poverty appears to have slowed down, halted or reversed in the wake of reforms in the period of globalization. This was partly due to disequalizing forces inherent in the reform programmes. Greater integration into the world economy meant a rise in the relative price of food that was imported/traded internationally. In India, Pakistan and Nepal there is evidence that this particularly affected the poor, the majority of whom were net buyers of food. The reforms often involved the removal of agricultural subsidies, causing a reduction in the growth of agriculture, the principal source of income for the majority of the population.

Globalization and Employment

Contrary to the expectation that greater integration into the world economy would lead to growth in employment, there appears to have been a sharp reduction. In Pakistan, annual growth in employment in manufacturing in the three years after the acceleration of reforms (that is, between 1987–88 and 1990–91) was −0.2 per cent while manufacturing output grew at an anuual average rate of 5.3 per cent, yielding an output elasticity of employment of −0.04.[28] In Bangladesh, employment in most major manufacturing industries, including jute textiles, cotton textiles, paper and steel, declined absolutely in the early 1990s.[29] In India the output elasticity of employment in manufacturing industries during the period 1987–92 was 0.23.[30]

That this represents an extraordinarily low degree of labour intensity in industrial growth can be gauged by comparing it with the output elasticities of employment in manufacturing in Korea:[31] during 1970–80, 0.67; during 1980–90, 0.45. By the 1980s Korea had been transformed into a high-wage economy by LDC standards. It is appropriate to consider its elasticity in the 1970s when comparing Korea with contemporary India. Employment elasticity in Indian manufacturing, on this basis, was only one third of that of Korea!

This phenomenon of sharply reduced labour intensity in industrial growth during the period of globalization needs careful analysis, but in the absence of suitable studies one can only surmise what its cause might have been. Integration into the global economy has created tremendous pressure for improved international competitiveness, that is, reduced unit labour costs. Many of the industries developed under the previous ISI regime incorporated concealed unemployed labour, especially in public-sector enterprises. Faced with the pressure to reduce their unit labour costs, these industries, often privatized, did all they could to reduce their concealed unemployment. Thus the head-count rate of employment growth became very slow even though labour absorption at constant intensity of employment may have increased at a reasonable rate. Once concealed unemployment is eliminated, the headcount rate of employment growth will be higher. Industries will have become more efficient by the end of the transition, but the transition has been marked by increased unemployment.

These countries should have exercised better management of the transition process. It was certainly efficient to improve the effectiveness of employment in industries, but the incrementally unemployed workers should have been protected either by public works programmes or by some form of unemployment insurance. It was certainly efficient to end the discrimination against producers of food and agricultural goods in the form of artificially depressed prices that was fostered under the ISI trade regime, but the adverse effect this had on the living standard of the poor should have been mitigated by carefully designed programmes: for example targeted income subsidies and targeted public distribution and public works programmes to supplement the earnings of poor households. Substantial public resources should have been committed to such programmes and policies, but the contractionary macroeconomic policy that was a part of the reform programme during the era of globalization ruled this out.

CONCLUSIONS

The main arguments of this chapter are summarized as follows. During the 1980s the South Asian countries followed many other LDCs in gradually moving away from the ISI strategy to become better integrated into the global economy. This course of action was more than justified in view of the inefficiencies and limitations of ISI as a development strategy.

These countries implemented extensive reforms of their trade regimes and a multitude of other policies and institutions at the behest of the multilateral development agencies. They achieved significant success in increasing their trade, both as a proportion of GDP and as a proportion of world trade. Trade among themselves, however, remained very restricted due to serious bilateral hostilities and tensions. All the countries had very limited success in attracting FDI. With few exceptions, these countries have not succeeded in breaking into the IT export market; they have also lagged behind the newly industrializing East and South-East Asian countries in adopting IT technology in their own industries.

Increased integration into the global economy has brought some growth, but this has not been robust enough to outweigh the periodic effects of adverse weather and/or political cycles. That increased integration has failed to produce a more powerful growth impulse is also due to the preoccupation of the reforms with allocative efficiency and neglect of the complementary measures needed to create a broader framework for growth. Three deficiencies stand out: (1) the lack of effective governance, leading to a failure to promote regional cooperation and to a failure to build a consensus in favour of an effective development strategy; (2) the failure to replace the discarded ISI system by an alternative system of incentives to invest in potentially worthwhile activities, and (3) the failure to promote investment in infrastructure and human capital.

Globalization has not allowed South Asia's progress towards poverty reduction to continue at its previous pace. Indeed it has often slowed down or temporarily reversed. This has been due to structural inequality being aggravated by the disequalizing forces unleashed by the reform packages that were adopted in the pursuit of global integration. It might have been possible to offset the adverse effects of these forces if the integration process and growth had been more robust.

Notes

1. Although there is no unambiguous way of defining South Asia, one widely used definition is that it consists of the member countries of the South Asian Association for Regional Cooperation (SAARC): Bangladesh, India, Nepal, Pakistan, Sri Lanka, Bhutan and the Maldives. The reason for excluding Bhutan and Maldives from the present analysis is that, apart from their minuscule size (together they account for less than 0.08 per cent of the population of the SAARC countries), information on them is very limited. There is also the question of whether Myanmar should be considered a part of South Asia, but it would make little sense to include it in a study of globalization, partly because of the lack of relevant data and partly because Myanmar is only just beginning to shed the autarkic economic strategy it has followed for decades.

2. All countries in this World Bank category had a per capita income of less than $725 in 1994, according to the World Bank's 'atlas method'. Of the 133 countries, each with at least a million people, included in World Bank (1996a), 51 belonged to this category.

3. The World Bank (1990) estimated that South Asia had 47 per cent of world's poor in 1985.

4. See Khan (1994) p. 53.

5. For an excellent account of the past development strategy in the Indian context see Bhagwati (1993).

6. The most detailed chronicles of policy reforms in individual countries are the World Bank's periodic country economic memoranda. For independent accounts of the Indian reforms from different perspectives, see Bhagwati and Srinivasan (1993) and Bhaduri and Nayyar (1996). For an independent account of the Bangladeshi reforms see Centre for Policy Dialogue (1995).

7. See World Bank (1996a).

8. These ratios are based on data in World Bank (1996b), pp. 216–17.

9. Between 1985 and 1994 the terms of trade declined by 13 per cent for Nepal, 25 per cent for Bangladesh, 10 per cent for Pakistan and 17 per cent for Sri Lanka. For India there was an improvement of about 9 per cent. See World Bank (1996a), p. 192.

10. Like most World Bank reporting of capital flows, the figures in Table 4.3 seem to refer to net flows of *capital* (that is, net of any withdrawal of past capital investment), but not net of repatriation of dividends and interest.

11. See the report entitled 'IT pact just around the corner, say US and EU' in *Asia Times*, 13, December 1996.

12. See 'Asia's Labour Pains' in *The Economist*, 26, August 1995.

13. See Lal (1996) for the sources of these arguments and for a study of the effect of IT on a sample of electrical and electronic goods manufacturing firms in India. Lal's very limited sample does not provide conclusive evidence of improved productivity through the use of IT. He attributes this to the time lag in the productivity effect of IT, whose application in the Indian industries studied by him has been recent.

14. The idea of the political cycle and the rates of growth in different periods of the cycle are from a paper by Amjad and Kemal (1996).

15. References to this topic are well known. Of particular interest is the recent paper by Wade (1996a).

16. The Bangladeshi case is perhaps extreme and is discussed in Khan (1996a).

17. See World Bank (1993c), p. 49 for details of discriminatory OECD protection against exports from LDCs, including South Asia.

18. See Harrison *et al.* (1995).

19. Evidence for the period up to the mid 1980s is analysed in Khan and Hossain (1989). For more recent periods see Ravallion and Sen (1994) and World Bank (1995c).

20. The headcount ratio simply shows the proportion of population in poverty, that is, below the poverty threshold. The poverty gap index – the ratio of the total income gap of all the poor to the total income required to provide everyone with just enough income to rise above the poverty level – is a composite measure of the number in poverty and the average extent of their poverty. The squared poverty gap also gives an indication of the distribution of income among the poor. See Ravallion and Sen (1994) for further explanation and additional references.

21. According to the data collected by the Agricultural Statistics Wing of the BBS, the average daily money wages of male agricultural labourers without food changed from Tk29.54 in 1985–86 to Tk42.25 in 1994–95. Between these two dates the rural consumer price index increased by 79.06 per cent (BBS, 1996). This means that at 1985–86 purchasing power, the daily agricultural wages in 1994–95 were Tk23.60 or 20.1 per cent lower than in 1985–86.

22. The problem of the worsening distribution of income in Bangladesh during the post–1985 period has two distinct dimensions: there was a fall in the average rural income relative to the average urban income, while intrarural inequality did not change significantly; and there was a rise in urban inequality. For evidence see the BBS estimates of rural and urban Gini ratios reported in World Bank (1995c).

23. Evidence cited here is from Tendulkar *et al.* (1996).

24. One might wonder about the impact of the earlier reforms, that of the early 1980s, on poverty. There is no evidence that the reduction in rural poverty was halted at that time, although the reduction in urban poverty was briefly halted in 1987–88 and 1988–89 (see Tendulkar *et al.*, 1996).

25. Tendulkar *et al.* (1996) carry out econometric analysis of Indian data to demonstrate the validity of the argument.

26. Evidence on poverty trends on Pakistan has been obtained from Amjad and Kemal (1996).

27. Official estimates of the headcount index are reported in Guru-Gharana (1996). The problem with the Nepalese estimates is that the poverty threshold does not appear to represent a constant standard of living, the number of observations are far too few and the assertion that poverty has been increasing does not appear fully convincing in view of the steady and significant growth in per capita

income, without any clear evidence of a sharp rise in the inequality of income distribution.

28. These official estimates of employment and output growth in manufacturing are quoted in Amjad and Kemal (1996).

29. See BBS (1996), p. 9.

30. This is estimated by fitting a double-logarithmic function to data on employment and output in manufacturing reported in World Bank (1995d). The elasticity coefficient is significant at the 1 per cent level.

31. The elasticities for the Republic of Korea are estimated in the same way as for India, based on data reported in different issues of The World Bank's *World Tables*.

5 Growth and Poverty in East and South-East Asia in the Era of Globalization

Azizur Rahman Khan

East and South-East Asia (ESEA) is the most populous of the regions into which the contemporary world economy is typically classified. In recent decades this has also been the most dynamic region of the world economy. This chapter analyses the performance of the region during the accelerated globalization of the world economy that has taken place since the beginning of the 1980s.[1]

Although the region has generally achieved a superior economic performance, progress has by no means been uniform everywhere. Four distinct categories can be identified among the main countries of the region.

The Republic of Korea and Taiwan represent the first tier of the newly industrializing economies (NIEs) of ESEA that adopted an outward-oriented strategy of development from the 1960s.[2] Hong Kong and Singapore are usually grouped together with Korea and Taiwan, but this study excludes these city states because they have long held the status of high-income countries.[3] Their inclusion in the group would not add much to the analysis, while their status as city states means that they are often considered atypical and unrepresentative.

In the next category are the second-tier NIEs of ESEA: Indonesia, Malaysia and Thailand. Their past development strategies incorporated many elements of import-substituting industrialization (ISI), but in the years immediately preceding and during the period of globalization they made significant adjustments to their development strategies in order to become better integrated into the global economy.

The third category consists of China alone as a unique case. China was more or less insulated from the world economy until about a decade ago, when it began a controlled transition towards greater participation in world trade.

In the fourth and final category, the Philippines will be used as an example of countries whose development strategies have produced different outcomes from those of the above mentioned ESEA countries. Until at least the middle of the 1990s its performance in terms of growth and distribution was dismal.

These four groups of countries represent the principal types of ESEA response to globalization, and together the seven countries represent a third of the population of the less developed countries (LDCs). The ESEA countries that are excluded from the study are Vietnam, Laos, Cambodia and North Korea.[4] The reason for their exclusion is that little relevant information about them is available, although it is known that in recent years Vietnam has made significant progress towards greater integration into the global economy. Furthermore its growth performance has also been very impressive, averaging 7.4 per cent per year between 1988 and 1995.[5]

As with the study on South Asia (Chapter 4), the beginning of the 1980s is identified as the approximate start of the acceleration of globalization. The main impetus for this was the removal of two major obstacles to the international movement of goods, services, capital and technology, namely the ISI strategy pursued by the LDCs and the highly autarkic policies of the centrally planned socialist economies.

All seven of the ESEA countries discussed here achieved high rates of growth in the 1970s (see Table 5.1), and all but China achieved a relatively high degree of integration into the world economy (as measured by their ratio of trade to GDP) in that period. With the exception of China and Taiwan, all the countries were hit by severe external imbalances around the beginning of the 1980s. Thus the period of globalization for these countries began with the implementation of stabilization and structural adjustment programmes. This often meant a short period of reduced growth, but apart from the Philippines they all succeeded in achieving a high average annual growth rate in the subsequent decade and a half. The growth rate of GDP actually accelerated in China and Thailand, and while it declined marginally to moderately in Korea, Taiwan, Indonesia and Malaysia, it remained very high everywhere by LDC standards. In the Philippines, the 1980s and the early 1990s turned out to be a period of sharply reduced growth in GDP. In this study Korea, Taiwan, Indonesia, Malaysia, Thailand and China – referred to as the ESEA-6 – are regarded as examples of economic success during the period of globalization on the evidence of their excellent growth performance based on their high and/or accelerated integration into the global economy.[6]

However, the record of these countries in poverty reduction is less uniform. In the 1970s the ESEA–6 made good progress towards the elimination of poverty but during the 1980s and early 1990s their progress was less uniform than in the past and by no means highly correlated with their growth performance.

The first section begins with a brief account of the performance of these ESEA countries in the period before the 1980s and 1990s. It goes on to discuss the nature of the imbalance they faced at the beginning of the period of accelerated globalization and the adjustments they made to overcome that imbalance. The second section discusses their growth and integration performance and the role that IT played in their success. Special emphasis is placed on the first-tier NIEs. The third section analyses income distribution and poverty reduction in the 1980s and 1990s. The final section summarizes the main conclusions.

THE ESEA PERFORMANCE RECORD

All the ESEA countries achieved very high rates of growth in the 1970s (Table 5.1). During this decade the slowest growing of the seven ESEA countries, China, achieved an annual growth rate that was higher than the average growth rate of the developing world as a whole (5.2 per cent per year) and nearly three fifths higher than the growth rate achieved by South Asia (3.5 per cent per year). The most rapidly growing of the seven countries - the first-tier NIEs - achieved historically unprecedented, double-digit growth rates.

The development strategies pursued by these countries before the 1980s were not uniform, but in the 1970s all had very high rates of investment, backed by very high rates of domestic saving (Table 5.2). By the end of the decade the rates of investment and saving in all the countries were substantially higher than the LDC average. Another shared characteristic was a high level of basic human capital development. As early as 1970 these countries had attained primary school enrolment rates that were far higher than those of other LDCs at comparable stages of development: 80 per cent in Indonesia, 89 per cent in China and over 100 per cent in Korea, Taiwan and the Philippines.[7]

Over time there has been an evolution in the interpretation of the remarkable success of the first-tier NIEs of ESEA and to date there does not seem to

Table 5.1   GDP growth rates for East and South-East Asian countries (per cent per year)

	1970–80	1980–90	1990–94	1995
Korea	10.1	9.4	6.6	9.0
Taiwan	10.0*	7.7	6.5	5.9
Indonesia	7.2	6.1	7.6	8.1
Malaysia	7.9	5.2	8.4	9.6
Thailand	7.1	7.6	8.2	8.6
China	5.5	10.2	12.9	10.2
Philippines	6.0	1.0	1.6	4.8

*For the 1963–80 period.
Sources: Lee (1994); Yu (1994); ADB (1993); China, State Statistical Bureau (SSB) (1996); World Bank (1995a, 1996a); IMF (1996).

Table 5.2   Domestic investment and saving rates for East and South-East Asia (percentage of GDP)

	Investment rate			Saving rate		
	1970	*1980*	*1994*	*1970*	*1980*	*1994*
Korea	24	32	38	15	25	39
Taiwan	30	30	24	n.a.	33	29
Indonesia	16	24	29	14	37	30
Malaysia	22	30	39	27	33	37
Thailand	26	29	40	21	23	35
China	28	35	42	29	35	44
Philippines	21	29	24	22	24	18

Sources: ADB (1993, 1994); China, SSB (1996); World Bank (1995a, 1996a).

be agreement on the nature of its various components.[8] It is, however, well documented that the key to their success was not an adherence to *laissez faire* policies pursued in a free market under conditions of free trade. The key element of their strategy was targeted support, through the provision of subsidized credit and other incentives, to industries identified as potentially profitable. The principal difference between the standard ISI strategy pursued elsewhere and the interventions made by these countries was that (1) ISI was highly arbitrary, resulting in randomly distributed rates of effective protection for individual activities, whereas the first-tier NIEs systematically promoted activities that were identified as worthwhile bets; and (2) unlike the ISI, these NIEs did not discriminate against exports. The protection they provided to targeted industries was outward looking in so far as the effective exchange rate for exports was frequently higher than the effective exchange rate for imports. These countries also avoided overt overvaluation of the exchange rate, which makes the adoption of universal quantitative restrictions on imports inevitable and promotes employment-restricting technology by underpricing imported capital equipment. Dependence on quantitative import controls was not so widespread and inflexible as to create serious supply rigidities and a totally arbitrary (unintended) system of effective protection.

The second-tier NIEs – Indonesia, Malaysia and Thailand – followed a strategy that was closer to ISI until late in the 1970s or early in the 1980s. But as Amsden's (1993) analysis of Thailand shows, support to industries during the ISI phase in these countries was carefully targeted to promote efficiency, and was not the arbitrary kind promoted by South Asia and many other parts of the developing world.

During the 1970s, growth in both groups of NIEs was poverty alleviating. In Korea and Taiwan this was in large part due to the initial egalitarian redistribution of land. Its effect was subsequently reinforced by the high employment intensity of growth and the wide access to human capital. In Malaysia and Thailand too growth during the 1970s was poverty reducing, largely because of widespread access to land, facilitated by the relatively large and elastic supply. In Malaysia's case, ethnically based redistributive measures might also have helped increase access to land. Furthermore growth was highly employment intensive in these countries. In Indonesia the incidence of rural poverty increased between 1970 and 1976 due mainly to a rise in the price of rice, the principal source of food energy for the poor, on which the country was import dependent. This was brought under control by an accelerated programme of self-sufficiency in rice and complemented by generally favourable policies towards agriculture and the rural economy. Ever since, growth has been associated with poverty reduction.

China's economy grew at a slower rate than the economies of the other six countries in the 1970s, although it achieved the highest rates of investment and saving. There was widespread inefficiency of resource use, but nonetheless the economy grew at a reasonably high rate due to the sheer volume of investment. Strongly egalitarian policies, often arbitrarily imposed at the cost of reduced incentive and efficiency, succeeded in keeping down discrepancies in income distribution, but low incomes led to widespread poverty.

The Philippines achieved a reasonably high rate of growth in the 1970s aided by a high rate of capital inflow after the first oil shock. But growth was not particularly poverty reducing due to the extreme inequality of agricultural land ownership and the adverse effect of its ISI strategy on employment growth.[9]

At different times in the late 1970s and early 1980s all the ESEA countries except China and Taiwan faced serious external imbalances (Table 5.3). Korea, Thailand and the Philippines, all oil-importing countries, faced the problem earlier, mainly because of the two oil shocks. Indonesia and Malaysia, both oil exporters, faced it later, after the oil boom came to an end. While the problem of external imbalance hit Korea, Indonesia and Malaysia, emergence in the case of Thailand and the Philippines was more gradual. In

Table 5.3   Current account deficit before official transfer for East and South-East Asia (percentage of GDP)

	Peak ratio and year	Three-year average ratio prior to peak	Average ratio 1987–89
Korea	8.4 (1980)	2.9	−5.8
Indonesia	7.5 (1983)	1.0	2.1
Malaysia	13.5 (1982)	2.4	−4.4
Thailand	7.7 (1981)	6.4	2.6
Philippines	9.1 (1982)	6.2	2.7

Source: World Bank (1995a).

all the countries the problem reached unsustainable proportions and forced them to adopt stabilization programmes and reform their trade regimes.

China's peak rate of external deficit was only 1.8 per cent of GDP (in 1980). The country had, however, embarked on extensive systemic reform in 1979, beginning with complete transformation of the organization and institutions of agriculture. By the middle of the 1980s the focus of China's reform programme had shifted to export-led growth and rapid integration into the global economy. Taiwan's long record of external surplus was broken only twice after the first oil shock, in 1975 and 1980. The impetus for the reform of the trade regime in favour of greater openness to imports and capital flows, however, came from the pressure exerted by trading partners in the advanced industrial countries.

Thus the accelerated globalization of the world economy in the 1980s coincided with the widespread reform of the trade regimes and economic policies in the ESEA countries. Korea and Taiwan liberalized imports, a policy that was feasible in view of the successful transition to adulthood of targeted infant industries that had been promoted in the previous decade. This also led to a massive restructuring of exports. The cornerstone of the continued strategy of export-led development was the maintenance of a high degree of international competitiveness.

The second-tier NIEs – Indonesia, Malaysia and Thailand – also undertook a large-scale liberalization of their trade regimes and completed their transition from ISI to export-led development policies. This again was feasible because of the relative efficiency of industries that had been promoted earlier in a targeted and coherent ISI regime. These countries also liberalized their investment policies, a reform that encouraged large inflows of foreign direct investment (FDI). The structure of exports was radically altered in the process of greater integration into the world economy and was facilitated by the maintenance of a high degree of international competitiveness.

By the mid 1980s China was also making a decisive transition to export-led growth by sharply shifting incentives in favour of exports while retaining many of the controls over and regulations governing trade and industry. Among the policies that had a major role in this transition were adjustments to the exchange rate, numerous forms of targeted support to export industries and vast liberalization of foreign investment.

Reforms in the Philippines during the 1980s were less effective. Its industries, developed under an indiscriminate ISI regime and suffering from a lack of competition, were not subjected to radical reform and the trade regime continued to discriminate against exports. A combination of political instability, ineffective attempts to stabilize the macroeconomic imbalance and failure to ensure international competitiveness led to a loss of the Philippines' share of the world export market and delayed its access to the benefits of the world economy until the early 1990s.

GROWTH AND INTEGRATION DURING THE 1980s AND 1990s

Integration into the Global Economy

This section considers how well the ESEA countries have succeeded in taking advantage of the increased globalization of the world economy since the beginning of the 1980s and the extent to which their increased integration into the world economy has contributed to their growth. Between 1981 and 1993 ESEA exports grew at an average annual rate of 11.2 per cent, compared with 5.3 per cent for the LDCs as a whole[10] and 5.4 per cent for the world as a whole (World Bank, 1996a, p. 80). During this period the ESEA share of FDI also increased rapidly. In 1994 it attracted 54 per cent of the FDI received by all LDCs (ibid. p. 84).

Tables 5.4, 5.5 and 5.6 highlight some of the features of the accelerated integration of the ESEA countries into the global economy. As seen in Table 5.4, of the first-tier NIEs, Korea continued to show an increase in its export/GDP ratio between 1980 and 1994 but Taiwan experienced a fall in this ratio. As already noted, Taiwan's export/GDP ratio in 1980 was unusually high. Indeed the annual growth rate of Taiwan's exports was well over twice the growth rate of world exports. The exports of the second-tier NIEs increased extremely rapidly, especially during the early 1990s. China's exports increased at a dramatic rate: between 1980 and 1994 China's export/GDP ratio quadrupled! The Philippines was the only country to experience slower export growth than the rest of the world, and it was only in the early 1990s that its exports began to grow rapidly.[11]

A second important feature of export growth is an increase in the share of manufactured exports and a fall in the share of primary exports. The first-tier NIEs already had a high ratio of manufactured exports to total exports at the beginning of the 1980s, the period of acclerated globalization, and since then there has been a further increase in the ratio. The change in the ratio of manufactured exports to total exports hides the remarkable change in the composition of manufactured exports that took place in the first-tier NIEs during this period. To illustrate, machinery and transport equipment as a proportion of total exports increased in Korea from 20.3 per cent in 1980 to 42.3 per cent in 1993, and in Taiwan from 24.7 per cent in 1980 to 44.2 per cent in 1993 (Table 5.4).

The second-tier NIEs have experienced a dramatic change in the composition of their exports in favour of manufactured goods, particularly the more sophisticated products. Exports of machinery and transport equipment as a proportion of total exports increased from 11.5 per cent in 1980 to 40.5 per cent in 1992 in Malaysia, and from nearly 6 per cent to over 27 per cent in Thailand (Table 5.4). The composition of China's exports has similarly changed: not only did manufactured exports rise sharply as a proportion of

Table 5.4   Growth and composition of exports from East and South-East Asia[1]

	Exports/GDP ratio		Growth rate of exports (% p.a.)		Manufactured exports as % of total exports		Machinery exports as % of total exports	
	1980	1994	1980–90	1990–94	1980	1993	1980	1993
Korea	34	36	13.7	7.4	90	93	20.3	42.3
Taiwan	48[2]	38[2]	13.1	8.0	88	96	24.7	44.2
Indonesia	24	34	5.3	21.3	3	48	0.5	4.5
Malaysia	58	90	11.5	17.8	19	65[3]	11.5	40.5[3]
Thailand	24	39	14.3	21.6	28	73	5.9	27.7
China	6	24	11.4	14.3	48	81	2.9	15.9
Philippines	24	34	2.9	10.2	37	76	2.1	18.7

Notes
1. Exports refer to exports of goods and non-factor services in the first two columns (except for Taiwan) and to merchandise exports only in the other columns. Growth rates are based on values at constant price, that is, current price values deflated by the relevant price indices.
2. Merchandise exports only.
3. 1992.
Sources: Taiwanese data from ADB (1993, 1996); China, SSB (1996); Data for manufactured exports and machinery exports are from World Bank (1993d); All other data are from World Bank (1996a).

total exports, between 1980 and 1995 machinery and transport equipment as a proportion of total exports increased from 4.7 per cent to 21.1 per cent (China, SSB, 1996, p. 581). The Philippines have also experienced a substantial diversification of exports, although there are important qualifications to the significance of this. Technologically advanced manufactured exports largely represent low-value-added activities carried out in export-processing zones that use a large proportion of imported inputs and have very limited linkage to the rest of the economy (Khan, 1997).

A third notable feature of export growth of the ESEA countries is a rise in the share of exports to other LDCs, especially those in Asia, and declining dependence on the OECD market for export growth (Table 5.5). Thailand and the Philippines are the only exceptions to this trend. In future the OECD countries are likely to grow at a much slower rate than the LDCs, especially the Asian LDCs, which are likely to continue to be in the front rank of rapidly growing economies. A shift of exports away from the OECD countries with slow growth in demand and towards faster growing economies will be favourable to the ESEA countries. This particular outcome is also directly related to policy reform in these and other LDCs during the period of globalization. In the past, these countries, with the exception of the first-tier NIEs, often allowed their domestic currencies to be artificially overvalued, a practice that

Table 5.5   Direction of trade of East and South-East Asia (percentage of exports of countries of origin)

	Destination					
	Asian LDCs		OECD		Other	
Country of origin	1985	1992	1985	1992	1985	1992
Korea	12.9	25.4	62.3	53.1	24.7	21.5
Taiwan	15.6	28.4	34.7	–	49.7	–
Indonesia	17.2	24.4	75.1	63.5	7.6	12.1
Malaysia	38.1	41.1	52.9	47.9	9.1	11.1
Thailand	27.1	21.9	52.8	59.9	20.2	18.1
China	38.2	53.5	39.4	32.9	22.5	13.6
Philippines	19.5	12.9	70.8	81.8	9.7	5.4

Source: ADB (1994).

Table 5.6   Indices of real effective exchange rates in East and South-East Asia (1985=100)

	1988	1990	1993
Korea	93.6	107.3	99.9
Taiwan	100.3	106.8	94.7
Indonesia	55.5	54.4	54.6
Malaysia	71.7	66.7	77.3
Thailand	79.3	83.5	78.9
China	79.9	68.0	73.8
Philippines	74.5	76.3	77.8

Source: ADB (1994).

made their exports to each other unattractive relative to exports from the OECD countries. As Table 5.6 shows, most of these countries have sharply reduced the value of their currencies in real terms since the middle of the 1980s.

As for FDI, while the ESEA countries as a group have attracted a very large and increasing share of total FDI going to all LDCs, the pattern has been vastly different among individual countries. The principal advantage of FDI is that, in addition to augmenting investable resources, it provides access to technology, management expertise and the international market. Korea and Taiwan were neither hospitable towards nor dependent on FDI during their early development. This pattern continued for Korea and was only moderately relaxed in Taiwan during the period of accelerated globalization. Their domestic savings rates were high enough for them not to depend on foreign capital. Korea preferred to acquire technological knowledge through licensing arrangements, while in recent years Taiwan has been more disposed towards direct participation by transnational corporations in selected industries.

FDI as a proportion of investment has generally been higher in the second-tier NIEs. The ratio has been particularly high for Malaysia (Table 5.7), although the most dramatic increase in FDI has taken place in China in recent years. In 1994 China accounted for 42 per cent of all FDI going to LDCs! None of the second-tier countries had a pressing need for FDI as a source of augmenting investable resources, rather the main reason for seeking FDI was to gain access to technology, management skills and the international market.

A major determinant of the success of the ESEA–6 in taking advantage of the globalizing world economy was their ability to maintain a high degree of international competitiveness by stabilizing the unit labour cost in foreign exchange, in spite of increasing real wages. This was achieved through the combination of a rapid increase in labour productivity, a low rate of domestic inflation relative to world inflation and adjustment to the exchange rate.[12] Labour productivity increased rapidly due to the emphasis placed by these countries on human capital investment and the overall incentive structure that guided investment towards socially profitable activities. Both groups of NIEs achieved substantially lower rates of inflation during the 1980s and 1990s than in the preceding decade (Table 5.8). China's inflation was higher during the 1980s and 1990s than previously; but the aggressive adjustment in the exchange rate allowed China to stabilise its unit labour cost in foreign exchange. The Philippines failed to stabilize its unit labour cost in foreign exchange because of its inability to improve labour productivity and to contain the rate of inflation.[13]

These countries were not only competing against others in the international market, they were also competing against each other. What prevented this

Table 5.7   Foreign direct investment as proportion of investment in East and South-East Asia[1]

	1981–85	*1986–90*	*1994*
Korea	0.5	1.3	0.6
Taiwan	1.5	3.5	2.4[2]
Indonesia	1.0	2.0	4.2
Malaysia	10.8	10.5	16.3
Thailand	3.2	5.9	1.2
China	n.a.	n.a.	15.5
Philippines	n.a.	n.a.	6.5

Notes:
1. Data for 1981–85, 1986–90 and 1993 (Taiwan) are FDI as a percentage of gross fixed capital formation. For 1994 the figures refer to the ratio of FDI to gross investment.
2. For 1993.
Sources: UNCTAD *World Investment Report* (various years); World Bank (1996a, 1996b).

Table 5.8   Annual rates of increase in the consumer
price index in East and South-East Asia

	1971–80	1981–90	1991–93
Korea	16.5	6.4	7.1
Taiwan	11.1	3.1	3.6
Indonesia	17.5	8.6	8.6
Malaysia	6.0	3.2	4.3
Thailand	10.0	4.4	4.3
China	1.1	7.5	9.4
Philippines	14.8	13.0	11.7

Source: ADB (1994).

from becoming a 'beggar-thy-neighbour' game was the fact that the individual countries restructured their production and exports according to the changing pattern of comparative advantage.

Economic Growth

The six ESEA countries that successfully integrated into the global economy all attained high growth in GDP during the period of economic globalization (Table 5.1). The Philippines, which failed to take advantage of the increased globalization, stagnated during the 1980s and its performance only began to improve in 1994.

During the 1980s Korea maintained an annual GDP growth rate that was almost as high as during the preceding decade. Taiwan's growth rate during the 1980s was significantly lower than in the previous decade, though still very high by international standards. During the early 1990s the growth rate of both these countries fell further, though remaining 3.6 times the world average! As noted earlier, for years Taiwan has had a per capita income that almost puts it in the World Bank's high-income-country classification. It is currently at top of the league of the upper-middle-income countries and is destined to be the next country to enter the top rank. However, while Korea and Taiwan have enjoyed unprecedented development achievements in many areas in the past, it is unlikely that their economies will continue to grow at their historical rates. Nonetheless their growth performance in the period of globalization must be regarded as remarkable by any standard.

Among the second-tier NIEs, Thailand experienced steady acceleration of GDP growth during the period of globalization. Its annual population growth rate is now down to 1 per cent and per capita income has been growing by more than 7 per cent a year. The GDP growth rates of Indonesia and Malaysia declined somewhat in the early to mid 1980s due to the short-term retrenchment effects of stabilization, but since then they have accelerated steadily.

China's growth performance during the era of globalization has been historically unprecedented. Never before has more than a fifth of humankind experienced a more than 10 per cent increase in GDP (about 9 per cent in per capita GDP), sustained over a decade and a half.[14]

The Philippines is the only ESEA country in our list not to conform to this pattern of high growth. In fact, during the period of globalization it experienced negative growth in per capita income and its per capita GDP was lower in 1995 than in the early 1980s.

The remarkable growth performance of the ESEA–6 during the period of globalization was the result of development strategies that cannot be analysed adequately in the present study. One might characterize them as extensions of the strategies used in the 1960s and 1970s, briefly outlined in the first section, with modifications necessitated by increased integration into the global economy. These modifications were efficiency augmenting: for the second-tier NIEs and China in particular, outward-looking reforms led to more efficient resource use. As the incentive to save and invest was kept as high as before, and targeted support to worthwhile industries remained intact, this led to high growth.

Information Technology

Globalization has been facilitated by the rapid spread of information technology. Activities that encompass the electronics industry, telecommunications and information services, including computers, semiconductors, software and information systems, have reduced the cost of international communication and facilitated the flow of information. IT has therefore emerged as a critically important factor in the accelerated process of economic globalization.

A recent World Bank study of the role of IT in the development of East Asia identifies three distinct aspects of its importance.[15] First, it is an industry whose output demand is highly income elastic and rapidly growing. If a country can obtain comparative advantage in some aspect of the industry, this is a very important source of export revenue. Second, IT makes an important contribution to increased industrial productivity by enhancing the efficiency of both management and technology. Third, IT can contribute to overall economic efficiency through modernization of the transport and communication infrastructure.

An important point about IT activities is that comparative advantage in some segment of it is feasible for countries with vastly different factor endowments and most of its components are 'footloose'. Some processes (for example the assembly of microelectronics and computer motherboards) can be undertaken in countries with abundant unskilled and semi-skilled labour, as happens in Malaysia and the Philippines; while other processes require more sophisticated skills, such as those available in Korea and Taiwan.

The appropriateness of using IT for the enhancement of production technology of course varies from one country to another depending on whether it is complementary to or competitive with other production factors. It is conceivable that certain IT-based production techniques will replace labour and hence be inappropriate for a labour-abundant LDC (for example Indonesia) but quite appropriate for an LDC that is well on its way towards comparative labour scarcity (as Korea and Taiwan appear to be).

Information on different aspects of IT adoption in LDCs is often not readily available. The evidence that is available suggests that the ESEA countries are among the foremost LDCs in terms of carving out a market share in the IT industry. In 1993 Korea and Malaysia respectively had 9.5 per cent and 7.5 per cent of the world export market in electronic microcircuits, 4.7 per cent and 8.6 per cent of the market for diodes and transistors, and 6.1 per cent and 2.6 per cent of the market for automatic data processing (ADP) peripherals. Korea had 3.1 per cent of the market for digital computers. Singapore and Hong Kong, the high-income ESEA economies, had large shares of the world market in these IT products. Thailand, China and the Philippines had also entered the world export market in IT products. Together all these ESEA countries had 31.4 per cent of the world export market in electronic microcircuits, 27.7 per cent of the market in diodes and transistors, 38.8 per cent of the market in ADP peripherals and 28.4 per cent of the market in digital computers.[16] Information is not available about Taiwan's share. Clearly the ESEA region had become the largest country group, outside the OECD, to produce and export IT products.

Table 5.9 summarizes the available information on some indicators of the extent of use of IT in four of the ESEA countries in 1989. Korea had clearly attained a high level of IT use by LDC standards and was already on the way to the level of use in some OECD countries. Taiwan may also have attained a comparable stage of development, although information is not readily available in this regard. The other ESEA countries were still at a comparatively low level of use of IT.

Within ESEA the strategy for IT development varies among countries. The Korean strategy is probably representative of that of the first-tier NIEs. In 1992 Korea adopted an IT master plan, which set the following targets: an increase of personal computers and terminals from 2.2 million to 10 million by 2001; an increase in the share of locally produced computers from 3 per cent to 50 per cent; development of 256-Mbit DRAM chips within three to four years; development of broad-band information service digital networks for cellular phones; and establishment of a centre to map out a standard linking code in Korean and other languages (Hanna *et al.*, 1996, p. 87). The strategy adopted for the achievement of these targets was similar to that used in the past for the development of industries, namely broad-range but targeted public support. The IT industry has been protected from competition from established producers abroad. However, it has been recognized that the domestic market is not sufficiently large to allow the efficient development of the industry. Thus the protection afforded is not inward-looking; support is extended to enable them to expand exports as well. Government procurement is used to guarantee a minimum market. R&D support from the public sector amounted to 64 per cent of total R&D in the industry in 1980, falling to 20 per cent in the early 1990s. The use of IT in government administration was promoted to encourage the expansion of domestic demand. Providing R&D tax incentives to the private sector, encouraging industries to automate and investing in the human capital required for R&D development are other measures that helped the development of the IT industry.[17]

In stark contrast to this comprehensive strategy of developing IT and using it to enhance productivity and efficiency throughout the economy, is the case of the semiconductor industry in the Philippines. In 1987 imported inputs amounted to 76.3 per cent of the value of exports of the IT industry. While the industry accounted for 10.2 per cent of exports, it contributed only 0.4 per cent of value added and 0.14 per cent of employment to the economy.[18] The low linkage between this industry and the rest of the economy was due to its development in enclaves under the auspices of FDI, attracted by incentives that were strong enough to induce their location in the country but insufficiently strong to promote their integration into the rest of the economy. While this development has brought other important benefits to the Philippines, semiconductor exports have contributed little to the economy.

Table 5.9   Indicators of information technology for East and South-East Asia, 1989

	Korea	Thailand	Malaysia	Philippines	Brazil	USA
Telephone lines per thousand persons	28.32	2.08	7.35	0.95	6.00	50.58
Per capita sale of telecom services ($)	92.87	14.53	33.54	8.44	8.40	442.35
Mainframe computers per million persons	222	n.a.	n.a.	n.a.	n.a.	8287
Per capita sale of data processing ($)	10.70	0.71	3.63	0.43	1.61	39.06
Per capita sale of information processing services ($)	9.40	n.a.	n.a.	n.a.	n.a.	414.00

Source: Hanna *et al.* (1996).

Malaysia perhaps represents an intermediate case in which the IT industry has been promoted by FDI but has been more successful in creating linkages between this industry and the domestic economy by encouraging a more rapid diffusion of IT use. Unfortunately there is insufficient information available to analyse this comprehensively.

TRENDS IN POVERTY

This section aims to determine the trends in the incidence of poverty in the ESEA countries during the 1980s and 1990s, the period associated with accelerated globalization. As shown below, poverty reduction has been less uniform among the ESEA countries than their growth performance.

Poverty is measured by the number of the population below some threshold per capita income or expenditure that is held constant over time. Such thresholds do not represent constant standards of living across countries. Although the thresholds are frequently anchored to a minimum acceptable level of nutrition, as indicators of the living standard they differ between countries for a variety of reasons, for example differences in the nutritional standards used between countries, intercountry differences in consumption patterns, and differences in the method of allowing for non-food needs when estimating the poverty threshold. Thus the levels of absolute poverty are not comparable between countries. Furthermore it is not clear that use of a uniform poverty threshold for all countries, had it been possible to do so, would have changed the findings.

The First-Tier NIEs

Korea and Taiwan are among the countries with the most egalitarian distribution of income and a low incidence of absolute poverty. Indeed the incidence of poverty, by any reasonable standard, had declined to very low levels in Korea and Taiwan by the early 1980s and there is little evidence that high growth in the period of globalization has been associated with increased inequality. For Korea the Gini ratio of income distribution is estimated to have declined from 0.389 in 1980 to 0.345 in 1985 and 0.336 in 1988 (Korea Labor Institute, 1992, p.126). The hourly real wage in industries increased at an annual rate of 9.3 per cent from 1982–90 (ibid., p. 65). Direct estimates of change in the distribution of income are not readily available for Taiwan, but real manufacturing earnings increased at an annual rate of 4.4 per cent between 1979 and 1985 and 9.4 per cent between 1985 and 1990 (ADB, 1994, p. 207). The unemployment rate in both these countries declined between 1985 and 1990 (ibid.). Although direct estimates are not available, it is almost certain that the incidence of absolute poverty, according to any reasonable criteria, has fallen in these countries.

The Second-Tier NIEs

Tables 5.10, 5.11 and 5.12 provide estimates of the trends in poverty in Indonesia, Malaysia and Thailand during the 1980s and early 1990s. The incidence of poverty in all these countries declined over this period although the extent and pattern of poverty reduction varied.

In Indonesia the incidence of poverty in both rural and urban areas declined steadily throughout the period under review. A notable feature of the trend is that between 1981 and 1987 – the period of stabilization and decline in GDP growth rate – poverty reduction took place at a faster rate than during the subsequent period of faster growth and more rapid integration into the global economy.

Successful reduction of poverty during the stabilization period was due to the fact that fiscal retrenchment concentrated on the capital-intensive sectors and government programmes had little adverse effect on employment growth. In addition the severity of retrenchment was limited due to the cooperation of donors and creditors, who allowed a continued inflow of net resources. In more recent years the fall in the rate of poverty reduction has been attributed to the isolation of the remaining poor in remote pockets of poverty that are not easily reached by public programmes.

The incidence of poverty in Malaysia has declined more rapidly than in the other NIEs. By the early 1990s poverty in urban Malaysia had become insignificant and poverty in rural areas had been reduced to a very low level. Poverty reduction during the early to mid 1980s – the period of stabilzation

Table 5.10   Trend in poverty incidence in Indonesia
(percentage of population below the poverty threshold)

	Rural	*Urban*
1980	28.4	29.0
1981	26.5	28.1
1984	21.2	23.1
1987	16.4	20.1
1990	14.3	16.8
1993	13.1	14.2

Note: These are estimates by the Central Bureau of Statistics. Poverty threshold refers to per capita expenditure based on the cost of 2100 kilocalories of food energy and a further mark up for non-food expenditure.

Table 5.11 Trend in poverty incidence in Malaysia
(percentage of population below the poverty threshold)

	Rural	Urban
1973	55.3	22.9
1984	27.6	6.5
1987	24.7	7.3
1989	13.0	2.2
1995	6.5	1.9

Note: Poverty threshold refers to RM33 per capita per month at 1970 prices, using the consumer price index in subsequent years.
Source: Samudram (1996).

Table 5.12 Trend in poverty incidence in Thailand
(percentage of population below the poverty threshold)

	Whole country	Villages
1981	23.0	27.3
1986	29.5	35.8
1988	22.8	26.3
1992	18.6	20.7

Note: Poverty threshold refers to an income level that provides adequate nutrition (along with other basic necessities).
Sources: Suganya and Somchai (1988); Medhi *et al.* (1992); Medhi (1996).

and reduced growth – was due to an improvement in income distribution. Accelerated growth from the late 1980s was not accompanied by a significant worsening of the distribution of income, so that the pace of poverty reduction was maintained.[19]

In Thailand the incidence of poverty increased during the period of increased globalization and declined thereafter. Over the period as a whole there was a substantial reduction in poverty, although some of the potential poverty-reducing effects of the sharp acceleration in growth were offset by increased inequality in the distribution of income. A recent study by Medhi (1996) reports that from 1988–90 about 36 per cent of the reduction in the headcount index of poverty that would have resulted from income growth, with unchanged distribution, was offset by the adverse change in income distribution. The same study reports simulation exercises that show that the radical reduction in effective protection in the late 1980s – directly deriving from Thailand's greater integration into the world economy – contributed to poverty reduction. Higher growth in the period of globalization also helped channel more resources into poverty-alleviating programmes. Since the mid 1980s the share of economic and social services in total public expenditure has increased rapidly, with a favourable impact on the poor.

China[20]

China embarked on a massive reform of the rural economy in 1979 and until the mid 1980s its remarkable growth was largely led by the growth of the rural economy. From the mid 1980s the focus of China's development strategy shifted away from the rural economy in favour of export-led growth, whereby the Chinese economy became rapidly integrated into the global economy.

There was a sharp decline in the incidence of poverty in rural China until the mid 1980s, but thereafter the rate of decline slowed dramatically and in the early 1990s it ground to a complete halt (Table 5.13), with a consequent rise in the absolute number in poverty. In urban China there was a steady fall in the incidence of poverty until the end of the 1980s, but in the 1990s this trend reversed. Overall China's poverty-reduction record during the period of increased integration into the global economy was poor, in sharp contrast to its remarkable growth performance during the same period.

The asymmetrical performance in poverty reduction in the pre–1985 and post–1985 period in rural China is largely explained by a fall in the growth rate of *personal* income (the variable that features in the poverty threshold).

Table 5.13   Trend in poverty incidence in China
(percentage of population below the poverty threshold)

| | Rural | | Urban | |
	Standard PIT	Low PIT	Standard PIT	Low PIT
1980	59.8	40.8	n.a.	n.a.
1981	48.3	30.3	44.3	20.1
1983	26.4	14.3	n.a.	n.a.
1985	24.5	14.0	26.2	12.7
1988	27.0	16.1	n.a.	n.a.
1989	n.a.	n.a.	17.7	7.4
1990	23.9	13.9	15.0	7.4
1991	n.a.	n.a.	12.2	4.7
1992	22.9	13.6	n.a.	n.a.
1993	23.7	14.1	n.a.	n.a.
1994	23.1	13.6	12.0	5.9

Note: PIT stands for poverty income threshold.
Source: Khan (1996c).

In the earlier period, personal income grew rapidly due to a high rate of growth of agricultural output and a sharp improvement in the agricultural terms of trade. The effect of growth was strong enough to outweigh the effect of moderately rising inequality in the distribution of personal income. In the later period the rate of growth of personal income declined drastically due to a fall in agricultural output and a decline in or stagnation of the agricultural terms of trade. The growth in personal income was no longer high enough to offset the effect of inequality, which continued to rise. Since most of China's poor are located in rural areas, the decline in the rate of rural poverty reduction affected China's overall poverty-reduction statistics.

Until the late 1980s the rate of growth of personal income in urban China was high enough to outweigh the effect of the moderate rise in inequality. Thereafter growth in personal income accelerated, but it could no longer outweigh the effect of what was now a sharp increase in the inequality of income distribution.

An important point emerging in the case of China is that the overall growth rate of GDP is a poor predictor of the growth rate of personal income, the variable that features in the estimation of poverty. This is due partly to macroeconomic policies concerning the rate of accumulation, and partly to a change in the sectoral terms of trade, which feature prominently in the transmission of aggregate growth to sectoral growth.

The unprecedented rate of industrialization in the era of China's integration into the global economy (1984–94) contributed to income concentration in two very important ways. First, the output elasticity of employment in manufacturing fell drastically, from 0.62 in 1978–84 to 0.27 in 1984–94. This was in spite of the fact that the growth in manufactured exports was mainly in labour-intensive products. The explanation of this paradox seems to lie in the initial condition of the manufacturing industries, mainly state and collective enterprises: in the past employment had been expanded beyond the dictates of efficiency as part of the social policy of guaranteed employment. Economic reforms aimed at integration into the world economy made it increasingly difficult to continue this system of social protection. Both state and collective enterprises, in their quest for greater efficiency and collaboration with foreign investors, began to shed surplus labour during the period of globalization and this process gained momentum once legal cover was gradually extended to it. The observed low output elasticity of employment was the sum of two divergent effects: (1) a fairly high output elasticity of employment measured at constant intensity of employment per worker; and (2) a rise in the intensity of employment due to a reduction of concealed unemployment in industry. The process was certainly efficiency enhancing and one could argue that its adverse distributional impact might have been mitigated by appropriate social policies, for example unemployment insurance and/or an accelerated public works programme. Second, growth was concentrated in the richer coastal and eastern provinces, regions that attracted the most FDI. These trends were closely related to the fact that reforms aimed at facilitating the integration of China into the world economy were not offset by policies to protect the unemployed and the poorer regions.

Some specific aspects of development policy deserve to be highlighted in connection with the disequalizing effects that were unleashed by China's greater integration into the global economy. The push for an ever higher rate of accumulation was an obstacle to the growth of GDP being transformed into growth of personal income. The change in the composition of public expenditure and credit away from the rural sector and towards the urban sectors of the richer provinces was detrimental to overall poverty alleviation. The policy of allowing the state and collective enterprises to shed under-employed labour was not matched by an adequate policy to protect the unemployed. While the official tolerance of migration should have benefited the poor, *de facto* discrimination against them has impeded their welfare.[21] Institutional changes to the provision of education and health services were not complemented by increased public funds that would allow the poor to gain access to these services.[22]

The Philippines

Because of its dismal growth performance until the early 1990s the Philippines is an unlikely country to have experienced a reduction in poverty. It is there-fore surprising that the incidence of poverty declined, albeit slightly, between 1985 and 1991 (Table 5.14). With the resumption of growth in 1994 there was more of an impetus for poverty reduction in urban areas. The relationship between growth, inequality and poverty has been different in different peri-ods. From 1985–88 real per capita GDP increased by 12 per cent. According to the Family Income and Expenditure Survey (1985, 1988, 1991) real con-sumption per capita was stagnant, indicating a failure to convert growth of aggregate GDP into improved living standards. The incidence of poverty nevertheless declined due to an improvement in the distribution of expendi-ture in rural areas. From 1988–91 there was almost no growth in per capita GDP and inequality in distribution increased. The result was an increase in the incidence of poverty.

Greater integration into the global economy, prompting a downward adjustment of the exchange rate, appears to have contributed to increased poverty in the Philippines. According to Balisacan (1996) a 5 per cent deva-luation increases the rural headcount ratio of poverty by 1.9 percentage points and the urban headcount ratio by 2.5 percentage points. Since agri-cultural products are more tradable than those of industry in the Philippines, the devaluation substantially raised rural prices. The resulting terms of trade improvement did not benefit the rural poor, who are largely landless workers

Table 5.14   Trend in poverty incidence in the Philippines
(percentage of population below the poverty threshold)

	Rural	Urban
1985	56.4	37.9
1988	52.3	34.3
1991	55.1	35.6
1994	53.7	28.8

Note: Poverty threshold is the one officially estimated by the Inter-agency Technical Working Group on Poverty Determination and is believed to be relatively high compared with the ones for Indonesia and Thailand.
Source: Balisacan (1996).

and small farmers, net buyers of food. The urban poor also faced a higher increase in food prices than in nominal earnings.

CONCLUSIONS

During the 1980s and early 1990s the ESEA–6 achieved a greater degree of integration into the global economy by increasing their share of world exports and FDI. The success of both tiers of NIEs in this task was strongly facilitated by the relative efficiency of the industries that their past development policies had promoted. This enabled them to compete internationally in a more liberalized trading system. Their ability to maintain international competitiveness was another critical element in ensuring their successful integration into the global economy.

The period of globalization also witnessed a high rate of growth for these economies as they maintained the positive elements of their past development policies and reinforced them further by the efficiency-enhancing reforms that were introduced as part of their programme of increased integration into the global economy. Strong emphasis on the IT industry, especially in the first-tier NIEs, was another important element of increased integration and higher growth. Their growth in the period of globalization was not associated with a significant increase in inequality of income distribution. As a consequence they all experienced a continued reduction in the incidence of poverty.

China's remarkable success in increasing its share of global trade and FDI was due to a sharp shift in its development policy towards exports and international competitiveness. The resulting improvement in the efficiency of resource use, combined with continuation of the high investment rate, led to a very high rate of growth in GDP. However, the process unleashed strongly disequalizing forces, which led to an increase in inequality and a halt to the reduction of poverty that China had experienced before its integration into the global economy.

The Philippines failed to take advantage of the process of globalization due to its inability to maintain international competitiveness and its failure to break out of the inefficient ISI regime sufficiently quickly. Political instability and the absence of a coherent development strategy led to a decline in the rate of investment and the prolonged stagnation of GDP, from which it has only recently started to recover.

It is useful to note that specific elements of globalization can have asymmetrical redistributive effects under different circumstances. Trade liberalization and exchange rate adjustment seem to have improved the distribution of income in Thailand but adversely affected the poor in the Philippines. It is also important to exercise caution in attributing the absence of favourable distributional trends in China and the Philippines during the period of globalization to these countries' increased integration into the world economy. In the case of China, the adverse distributional effects are transitional and due to the initial distortion of its industries. This could have been offset by compensatory policies during the transition period.[23] In the Philippines the main cause of persistent poverty is slow growth. Greater integration into the global economy would almost certainly have contributed to higher growth in the Philippines.

Notes

1. This chapter employs the same notion of globalization as Chapter 4 on South Asia. As is stated in that chapter, the world economy has been gradually moving towards greater integration for a long time, but the process accelerated at the beginning of the 1980s. What is often referred to as the 'period of globalization' in this chapter should more accurately be called, as indeed it is from time to time, 'the on-going period of accelerated globalization of the world economy'. This longer phrase is often replaced by the shorter one in the interest of brevity.

2. As will be discussed later, their outward-looking strategy did not mean that they rejected protection in favour of free trade. It was outward looking in the sense that there was an absence of discrimination against exports. In the promotion of targeted industries there was no discrimination in favour of industries that sold their products in the domestic market relative to industries that sold their products abroad.

3. The World Bank classifies these two territories as high-income countries (HICs). According to World Bank (1996a), the per capita GNPs of these territories are close to or above that of the median of the 25 HICs that have at least one million people each. Indeed Taiwan would be included in the group of HICs, according to the World Bank classification, if it were recognized as a country, though it would rank second last in the group. Its per capita income in 1994 was 54 per cent

of that of Hong Kong and 52 per cent of that of Singapore. Note that the United Nations includes Hong Kong and Singapore in the category of 'developing countries', a classification with which the authorities in these countries seem to agree.

4. There is no unanimity of view as to whether Myanmar should be designated as part of South Asia or South-East Asia. Even if one were to consider it part of South-East Asia, it would not make sense to include it in the present study because of the absence of relevant information and because of its long-term adherence to autarkic policies from which it is only now beginning to emerge. The ESEA region in this chapter excludes the Pacific Islands (including Papua New Guinea).

5. According to the IMF (1996, p.123).

6. As shown later, Taiwan was the only country in this group to experience a reduction in the ratio of exports to GDP during the period of globalization. All the others succeeded in increasing their export/GDP ratios. The reduction in Taiwan's export GDP ratio started from a very high base and the ratio has remained very high in recent years.

7. The primary school enrolment rates were 67 per cent for South Asia and 68 per cent for North Africa and the Middle East. For Latin America, which was considerably richer at the time, it was 95 per cent. All these data are from World Bank (1995a).

8. For various interpretations of this experience see Amsden (1979), Wade (1990, 1996) and World Bank (1993b).

9. See Khan (1997) for an account of the Philippines experience.

10. Estimates of the export growth of the non-ESEA LDCs are not available, but growth was clearly much lower.

11. For an account of the poor performance of the Philippines in this and other regards see Khan (1997).

12. The underlying analytical model and the evidence for Korea and Malaysia can be found in Mazumdar (1993). Evidence for China is provided in Khan (1996d).

13. This is documented in Khan (1997).

14. Admittedly, as shown in the next section, this average growth was not shared equally by all the 1.2 billion people of China.

15. See Hanna *et al.* (1996). The report provides case studies of IT in Japan, Korea, Taiwan, Hong Kong and Singapore.

16. This information is from Chapter 2 of this volume.

17. See Hanna *et al.* (1996, pp. 90–2) for an account of the Korean strategy.

18. See Krugman *et al.* (1992, p.12) for this information. Unfortunately more recent information is not available.

19. See Samudram (1996) for some of the evidence.

20. The analysis of poverty trends in China is based on Khan (1996c), which provides detailed evidence that can not be reproduced here for reasons of space.

21. There has been a very large flow of migrants out of rural areas into cities, where in the past migration was controlled by the strict enforcement of residence permits. This enforcement has been relaxed, but the migrants have not been granted access to public resources such as subsidized education, health services and housing.

22. In the past these services were provided by collective institutions. The dismantling of these institutions has not been followed by adequate provision of services by local government or other bodies.

23. Admittedly these compensatory policies might have affected the pattern of globalization. It is possible that a policy of greater regional balance in public

investment would have affected the volume and pattern of FDI. Similarly a policy of greater social protection might have reduced the rate of accumulation and growth.

6 The Impact of Globalization on Africa

S.M. Wangwe and Flora Musonda

Africa is the least-developed continent in the world today, as is evident from the low levels of per capita income in many African countries. Among other things there is a lack of infrastructure, including telecommunication linkages with the outside world and within Africa, low levels of technological innovation, low expenditure on research and development (R&D) and inadequate social services.

This chapter examines the position of Africa in the globalizing economy. The first section deals with structural adjustment programmes aimed at opening up Africa to the global economy. The second section investigates diverse aspects of marginalization in trade, investment (including foreign direct investment) and information technology. The third section looks at factors that are influencing Africa's integration into the global economy; and the fourth at globalization's effects on growth, poverty and employment in Africa during the 1980s and 1990s.

LIBERALIZATION AND STRUCTURAL ADJUSTMENT

Most African countries have introduced and implemented economic reforms in the form of structural adjustment programmes (SAPs), and these reforms are clearly related to globalization. Trade liberalization, for example, is a structural-reform measure that in many cases serves to open up the economy, but it also brings stiffer competition. In turn globalization can further stiffen competition, so it is difficult to determine which portion of the effect is brought about by SAPs and which by globalization. We shall summarize the salient features of SAPs and globalization to pin down some important interrelationships.

In Africa, governments introduced SAPs in response to economic crises resulting from external and internal factors. The external factors included price hikes in petroleum, cyclical deterioration in terms of trade, droughts, wars and political upheavals. The internal factors included inappropriate policies such as overvalued domestic currencies, which penalized exports, subsidized imports and distorted factor market prices, slowing down overall growth. An over-extended public sector was evident in a large and inefficient civil service and direct government involvement in the production of goods and services through myriads of money-losing public corporations. The losses of public corporations caused large budget deficits, which were financed by printing currency (*seigniorage*), leading to high inflation. An inward-looking trade policy of import substitution, supported by the widespread use of tariff and quantitative barriers to protect uncompetitive manufacturing enterprises, stifled any innovative response to global competition. Excessive use of price controls to tinker with market forces and a corrupt bureaucracy emphasized licensing rather than market forces to achieve allocative efficiency. This fuelled rent-seeking activities and discouraged agricultural production. Governments controlled inefficient fiscal and tax structures by making disproportionate use of public debt (issue of treasury bills), interest-rates fixing and directed credit.

Financial liberalization has failed to improve the capacities of the fragile financial institutions. Foreign banks have been slow to finance development in those countries where they have been allowed to operate. Bank insolvencies and weak supportive infrastructures persist, and they have delayed the development of an efficient financial system.

The counterproductive policies pursued under the economic reform programmes have led to poor performance in the manufacturing sector. For instance the devaluation of national currencies has made imports more expensive, thereby raising the cost of production. Trade liberalization has compounded the problems of domestic industries. Cheaper imports from technologically advanced developing countries, especially South-East Asian countries, have made rapid inroads into the African basic consumer-goods markets (Bagachwa *et al.*, 1995; UNIDO, 1996). Manufacturers' associations in Ghana, Nigeria and Zambia have complained of dumping and unfair competition. In some cases external reforms have led to excessive competition among both large- and small-scale firms, and this competition has threatened their profit margins and lowered their sales volumes. In other cases reforms have resulted in plant closures, especially in less competitive, small-scale activities such as soap making, shoe making, textiles, and tie-and-dye-cloth industries (the latter are usually undertaken by women; the clothes are tied and coloured with the dye). Trade liberalization has also encouraged trading activities and discouraged investment in long-term productive activities.

On the other hand import liberalization has given some small-scale and informal-sector firms access to raw materials, tools and spare parts. This has been especially true of small-scale retail, tailoring, food and woodworking enterprises. Import liberalization has also generally improved the supply of goods.

African governments' capacity to manage their economies deteriorated during the economic reforms, and the past policies of many countries undermined the private sector's ability to make up for the diminished role of the state in the economy. Where the private sector is strong, it is dominated either by ethnic minorities (such as Asians in East Africa and whites in South Africa) or by subsidiaries of transnational corporations. Whether international linkages created by the non-indigenous private sector will improve domestic economies is unclear. The strength of the indigenous private sector can be improved if African governments take a more active role in enhancing its capacities, if the public sector is streamlined, and if better cooperation between the private and the public sector is ensured.

Preliminary assessments indicate that African countries' responses to SAPs differ, depending on a number of factors, such as the situation that prevailed before the reforms, the speed, intensity and sustainability of the reforms, resource endowments and financial inflows to complement domestic resources.

THE MARGINALIZATION OF AFRICA

The SAPs have failed to integrate Africa effectively into the global economy. The weakness of Africa's global integration is evident in its falling share of world trade, investment and IT. In this section we examine these three aspects of the marginalization of Africa as they pertain to its main regions: East, West, Southern and North Africa.

Trade

Africa's current position in the global economy is characterized by a small and declining share of world trade, and concentration on the production of primary exports and importation of non-primary products. Africa's share of world trade varied from 4.1 per cent to 4.9 per cent from 1960–65, fluctuated around 4.4 per cent during the 1970s and declined to 2–3 per cent in the 1990s. Its share of world exports fell from 4.7 per cent in 1975 to 2.0 per cent in 1990; the share of the least developed African countries suffered a more drastic fall, from 0.6 per cent to 0.2 per cent (UNIDO, 1993).

Table 6.1 gives four indicators of export growth: share of exports in gross domestic product (GDP), growth rate of exports, share of manufactured exports, and share of machinery exports. Between 1980 and 1994, although the share of exports in GDP increased somewhat in many countries, it actually declined in others, such as Algeria, Congo, Nigeria, Togo, Uganda and Zambia. Similarly export growth was negative for Côte d'Ivoire, Nigeria, Tanzania and Zambia in the 1980s, and for Algeria, Cameroon, Côte d'Ivoire, Mauritania and Togo in the 1990s. In the 1980s Mauritius was the

Table 6.1   Indicators of export growth for selected African countries

	Exports as % of GDP		Growth rate of exports (% per year)			Manufactured exports (% of total exports)		Machinery exports (% of total exports)		
	1980	1994	1970–80	1980–90	1990–94	1980	1993	1970	1980	1991
East Africa:										
Kenya	28	39	−2.2	4.3	0.4	12	29	0.3	0.7	10.6[1]
Tanzania	14	24	−6.8	−1.8	10.0	14	n.a.	n.a.	0.6	2.6[2]
Uganda	19	8	−10.5	2.3	5.3	3	1	n.a.	2.7	0.5
West Africa:										
Benin	23	27	−5.3	−2.2	1.9	8	11	n.a.	n.a.	n.a.
Côte d'Ivoire	35	47	3.2	−1.0	−1.2	n.a.	16	1.1	n.a.	2.1
Ghana	8	25	−8.0	2.5	7.5	1	24	0.1	n.a.	0.2
Malawi	25	29	3.9	2.5	0.4	7	4	0.2	0.1	0.2
Mauritania	37	43	−5.3	3.4	−3.8	2	1	0.4	1.4	0.2
Nigeria	29	22	1.4	−0.3	1.7	0	2	n.a.	0.1	0.1
Senegal	28	36	−1.3	2.8	1.4	15	22	4.2	3.0	2.1
Togo	51	30	1.5	0.6	−13.6	11	9	2.0	1.7	1.0
Southern Africa:										
Lesotho	20	15	n.a.	4.1	10.6	n.a.	n.a.	n.a.	n.a.	n.a.
Mauritius	51	59	6.0	10.4	4.6	27	90	0.1	2.8	2.0
Zambia	41	34	−0.5	−3.3	13.7	6	9	n.a.	n.a.	n.a.
Zimbabwe	30	39	2.8	5.4	4.5	38	38	n.a.	1.9	1.8
North Africa:										
Algeria	34	24	1.1	4.1	−0.4	0	4	1.6	n.a.	0.7
Morocco	17	22	−0.6	5.6	2.1	23	57	0.5	0.6	5.9
Tunisia	40	45	0.2	5.6	5.9	36	75	0.4	2.3	8.1

Notes:
1. 1990.
2. 1989.
Sources: World Bank (1993d, 1995a, 1996a).

only African country with an export growth rate that exceeded 10 per cent. African countries' shares of manufactured exports were quite low, with the exception of Kenya, Mauritius, Senegal, Tunisia and Zimbabwe. Zimbabwe's share remained constant between 1980 and 1993.

Finally, the shares of machinery exports were very low for all countries except Cameroon, Kenya and Tunisia. These very low shares suggest that Africa's competitiveness has lagged behind relative to the rest of the world. The rates of productivity growth and technological learning and innovations have been much lower in Africa than elsewhere.

Variations across subregions show no clear pattern. Generally, export growth in the 1990s has been faster for Southern Africa (and the shares of manufactures in GDP have also tended to be higher) than for other regions.

Since independence the commodity structure has remained relatively unchanged, as reflected in the indices of concentration and diversification for 1970 and 1990 (Table 6.2). Heavy dependence on primary commodities persists. However changes in the structure of exports, such as an increase in manufactured exports, may be important for inducing technological advancement, tapping dynamic comparative advantage and increasing productivity.

Table 6.2   Diversification and product concentration indices for the exports of selected African countries, 1970 and 1990

	Number of commodities exported[1]		Diversification index[2]		Concentration index[3]	
	1970	1990	1970	1990	1970	1990
East Africa:						
Kenya	17	123	0.918	0.806	0.499	0.309
Tanzania	49	74	0.848	0.832	0.255	0.262
Uganda	28	26	0.916	0.948	0.596	0.699
West Africa:						
Côte d'Ivoire	81	130	0.863	0.856	0.422	0.312
Gabon	21	39	0.883	0.913	0.500	0.770
Ghana	24	56	0.941	0.907	0.752	0.377
Nigeria	83	117	0.875	0.915	0.583	0.952
Senegal	82	92	0.793	0.857	0.311	0.280
Southern Africa:						
Mauritius	9	101	0.968	0.711	0.93	0.338
Zambia	22	45	0.963	0.932	0.952	0.823
Zimbabwe	–	165	–	0.782	–	0.327
North Africa:						
Algeria	76	85	0.831	0.883	0.652	0.554
Egypt	87	154	0.784	0.700	0.442	0.440
Morocco	84	155	0.816	0.756	0.292	0.166
Tunisia	70	174	0.754	0.668	0.260	0.200

Notes:
1. Refers to those commodities whose exports were greater than $50 000 in 1970 and $100 000 in 1990 or contribute more than 0.3 per cent to the total exports of the country.
2. Share of the most important commodities in total national exports.
3. Hirshman index normalized to yield values between 0 and 1 (maximum concentration).

Sources: UNCTAD (1984, 1991); ECA secretariat.

Commodity prices have rebounded, and projections suggest that some upward pressure will be exerted for the next few years. Although supply constraints have prevented some African countries from benefiting from the higher commodity prices, they will have to make every effort to increase their export volumes and thus increase their export earnings. However, the African countries must use the increased revenues to enhance the productive capacity of their economies and to improve their international competitiveness. They must also diversify their economies, particularly their exports, because the high commodity prices might not be sustained.

With liberalization of world trade and the increased interdependence of national economies, the African countries can expect stiffer competition from other producers of manufactured exports and primary commodities. Unless they take appropriate measures, the African countries may continue to lose world-market share to other countries, even in traditional export commodities such as cocoa, palm oil and coffee. Given that the diversification of production and exports is a medium- to long-term undertaking, the African countries will have to improve their international competitiveness in traditional exports too. This will require appropriate macroeconomic and sector policies – namely competitive exchange rates and measures to reduce the domestic costs of production – as well as improved competitiveness in non-price factors such as more efficient marketing services, and this includes using the information highway, discussed below.

The preferential trading arrangements with the European Union and through the General Agreement on Tariffs and Trade (GATT) that African countries achieved through the Lomé Convention are now under attack. Implementation of the Uruguay Round accord is likely to cause a phasing out of these preferences. Although the overall gain from Uruguay Round of trade negotiations is estimated at $213 billion, Africa (excluding Egypt and Libya) is likely to lose $2.6 billion a year (see Martin and Winters, 1995).

Investment

The small manufacturing base and poor export performance noted above are consistent with the low rate of investment in Sub-Saharan Africa. The levels of private and public investment have been modest, even in African countries with the most successful reforms. Investment as a percentage of GDP declined significantly between the 1970s the 1990s, from nearly 26 per cent to a little over 16 per cent (Table 6.3). Contributing to the investment decline was the drying up of external funding in the early 1980s. The fall in gross domestic investment mirrors the decline in the gross domestic savings rate: public savings declined by an average of 2 per cent a year. Public investment in infrastructure and the social sector has deteriorated since the start of the economic reforms as has investment in science and technology

Table 6.3 Public and private investments in Sub-Saharan Africa, 1970–94 (weighted averages, percentage of GDP)

	1970–79	1980–89	1990–94
Private	12.2	9.8	10.0
Public	13.6	9.5	6.3
Total	25.8	19.3	16.3

Source: IFC (1995).

institutions, telecommunications, power generation, general education and universities.

The sustainability of economic reforms and the credibility of government policy regimes are important for inducing investment in medium- and long-term development. The donor community and international financial institutions (IFIs) have been providing credibility to African governments during the economic reform, but what is required to gain investment is macroeconomic stability. Debt relief and selective financing might be more effective in achieving genuine macroeconomic stability than IFI-imposed trade policy regimes.

Despite liberalization of the investment codes of many countries, Africa is marginalized in terms of FDI inflows (Table 6.4). Most FDI in Africa is concentrated in a small number of countries that are endowed with natural resources, especially oil. Sub-Saharan Africa has failed to attract much FDI. The bulk of external resource flows into the region is accounted for by grants and official loans, with FDI accounting for only 12 per cent of the total in 1993 (UNCTAD, 1995a, 1995b). If the recent surge of FDI in Angola and Nigeria is excluded, the region as a whole recorded a decline in FDI inflows in 1994. In recent years the International Finance Corporation (IFC) has established several programmes, for example the African Project Development Facility and the African Enterprise Facility. However the IFC's investments in Africa in 1994 averaged only $600 000, compared with an average of $12.3 million elsewhere. By 1994 the share of Sub-Saharan Africa in IFC investments was about half that of the 1970s and 1980s (Helleiner, 1996).

Africa's share of FDI in the developing-country total fell from 11 per cent during 1986–90 to 6 per cent during 1991–93, and to 4 per cent in 1994. Net resource flows to Africa dropped sharply, from $24.1 billion in 1992 to $19.0 billion in 1993 – a fall of nearly 21 per cent. This was largely accounted for by a decline in bilateral development finance. The decline in official development finance was not compensated for by increases in private capital flows or export revenues. In effect, the decline contributed to a contraction in imports, such as occurred in 1993.

Table 6.4 Net foreign direct investment in Africa ($ million), current prices

Region	1980	1985	1986	1987	1988	1989	1990	1991	1992	1993	1994
Sub-Saharan Africa	−730 (−112.3)	780 (35.4)	568 (34.2)	1 212 (59.1)	1 089 (44.1)	2 473 (61.3)	809 (44.4)	1 897 (77.7)	1 571 (57.7)	1 713 (59.2)	3 116 (68.0)
Sub-Saharan Africa excl. South Africa	40 (6.1)	1 280 (58.2)	688 (41.4)	1 372 (66.9)	991 (40.2)	2 463 (61.0)	814 (44.6)	1 905 (78.0)	1 576 (57.9)	1 721 (59.4)	3 111 (67.9)
West Africa	−472 (−72.6)	464 (21.1)	91 (5.5)	791 (38.6)	444 (18.0)	1 988 (49.2)	703 (38.6)	883 (36.2)	1 022 (37.5)	1 538 (53.1)	2 353 (51.4)
East Africa	78 (12.0)	13 (0.6)	28 (1.7)	45 (2.2)	−2 (0.0)	61 (1.5)	57 (3.1)	20 (0.8)	21 (0.8)	25 (0.9)	72 (1.6)
Central Africa	223 (34.3)	390 (17.7)	184 (11.1)	153 (7.5)	171 (6.9)	−129 (−3.2)	−11 (−0.6)	−67 (−2.7)	30 (1.1)	−11 (−0.4)	−42 (−0.9)
North Africa	80 (12.3)	1 421 (64.6)	1 093 (65.8)	838 (40.9)	1 378 (55.9)	1 565 (38.8)	1 014 (55.6)	544 (22.3)	1 152 (42.3)	1 182 (40.8)	1 464 (32.0)
All Africa	−650	2 201	1 661	2 050	2 467 (8.9) (1.2)	4 037 (14.1) (2.0)	1 823 (5.3) (0.9)	2 441 (6.0) (1.5)	2 723 (5.0) (1.6)	2 895 (3.9) (1.4)	4 580 (5.4) (2.1)

Notes: Figures in parentheses are percentages of the total for African countries; percentages for All Africa are developing-country and world totals.
Source: World Bank (1996e).

Information Technology

Overall, investment in technology in the form of R&D is very low in Africa and has been declining. Africa spent only 0.33 per cent of its GDP in investment in technology in 1970. This ratio fell to 0.29 per cent in 1990 (see Table 7.9, Chapter 7). With the exception of South Africa, the African countries' expenditure on telecommunications equipment in 1986 represented only 0.7 per cent of world spending. Moreover, only a few countries are the main spenders: Algeria, Libyan Arab Jamahiriya, Kenya, Zimbabwe, Nigeria, Morocco, Côte d'Ivoire and Tunisia. The low GDP levels and poor growth rates of most African countries (see Table 6.6) have resulted in poor telecommunications infrastructure and low teledensity levels. The African telecommunications network is growing very slowly by international standards. South Africa is the only country with good telecommunications. Table 6.5 compares the state of telecommunications in South Africa with that in the rest of Africa. The most striking indicator is teledensity; teledensity in South Africa is 9.5 main lines per 100 people whereas in the rest of Sub-Saharan Africa it is only 0.5. About 33 per cent of Africa's main lines and nearly 84 per cent of all cellular subscribers are in South Africa. North Africa is much better off than Sub-Saharan Africa in terms of main lines and teledensity, but it has a much smaller proportion of cellular subscribers.

The lack of software in local African languages is a serious problem even in South Africa, which is relatively more advanced. Some countries have attempted to apply local languages to computer technology. Ethiopia, for example, has searched for a reliable means of fully exploiting computer capability in the national language and thereby enhancing IT applications in all sectors of the economy.[1]

Access to IT is influenced, *inter alia,* by purchasing power as well as by education and computer literacy. Economically disadvantaged groups are less likely to be able to afford to buy computer hardware. To the extent that women are underrepresented in the education system, they are likely to lack

Table 6.5   Comparison of South Africa's telecommunications infrastructure with the rest of Africa, 1995*

Indicator	South Africa	Sub-Saharan Africa	North Africa
Main lines (millions)	3844.5 (32.5%)	2628.1 (22.2%)	5363.6 (45.3%)
Teledensity (main lines per 100 people)	9.5	0.5	4.2
Cellular subscribers	520000 (83.9%)	63554 (10.3%)	36000 (5.8%)

* Percentage of African total is given in parentheses.
Source: ITU (1996).

access to its technology. In addition the information highway is inherently exclusionist in its use of culturally determined symbols, images, sounds and language (see Marcelle, 1996).

Factory automation and computerization are uncommon in African industries, and this is preventing the industries from becoming internationally competitive. Most African countries rely on the importation of such IT as numerically controlled machine tools (NCMTs), which are used mainly in the defence industry.[2]

Locally manufactured computer hardware is extremely rare.[3] Government policies have also hindered the use of computers in Africa in the past. For example, from 1974 to the 1980s Tanzania banned the importation of computers on the pretext that they were luxury items. Some countries have resisted connection to the information highway because of the undesirable information that can be accessed. Thus a country may voluntarily exclude itself from enjoying the benefits of new technology (Ramani, 1996).

The Uruguay Round accord formalized and universalized standards for the protection of intellectual property rights (Correa, 1996). The implication of this for developing countries is that access to existing computer programmes will become more costly when the scope for 'pirating' is reduced. Pirating is evident in many African countries, although it is difficult to give accurate figures. Pirated software (including diskettes) is available at lower cost. In addition, patenting will make the underlying ideas and concepts involved in software preparation difficult to access, thus raising barriers to entry into the semiconductor industry.

We can conclude that the marginalization of Africa in terms of IT occurs through:

- An inability sufficiently to increase the stock of IT hardware in Africa.
- The low capacity to develop appropriate software.
- The ineffectiveness and unreliability of the telecommunications systems, a situation that is aggravated by their unequal distribution between and within countries, especially between urban and rural areas.
- A lack of skill in developing and making effective use of IT.

Electronic Networking

Despite these constraints, more than half of African countries have some form of e-mail service and a gateway to the Internet. However infrastructure is poor, and access to low-cost electronic communications is confined mainly to capital cities. Only Mauritius, Senegal and South Africa have these facilities outside their capitals (see Jensen, 1996).

A commercial, up-to-date communications system for Zambia's business and professional community (Zamnet) operates from the University of

Zambia. It began by offering an e-mail service, free of charge, to non-commercial organizations such as non-governmental organizations, health and education institutions and United Nations agencies. Zamnet now offers the opportunity to browse on the World Wide Web, as well as network news and file transfer. At present Zamnet has more than 600 full Internet accounts. The service is concentrated mostly in Lusaka and the Copperbelt.

Information from Zamnet's database of hotels and lodges in Zambia, for example, can be downloaded by any Internet user interested in accommodation in that country. A construction company has found the network useful for obtaining information on low-cost housing in other parts of the world. Banks are using Zamnet for the import declaration form system – the network provides a rapid means of communication between themselves, the Ministry of Finance and the Bank of Zambia. Commercial rose growers are using it to keep in touch with market developments in Europe.

Zamnet services in Zambia have scope for further expansion. A potential source of business is Telcom 2000, a fibre-optic system primarily intended for improving communications in farming communities, especially in remote areas. However, the use of Zamnet has been constrained by insufficient telephone lines, a small Internet link and the computer illiteracy of the general population.

Kenya too has Internet services. Two of Kenya's major Internet providers launched their services in April 1996, although the Kenya Post and Telecommunications' (KP&T) announcement of Internet availability and providers was not due until early May 1997. According to the latest count, eight Nairobi-based companies are or will soon be providing full e-mail and Internet services.

South Africa has five network operators, all of which aim to expand their business in Africa. Telkom SA Limited is the dominant operator with 3.7 million main exchange lines in operation. Eskom is the national supplier of electricity. It has its own telecommunications network and cooperates with several African countries. Transtel is the telecommunications subsidiary of Transnet, South Africa's government-owned railway and transport company. Transtel is currently expanding to link all its African operations via satellite. South Africa has two competing cellular operators: MTN and Vodacom.

Subscription charges for access to Internet vary considerably across the different subregions of Africa. For example in Southern Africa these charges range from $10 to $100 per month, which is a fairly high sum relative to the average per capita income in most African countries. This means that even if computers are available, access to them is likely to be limited to a few people (see Jensen, 1996).

Regional Cooperation

Some modest initiatives at regional cooperation in electronic networking are underway. The first African regional grouping for the provision of Internet infrastructure has been established in Nairobi (Kenya) as a focal point for the East African Internet Association. It plans to provide shared services to its members in Kenya, Tanzania and Uganda.

The Trade Information Network (TINET), the Automated System for Customs Data (ASYCUDA), the Advanced Cargo Information System (ACIS) and the Regional Telecommunications Programme are useful beginnings in regional cooperation. TINET deals with trade data bases and has links to local points in other countries of the Common Market for Eastern and Southern Africa (COMESA). ASYCUDA deals with customs information in the member countries. In 1996 COMESA launched a third regional programme to coordinate and upgrade the telecommunications systems in the region.

The Southern African Development Community (SADC) is involved in shared telecommunications networks. SADC has outlined plans to link its member countries via a computer-based network for the exchange of geological and mining information. The government of France has contributed $500 000 towards the cost of hardware, software and training. Under the auspices of the Pan-African Geological Information System (PANGIS), SADC geologists have teamed up with the International Centre for Exchange in the Geosciences (CIFEG) – a branch of the French geological department – to pool regional bibliographical information on geology and mining for a database to be hosted by SADC's mining-sector coordinating unit in Lusaka. The network will provide potential investors with information on geological and mining resources. It will also enable Southern African states to exchange data and information electronically with other parts of Africa that have access to the PANGIS network.

Another good example of regional cooperation in IT is the digital loop that is being provided by a phased-development programme in Botswana. This programme is designed to provide a gateway to the rest of the world through Namibia, in addition to those through South Africa, Zambia and Zimbabwe.

It would be to Africa's great advantage if a number of countries coordinated their incipient software and hardware programmes with common suppliers in order to ensure larger production runs and consequent cost reductions. Regional cooperation can ensure consolidation of resources to undertake research and development (R&D). Local solutions to local problems can be found through the sharing of national experiences.

FACTORS INFLUENCING AFRICA'S INTEGRATION

Several factors have contributed to the marginalization of Africa in the globalization process. The first was the colonization of Africa by Belgium, France, Germany, Portugal and the United Kingdom. These colonial masters ensured that the occupied countries were very closely linked to the governing economies rather than to the rest of the world or to other African countries. The colonies were deprived of adequate infrastructure, education, clean water, health care and so on. After independence, many African leaders tried to reverse the colonial legacy of dependence by adopting inward-looking manufacturing policies, but a protective environment was not particularly conducive to developing the national capabilities needed to attain international competitiveness.

The marginalization of Africa in terms of investment is largely explained by political instability and the poor quality of its supportive infrastructure. It is generally believed that successful attraction of FDI lies in the incentives and investment environment a country has to offer, including a favourable national regulatory framework. Positive macroeconomic indicators also help determine the magnitude of investment flow.

Collier (1995) cites four main factors in Africa's marginalization: insufficient reforms, insufficient scale and low-level traps, a high-risk environment and weak restraints. The thesis of insufficient reforms is that though the reforms implemented to date may have substantially narrowed the gap in economic incentives between Africa and elsewhere, they have not eliminated it. The thesis of insufficient scale and low-level traps is that Africa has relatively small markets and scales of production as well as fewer human resources. Another major obstacle to successful integration is the perception that Africa's investment environment is more risky for private agents than that of Asia, for example. Africa is subject to the risks and shocks associated with frequent policy changes. Weak agencies of restraint indirectly account for the high-risk environment: the weakness of the armed forces means that government policies can change without notice; the weakness of the central bank means that macroeconomic policy can change abruptly; the weakness of audits means that taxes can change abruptly. Weak agencies of restraint also directly contribute to marginalization: weakness of the accountancy department implies that the financial system is rudimentary, often supplying only trade credit.

GLOBALIZATION'S EFFECTS ON GROWTH, INCOME AND EMPLOYMENT

This section examines the growth performance of selected African countries and the incidence of poverty and unemployment in the era of accelerated globalization – the 1980s and 1990s. Table 6.6 compares the annual rates of growth in these African countries in the 1970s, 1980s and 1990s. The growth rates were higher in the 1970s than in the subsequent periods for Algeria, Côte d'Ivoire, Kenya, Lesotho, Malawi, Mauritius, Nigeria, Togo and Tunisia, while growth rates improved during the 1980s and 1990s for Benin, Ghana and Mauritania. For Tanzania, the growth rate remained more or less unchanged throughout the period

Africa's economic performance has been unpromising for a long time. The rate of growth of per capita GDP has remained low both in absolute terms and relative to that of other developing regions. All the African sub-regions experienced relatively high growth rates during the 1960s, however the momentum slowed over the years. Since the 1970s most of the subregions have consistently recorded GDP growth rates that are below the population growth rates. The aggregate GDP growth rate for Africa declined from 3.6 per cent during 1970–80 to 2.5 per cent during 1980–90 and 1.7 per cent

Table 6.6   GDP growth rates for African countries (percentages)

	1970–80	*1980–90*	*1990–94*
East Africa:			
Kenya	6.4	4.2	0.9
Tanzania	3.0	3.8	3.1
Uganda	–	3.1	5.6
West Africa:			
Benin	2.2	2.6	4.1
Côte d'Ivoire	6.8	−0.1	−0.2
Ghana	−0.1	3.0	4.3
Mauritania	1.3	1.7	3.6
Nigeria	4.6	1.6	2.4
Senegal	2.3	3.2	0.0
Togo	4.0	1.8	−3.4
Southern Africa:			
Lesotho	8.6	4.3	6.1
Malawi	5.8	2.7	−0.7
Mauritius	6.8	6.5	5.3
Zambia	1.4	0.8	−0.1
Zimbabwe	1.6	3.5	1.1
North Africa:			
Algeria	4.6	2.9	−0.6
Morocco	5.6	4.2	1.7
Tunisia	6.8	3.3	4.5

Sources: World Bank (1995a, 1996a).

during 1990–94 (Table 6.7). The decline was more marked in the case of the Maghreb countries and the net oil exporters. For instance growth in the Maghreb, which was nearly 4 per cent in the 1970s, fell to 1.4 per cent during 1990–94.

Cornia *et al.* (1992) argue that the orthodox adjustment policies that were applied on a massive scale in Africa during the 1980s have failed to contribute to the achievement of long-term development objectives, which have also been hindered by the presence of persistent macroeconomic imbalances and too much emphasis on demand rather than supply management.

The situation regarding poverty alleviation is also not encouraging.[4] Poverty tends to be worst in rural areas, even allowing for the often substantial differences in the cost of living between town and countryside. The problems of malnutrition, lack of education, low life expectancy and substandard housing are also generally more severe in rural areas.

Despite the distributional concerns of many African governments, the objective of reducing income inequalities has not been achieved. Income

Table 6.7   Real GDP annual growth rate by African sub-regions at constant prices and exchange rates, 1970–94 percentages)

Sub-Region	*1970–80*	*1980–90*	*1990–94*	*1994*
ECCAS	2.7	1.9	−3.7	−2.6
ECOWAS	4.2	2.1	2.0	1.7
Maghreb	3.7	1.9	1.4	2.0
PTA	1.1	3.2	2.0	2.9
Franc Zone	4.3	1.7	0.2	1.3
Net oil exporters	4.1	2.5	1.6	1.2
Net oil importers	2.5	2.5	1.9	3.5
All RMCs	3.6	2.5	1.7	1.9

Notes: ECCAS = Economic Community of Central African States (Burundi, Cameroon, Central African Republic, Chad, Congo, Equatorial Guinea, Gabon, Rwanda, Sao Tome and Principe, and Zaire); ECOWAS = Economic Community of West African States (Benin, Burkina Faso, Cape Verde, Côte d'ivoire, Gambia, Ghana, Guinea Bissau, Liberia, Mali, Mauritania, Niger, Nigeria, Senegal, Sierra Leone, and Togo); Maghreb = Algeria, Libya, Mauritania, Morocco and Tunisia; PTA = Preferential Trade Area of Eastern and Southern Africa (Angola, Burundi, Comoros, Djibouti, Ethipia, Kenya, Lesotho, Malawi, Mauritius, Mozambique, Namibia, Rwanda, Seychelles, Somalia, Sudan, Swaziland, Tanzania, Uganda, Zambia, Zimbabwe); Franc Zone = Benin, Burkina Faso, Cameroon, Central African republic, Chad, Comoros, Congo, Côte d'Ivoire, Equatorial Guinea, Gabon, Mali, Senegal, Niger, and Togo; Net oil exporters = Algeria, Angola, Cameroon, Congo, Egypt, Gabon, Libya, Nigeria and Tunisia; RMCs = regional member countries of the African Development Bank. The 1994 figures are preliminary estimates.
Source: African Development Bank (1995), p. 16.

inequalities, which were quite large in the mid-1970s, have perhaps changed somewhat in character but they have not diminished. The stabilization policies of the 1980s led to a narrowing of the rural–urban income gap in most cases, but they did not result in an overall decline in income inequality, as income differentials within both urban and rural areas have accentuated (Cornia *et al.*, 1992).

The trends in income distribution are also discouraging. Table 6.8 shows the income shares of the top 20 per cent and bottom 20 per cent of the population for a few of the African countries for which data are available. For Kenya, Tunisia and Uganda, the share of the top 20 per cent improved between the 1970s and 1980s whereas that of the bottom 20 per cent either remained constant or increased marginally.

The data on real wages also reveal worsening trends. Real wages in manufacturing fell throughout the 1980s in 12 of the 15 countries for which data were available (ILO, 1995b). For example the minimum wage declined by 72 per cent in Zaire between 1984 and 1988, by 30 per cent in Niger between 1980 and 1987, and by at least 25 per cent in Nigeria between 1986 and 1990 (see Jespersen, 1992).

The decline in real wages did not promote employment expansion during the 1980s. Instead the growth rate of formal employment in Africa fell from 2.8 per cent in 1975–80 to 1 per cent in the 1980s (ILO–JASPA, 1989). The SAPs discussed above led to a decline in public-sector employment in the 1980s. Private-sector employment fell because manufacturing shrank after import liberalization – wage employment in manufacturing declined at an estimated rate of 0.5 per cent a year in the 1980s (ILO, 1995b). Table 6.9 shows that during the 1980s many African countries experienced stagnating or declining rates of growth in employment. An important source of the unemployment problem in the African countries is the large reserve of under-employed labour outside the modern sector. Diminishing job opportunities

Table 6.8   Trends in income distribution in selected African
countries percentage of income

	Income share of top 20 per cent		Income share of bottom 20 per cent	
	1970–75	*1989–94*	*1970–75*	*1989–94*
Egypt	48	41	6	9
Kenya	60	62	3	3
Tanzania	53	45	5	7
Tunisia	42	46	6	6
Uganda	47	48	6	7

Source: World Bank (1996d).

Table 6.9   General employment levels in selected African
countries (percentage change over the period)

	1983–87	1987–91	1983–91
Moderately growing			
employment levels:			
Algeria	14	15	20
Botswana	49	48	122
Kenya	16	14	32
Malawi	5	15	21
Mauritius	32	12	47
Seychelles	11	21	34
Zimbabwe	5	15	20
Declining employment			
levels:			
Benin	−4	−33	−36
Burundi	22	−10	10
Central African Republic	1	−27	−26
Ghana	26	−45	−31
Niger	37	−14	19
Stagnating employment			
levels:			
Côte d'Ivoire	−6	−5	−11
Gambia, The	−1	8	7
Senegal	−26	50	12
Swaziland	5	10	16
Zambia	−1	8	7

Source: ILO-JASPA (1995).

in the modern sector and the depressed state of rural economies have discouraged migration, which suggests that open unemployment may now pre-
vail even in rural areas. The urban informal sector, which offered an outlet for
the urban and rural unemployed, is also becoming saturated. It generates
mainly 'survival' jobs of extremely low productivity and income.

CONCLUSIONS

This chapter has discussed the contribution of globalization to Africa's
marginalization. We have demonstrated that Africa is only weakly integrated
into the global economy and that its integration is not on terms determined by
Africa. The marginalization of Africa is evident from its falling share of world
trade, investment and information technology. This process can be explained

in terms of historical developments, the policies that African countries have pursued, and the inadequate economic and social infrastructure.

The economic reforms adopted in many African countries in the 1980s and 1990s have exhibited a variety of relationships and interactions with the globalization process. The results of the SAPs have varied from country to country, and their full effects are not yet known. However there are indications that these reforms can improve Africa's position in the globalization process. In particular, policies relating to macroeconomic stability, trade and investment regimes, and transport and communications infrastructure can enhance Africa's integration into the global economy.

African governments also need to formulate national technology policies to create an environment in which the economic and social benefits of information technology can be realized. The international competitiveness of Africa is unlikely to improve without increased use of information technology in economic and social activities. The private sector should be encouraged to use information technology in production systems. This can be done by removing or reducing import duties on computers in order to make them more affordable – computers are still quite expensive in Africa because of these import duties and also because of value added and sales taxes.

The main issue for further research is how Africa can redefine its position in the world economy in ways that are consistent with its medium- and long-term development objectives. Further research is needed to determine the options open to Africa and the opportunities that could be created by effective use of information technology in the pursuit of greater interdependence and greater integration into the global economy.

Notes

1. The Ethiopian government established a National Computer Centre (NCC) in 1987 under the Ethiopian Science and Technology Commission. The NCC developed application software packages in Amharic (for example an Amharic operating system, 'AGAFARI', and Amharic publishing, 'MAHTEME') and encouraged the use of PCs in the local language for word processing, databases, desktop publishing, statistical analysis, spreadsheets and so on. To make personal computers operational in the Amharic language, an add-on device was developed. In addition, printer chips for Amharic are also available.
2. In Zimbabwe, NCMTs are imported for use in the manufacture of components for transport equipment, mining machinery and weapons. They are also used to produce such precision items as diesel engines for railways and trucks, and components of agricultural and mining machines, often for export to neighbouring countries such as Kenya, Tanzania and Zambia.
3. Some local efforts in the manufacture of computers include assembly operations for personal computers in Cameroon, Zimbabwe and Kenya, minicomputers in

Côte d'Ivoire and microcomputers in Morocco. In 1996 two international computer firms set up computer assembly projects in Zambia to accelerate the pace of computerization: Cellcome Computers set up a ZK445 million assembly plant for its DCS computers in Lusaka, while Quantum Technology (Africa) is planning a ZK2.2 billion computer assembly facility. Cellcome is primarily targeting the Zambian market, but Quantum has a wider market projection for domestic users and for the Common Market for East and Southern Africa (COMESA).

4. According to the World Bank (1990), nearly half of the world's poor live in South Asia; Sub-Saharan Africa has about one third fewer poor, although in relation to the region's overall population its poverty is roughly as high.

7 Regional Perspectives: An Overview

A.S. Bhalla and Albert Berry

Our main concern in this volume is to examine the effect that globalization and information technology (IT) are having on developing countries. Some analysis of industrial countries is also presented for completeness and as yardstick against which the impact of globalization on developing regions can be considered. If there is one thing that the earlier chapters have suggested, it is that the impact of globalization and IT vary considerably across regions and national boundaries. For simplicity, and despite the significant variations within them, this overview uses the same conventional designation of regions applied throughout the rest of the volume, namely South Asia, East and South-East Asia, Africa, Latin America and the OECD countries.

The conditions prevailing at the time of accelerated globalization varied from one region to another.[1] In Africa, for example, the conditions in terms of global integration were much less favourable than those in Asia and other regions (see Collier, 1995; Mosley, 1996), including low growth (lower than in the other regions), caused in part by poor macroeconomic policies; a weak performance on the part of the agricultural sector, in which the bulk of the population is engaged; inadequate support by aid donors with respect to agricultural research and extension systems; depressed and declining commodity prices, leading to worsening terms of trade; and unsustainable levels of debt. Particularly weak governance/severe corruption contributed to the poor average performance of two of the states, Nigeria and Zaire, despite the fact that they have the greatest volume of exploitable natural resources.

The debt problem severely plagued Latin America from the early 1980s, but the countries of both South-East and South Asia suffered far less from this. Foreign banks stopped lending to Latin American countries following the Mexican government's inability to service its debt in 1982. No such capital supply shock had hit the Asian countries until 1997, when the Thai *baht* came under attack as the country's large fiscal and balance of payments deficits worried the international financial community. With impressive speed the pressure moved to Malaysia, Indonesia, Republic of Korea and Hong Kong. There was concern (*The Economist*, 15 November 1997) that if the banking reform in the affected countries did not proceed quickly and effectively the crisis in South-East Asia could drag China and Japan down

168

with it. This new contagion highlights one of the risks of an interconnected world financial system–the greater vulnerability of banks and countries to attacks which would not pose a threat to them in a less open system. For the open system to function well, the agents and institutions must be both more careful and better regulated. It remains to be seen how quickly and success-fully the needed institutional improvements can be made.

The above differences in the conditions prevailing at the beginning of the 1980s partly explain the wide variations in the level and rate of integration of different regions and individual economies into the global economy.

REGIONAL DIVERSITY IN GLOBAL INTEGRATION

In terms of the two frequently used indicators of globalization – the ratio of exports to GDP and the ratio of FDI to GDP East and South-East Asia (ESEA) is now the most integrated region, but it is noteworthy that this status has only recently been achieved. Judging by the (current price) export/GDP ratio, Sub-Saharan Africa was the most integrated of the major regions as recently as 1980,[2] a year in which no less than 30 per cent of its GDP was exported (reflecting in part the high price of Nigeria's oil exports) (Table 7.1). During the 1970s all of the four major developing regions experienced sig-nificant increases in this ratio (though its absolute level remained quite low for both India and China), as did the industrial countries. As a result the world figure rose sharply from 14 per cent to 22 per cent. It was during the 1980s, however, that regional trends diverged dramatically. The export ratio fell in both Sub-Saharan Africa and Latin America, then recovered to end the decade at about where it started; that of South Asia edged up a little, while that of East Asia continued its dramatic increase to equal the African figure. Changes in relative prices were central to some of these trends. Thus the big increase in Sub-Saharan Africa's current price export/GDP ratio in the 1970s was entirely explained in this way – in fact the corresponding constant price ratio was falling. Since 1980 the current price ratio has fallen somewhat, but the constant price ratio has changed very little. The contrast is more extreme for Latin America: the current price ratio rose in the 1970s then showed little net change until 1994, despite a fall in the mid 1980s, whereas the constant price ratio fell very sharply in the 1970s and has risen nearly as much since then. East Asia's performance has been unequivocal by both measures, showing a continuing increase since 1970. By the early 1990s South Asia and Latin America were exporting around 15 per cent of their output, while Sub-Saharan Africa and East Asia exported close to 30 per cent. Interestingly, the dramatic increase in the export ratio of non-communist East Asia was virtually mirrored a few years later by that of China.

Table 7.1   Exports of goods and non-factor services as a percentage of GDP

	1960	1965	1970	1980	1985	1987	1990	1994
Low- and middle-income								
economies, by region	–	13	13	23	–	20	24	22
Sub-Saharan Africa	–	23	20	30	–	25	29	27
East Asia	–	7	6[1]	–	–	31	31[1]	28[1]
South Asia	–	6	5	8	–	8	9	13
Middle East & North Africa	–	19[2]	29	–	–	–	–	–
Latin America and the Caribbean	–	13	13	16	–	12	15	15
Low-income	7	7	7	13	10	13	18	19
India	5	4	4	7	6	7	8	12
China	4	4	3	6	11	13	18	24
Other	17	16	13	20	14	20	24	17
Middle-income	17	17	–	–	26	22	25	23
Lower middle-income	15	15	–	–	23	22	28	–
Upper middle-income	18	20	15	28	28	22	24	–
High-income	–	13	14	22	–	19	20	–
World	–	12	14	22	–	19[3]	20	–

Notes:
1. Includes the Pacific.
2. Includes Europe.
3. Total reporting economies.
Sources: World Bank (1984, 1987, 1989, 1991, 1992, 1993a, 1995a, 1996a).

A different perspective on international economic integration can be gained by looking at the share of manufactured goods in total exports (Table 7.2). Africa has the lowest share of manufactured exports of all the developing regions, that of Latin America and the Caribbean is at an intermediate level, while those of South Asia and East Asia are substantially higher.[3]

The composition of manufactures varies considerably across regions. Although in both subregions of Asia the share of manufactured goods in merchandise exports is high, the manufactured exports of South Asia are much less sophisticated than those of East Asia. A large proportion of exports, particularly those from Bangladesh, India and Pakistan are low-skill, rudimentary, labour-intensive goods such as textiles and garments, and processed versions of raw materials such as cotton and jute. On the other hand the ESEA countries have moved far in the direction of sophisticated, capital-intensive (higher value-added), high-tech manufactures. Meanwhile, China has become a major exporter of labour-intensive manufactures.

The World Bank (1996b, p. 23) uses the share of manufactured exports as a proxy variable to indicate 'countries' access to learning and technology

Tablez 7.2 Manufactured exports as share of total exports, by region (percentages)

	1980	1985	1990	1991	1992	1993
Sub-Saharan Africa:						
WB estimates	11.3	17.7	21.3	23.4	38.0	39.2
Our estimates	9.5	11.5	16.2	16.6	n.a.	n.a.
Middle East & North Africa:						
WB estimates	20.8	29.1	45.7	41.5	44.6	42.4
Our estimates	4.7	9.6	15.3	13.8	15.8	13.0
Latin America & the Caribbean:						
WB estimates	25.0	29.9	28.6	30.0	35.8	34.9
Our estimates	15.9	17.7	29.0	21.6	31.3	n.a.
South Asia:						
WB estimates	47.5	55.2	77.7	67.4	76.6	76.9
Our estimates	52.4	55.3	71.0	73.5	75.2	n.a.
East & South-East Asia:						
WB estimates	26.1	32.0	50.9	57.1	55.4	55.0
Our estimates						
Exc. Japan & Hong Kong	34.0	45.2	63.5	65.5	67.4	55.7
Inc. Japan & Hong Kong	68.6	76.3	82.7	70.7	84.5	64.7

Note: Data refer to merchandise exports.
Sources: Our estimates are based on World Bank (1993d). World Bank (WB) estimates were supplied by the World Bank and refer to the data used for World Bank (1996b). (These estimates are not fully reported in World Bank (1996b) and were supplied by the Bank on special request.)

transfer gains and ability to produce at world standards'. Given the lack of robustness and comparability of data on this share (see note 3), this proxy can be quite misleading. A more appropriate indicator of learning and the effects of modern technology is the share of manufactured exports that fall in the category of higher value-added products, for example machinery. The data in Table 7.3 show the substantial lead enjoyed by East and South-East Asia (excluding China) in this regard (over 40 per cent in the early 1990s), followed by Latin America (averaging about 10 per cent), South Asia (around 5 per cent), the Middle East and North Africa (about 3 per cent) and Sub-Saharan Africa (less than 2 per cent).[4]

FDI as a percentage of GDP is another frequently used index of globalization. Table 7.4 presents estimates of an FDI index – the ratio of a country's

Table 7.3   Share of machinery exports in total exports, by region (percentages)

	1980	*1985*	*1990*	*1991*	*1992*	*1993*
Sub-Saharan Africa	n.a.	0.9	1.0	1.7	1.7	n.a.
Middle East & North Africa	1.1	2.7	2.9	2.8	3.6	3.6
Latin America	6.0	5.1	10.7	5.6	12.9	6.8
South Asia	5.4	4.3	5.0	4.8	4.6	n.a.
East & South-East Asia						
Inc. China	5.5	4.7	11.2	13.2	14.9	12.8
Excl. China	34.8	44.7	44.2	41.4	45.8	40.0

Source: World Bank (1993d).

share in total world FDI to its share of total world GDP (for details see Bhalla and Bhalla, 1997). An FDI index of 1 implies that the investment flow as a proportion of world FDI is proportional to the region's share in world GDP; a value above 1 shows a relative attractiveness for FDI inflows. Here both the Asian regions have a relatively high score, with Latin America a little behind and Africa substantially so (the 1990 figure for Africa clearly seems to be wrong). The limited attractiveness of Africa for FDI inflows is reflected in its low ratio: Africa's share has been declining, along with that of Latin America (Figures 7.1 and 7.2).

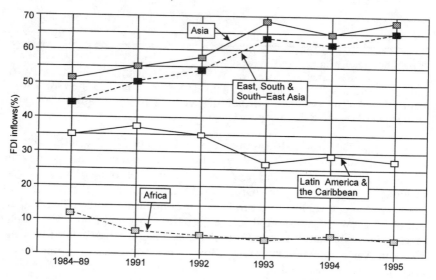

Note: FDI inflows from within the regions are included.

Figure 7.1   FDI inflows as a percentage of the total for developing countries

Source: Based on data in UNCTAD (1996).

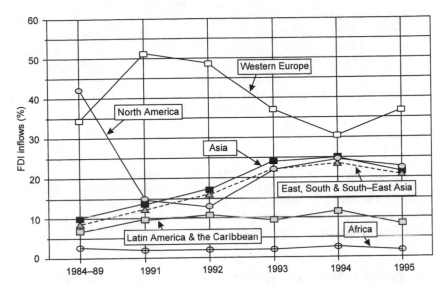

Note: FDI inflows from within the regions are included.

Figure 7.2   FDI inflows as a percentage of the total for all countries
Source: Based on data in UNCTAD (1996).

Table 7.4   GDP-weighted index of inward and outward FDI flows, by region[1]

	Inward FDI flows			Outward FDI flows		
	1986	1990	1994	1986	1990	1994
Africa	0.96	6.7	1.82	n.a.	n.a.	n.a.
South Asia	0.17	0.14	0.33	n.a.	n.a.	n.a.
East & South-East Asia	1.88	2.05	3.63	n.a.	0.67	2.14
Australasia	3.07	2.87	2.13	n.a.	0.73	2.26
Latin America & the Caribbean	1.05	2.00	1.80	n.a.	1.00	0.33
Western Europe	1.17	1.66	1.00	n.a.	1.95	1.62
North America	1.42	1.03	0.88	n.a.	0.49	0.77

Notes:
1. Some ratios are based on incomplete data and may be wrong, as seems to to be
   the case for the Africa ratio for 1990. These ratios are therefore more illus-
   trative than definitive.
2. Excluding Taiwan.
Sources: UN/UNCTAD *World Investment Reports* (various years); World Bank,
World Development Report (various years)

While most geographical regions are being increasingly integrated into the world economy, Sub-Saharan Africa has thus been left out of this process. Its export/GDP ratio has shown little net change for 15 years and its share of the FDI going to the developing countries has fallen. In contrast the ratio of aid to GDP in Africa is much higher than in other regions and has risen markedly, from 3.4 per cent in 1980 to 12.4 per cent in 1994. The corresponding ratios for South Asia were 2.4 per cent and 1.4 per cent, East Asia 0.7 per cent and 0.8 per cent; and Latin America and the Caribbean 0.3 per cent and 0.3 per cent (see World Bank, 1996a). While foreign aid to Africa increased, the FDI/GDP ratio declined from about 2.4 per cent per annum during 1984–89 to about 1.5 per cent in 1995. In contrast, that of Asia more than doubled (from 10 per cent to 21.6 per cent) while that of Latin America and the Caribbean rose more slowly (rising from 6.7 per cent to 8.4 per cent) (see UNCTAD, 1996). Thus aid became the only major channel through which foreign investment and technology entered Africa.

THE IMPACT OF GLOBALIZATION

Growth and Productivity

The protagonists of globalization argue that liberalization of trade and investment, the shift to a more market-based economy and deregulation of industrial and trade policies should improve the allocation of resources, raise productivity, improve international competitiveness and enhance growth. That this has not yet happened at the world level can be partly attributed to the slow growth of the GDP and exports of the high-income countries in the early 1990s (see Table 7.5 and Appendix Table 7.1) and to the economic woes of the countries of the former Soviet Union. It is more helpful to look at those countries and regions that have gone far enough with the introduction of the new policy to provide a meaningful test of its merits, though there would be arguments as to which countries fall into this category. In any case the growth rates for all regions outside Asia were much faster during 1966–73 than during 1974–90 and 1991–93 (Table 7.5). The growth rates for South Asia were about the same in the early 1990s as in 1966–73 but slower than during 1974–90. The forecasts for all the regions show that growth rates during 1995–2005 will be much lower than those during 1966–73. Only in East and South-East Asia has growth during the past decade surpassed the earlier record. The World Bank also forecasts that all regions will have much lower growth rates during 1995–2005 than in 1966–73. It is possible that the failure of both labour productivity and growth to increase during the past decade, when the globalization process accelerated, was due to continued imperfections in the factor and product markets and to the wide disparities

Table 7.5   GDP growth rates, by region (annual growth in percentages)

	1966–73	1974–94	1991–94	1995 (estimated)	1996–2005 (forecast)
Industrial countries					
GDP	4.7	2.7	1.6	2.4	2.8
GDP per capita	3.8	2.1	0.9	1.8	2.4
Latin America and the Caribbean					
GDP	6.4	2.6	3.6	0.9	3.8
GDP per capita	3.7	0.4	1.6	−0.7	2.2
Sub-Saharan Africa					
GDP	4.7	2.2	0.7	3.8	3.8
GDP per capita	2.0	−0.7	−2.2	1.1	0.9
Asia					
GDP	5.9	6.8	7.7	8.2	7.2
GDP per capita	3.3	4.9	6.0	6.7	5.8
East Asia and Pacific					
GDP	7.9	7.9	9.4	9.2	7.9
GDP per capita	5.1	6.2	8.0	8.0	6.8
South Asia					
GDP	3.7	4.9	3.9	5.5	5.4
GDP per capita	1.3	2.7	1.8	3.6	3.7
Middle East and North Africa					
GDP	8.6	1.4	2.4	2.5	2.9
GDP per capita	5.7	−1.8	−0.3	0.1	0.4
Europe and Central Asia					
GDP	6.9	3.3	−9.0	−0.7	4.3
GDP per capita	5.8	2.3	−9.3	−0.8	3.7

Source: World Bank (1996b).

in the degree of global integration. Perhaps the earlier import-substitution model had advantages over the new one in areas such as the promotion of learning-by-doing and the encouragement of high investment rates.

The regions that have experienced rapid growth also account for a high share of total FDI inflows, especially East and South-East Asia. Interestingly this positive relationship between FDI and growth does not extend to the OECD (industrial) countries, which account for the bulk of the FDI inflows that do not go to East and South-East Asia.

The protagonists of globalization have argued that without it growth rates during the 1980s might have been even lower. Even if one assumes that faster growth results from globalization (as in ESEA for example), it may be more the result of industrial and trade policies adopted in the earlier periods (see Chapter 1).

Poverty, Income Distribution and Employment

Developing Countries

There are large economic and social disparities among the countries and regions of the world. Per capita income in Sub-Saharan Africa (in terms of purchasing power parity) is only about one twelfth that of the industrial countries, while that in South Asia is about a tenth (Table 7.6). Such social indicators as literacy rates, life expectancy and the human development index[5] also vary widely among regions (Table 7.7). Life expectancy in 1993 was just 51 years in Sub-Saharan Africa compared with over 74 years in the industrial world and close to 70 years in some developing regions. Among the developing regions the overall human development index (HDI) is highest in Latin America and the Caribbean, followed by ESEA. Both these regions also show higher rates of literacy and life expectancy than South Asia and Sub-Saharan Africa.

Over the last couple of decades, during which the effects of globalization (reflected in increases in average trading ratios for the world in general and developing countries as a group) and the new wave of technological change have been felt, income disparities have widened in two areas of particular concern. First, certain regions or countries have tended to slip back in the global income parade. Sub-Saharan Africa has lost ground in both relative and absolute terms, with per capita GDP falling by about 24 per cent over 25 years. Despite the increasing participation of the developing countries in world trade, growth is not evenly distributed among them. Three quarters of the aggregate increase in the ratio of trade to GDP has occurred in just 10 developing countries – the ratio has fallen in 44 of 93 developing countries over the last decade (World Bank, 1996b, p. 21). The ILO (1995a) points out

Table 7.6   Ratio of share of world income to share of world population, by region

	1960	1989	1989 as ratio of 1960
Sub-Saharan Africa	0.27	0.13	0.48
South Asia	0.16	0.12	0.75
ESEA (exc. China)	0.19	0.29	1.53
Latin America	0.66	0.52	0.79
All developing countries	0.23	0.20	0.87
Least developed countries	0.15	0.06	0.40
Industrial countries	2.67	3.68	1.38

Source: Stewart (1995).

Table 7.7   Human development index, by region (reference year 1993)

	Adult literacy rate (%)	Real GDP per capita (PPP $)	Life expectancy (years)	(HDI)[*]
Sub-Saharan Africa	55.0	1 288	50.9	0.379
South Asia	48.8	1 564	60.3	0.444
East Asia	81.0	2 686	68.8	0.633
East Asia (exc. China)	95.9	8 336	71.3	0.877
South-East Asia & Pacific	86.0	3 216	63.7	0.646
Latin America and the Caribbean	85.9	5 756	68.5	0.824
Industrial countries	98.3	15 136	74.3	0.909
World	76.3	5 428	63.0	0.746

[*]Human development index.
Source: UNDP (1996), p. 209.

that the overall developing-country share of world trade scarcely changed between 1970 and 1991: the remarkable increase in the share of the Asian countries from 4.6 per cent to 12.5 per cent was offset by a corresponding decline for other developing countries. The 1990s have witnessed a surge of private capital flows to developing countries – both FDI and other types of capital – but official flows have dwindled. However these flows, like the growth of trade over a longer period, have been highly concentrated among a few countries: half of the developing countries receive little or no FDI, and in a third of them the ratio of FDI to GDP has fallen over the last decade (ibid). Africa's share of net private capital inflows from 1989–95 was just 4.2 per cent.

The World Bank (ibid.) is inclined to blame poor policy in many developing countries for keeping them out of the export and capital inflow bonanzas.[6] Easterly et al. (1993) and UNCTAD (1996), in contrast, attribute more blame to external circumstances. Clearly the impact of declining commodity terms of trade has been severe in many countries. The benefits of trade for the least developed countries have been curtailed during the last 25 years by a cumulative decline of about 50 per cent in their terms of trade (Berry et al., 1997, table 4), which offset much of the quantum increase in exports, especially during the early 1990s. Also limiting the benefits of export expansion was the heavy pressure of debt whose servicing precluded the export earnings from being used to import developmental goods in the degree which would have been desirable.

A second distribution-related concern flows from the fairly general trend towards intracountry increases in inequality in the developing world during the recent phase of globalization. At the same time the wide regional differences in levels of income inequality that existed before this phase appear to have worsened somewhat. The already extreme inequality has further widened in most of the Latin American countries (see Chapter 3, and Berry, 1997b); a similar trend, albeit with lower absolute levels, has characterized South Asia (see Chapter 4). Although information on Africa is scant and generally not very reliable, the situation in that region seems to be similar, judging by the increased income dispersion reported for Ethiopia, Ghana, Nigeria and Tanzania by Demery *et al.* (1995). Increased openness and trade are widely hypothesized to have amplified wage differentials between skilled and unskilled or less skilled workers in these and other regions. This situation contrasts with that of East Asia, where wage differentials and income inequality narrowed during the 1960s and 1970s, although some concentration has occurred in more recent years (Berry *et al.*, 1997). Most of countries in this region have relatively low levels of income concentration, and were able to keep them low during the periods of rapid growth and rising trade ratios. In Korea the level of concentration fell further, it may have done so in Indonesia as well; in Malaysia it did not worsen significantly; in Thailand it worsened to the point of cancelling out some of the potential poverty reduction associated with rapid growth (Chapter 5).

East Asia vs. Latin America

What explanation can be given to the divergent experiences across the regions, and especially between Latin America and East and South-East Asia (ESEA)? In the simplest theory, openness and trade are posited to raise the demand for unskilled labour and thus their wages in developing countries relative to those of skilled workers. However the Latin American experience of widening wage inequality in the late 1980s and early 1990s, together with a considerable amount of less systematic evidence from other parts of the developing world, is inconsistent with this argument.

Various interpretations of the tendency towards increasing inequality and divergence among the regions have been advanced. The inequality trend may be substantially due to the process of globalization; but it could also be due to elements of the economic reform packages that have been so widely implemented in order to achieve structural adjustment, or to the pace and character of technological change. Wood (1997) speculates that the reasons for differences across regions may include faster growth of the supply of skilled labour in East Asia, differences in natural resources (Latin America is better endowed with natural resources) and more regulated labour markets in Latin America.

If trade does play a significant role in the noted outcomes, the effects of the increases that have occurred may differ significantly according to the composition of a country's exports and imports and when the expansion occurred. Wage differentials narrowed in Korea and Taiwan in the 1960s, when many of the exports were labour intensive and when the market was not crowded by competing low-wage suppliers. Those differentials widened in Latin America during the 1980s, and 1990s. Most of the countries of this region do not have a very labour-intensive export basket, and were they to compete in that market they would be up against China and other low-income countries of Asia at a time possibly characterized by a new technology bias against unskilled labour (Wood, 1997), though as we argue below there is no clear evidence in support of the latter bias.

Although growth is normally vital for poverty reduction, the level of and changes in inequality also matter. Poverty often responds faster to growth where inequality is lower: intuitively, if many people are bunched closer to the poverty line, growth tends to pull them more quickly out of poverty than it does in societies where income distribution is polarized and many of the poor are a long way from the poverty line. Bringing such people closer to (but still not above) the poverty line may be as useful as raising others above it, but their being very poor in the first place often signals a lack of immediate economic potential and a lack of political voice, which together may imply that they will not systematically share the fruits of overall growth. Without efforts to redistribute, poverty reduction will be sluggish in many countries even when income does grow – as was the experience of a number of Latin American countries over the last decade and one that may be in store for India and a number of African countries in the future.

In the developing countries open unemployment is a less frequent and obvious outcome of low demand for various categories of labour than is the case in industrial countries. Such changes are more likely to show up in the widening wage and income differentials discussed above.

Industrial Countries

The effects of globalization on employment and income distribution in the industrialized countries are usually assumed to be manifested either through the importation of labour-intensive manufactures from developing countries and the FDI that moves to those countries, or through the rapid technological change that has contributed significantly to the latest phase of globalization and to a considerable extent is necessitated by the need to remain competitive with other countries. There is controversy over whether trade and FDI are significant factors in explaining unemployment or reduced demand for low-skilled labour in the OECD countries. The main competing argument is that recent technological change has been heavily labour displacing (see ILO, 1995a; OECD, 1994). While there is some truth in this, there is no clearcut empirical evidence to suggest that the use of information technology in recent years has reduced employment in the North (see below). It is widely believed that the much higher unemployment in the industrialized countries of continental Europe compared with the United States is due to the more flexible labour market in the latter, which makes labour mobility and sacking easier than in Europe, and which also makes it easier for wage reductions to occur. Accordingly, the general view is that a declining demand for less-skilled labour, whatever its origins, leads to rising unemployment in continental Europe while showing up in increasing wage differentials and income inequality in the United States.

Wood (1994) argues that growing unemployment in the North is caused by the expansion of imports from the South. Krugman and Lawrence (1994), on the other hand, argue that trade is not a very important factor in explaining both the unemployment of the unskilled in the United States and the widening differential between the earnings of skilled and unskilled workers. Analysing the US data on the employment and earnings of high-school dropouts, high-school graduates and those with some college education, Lawrence (1996) reports that the wage differentials between skilled and unskilled workers increased by about 15 per cent during the 1980s,, and estimates that the trade factor accounted for only 10 per cent of this increase. On the other hand, the effect of technological and organizational changes involving the replacement of unskilled by skilled workers is estimated to account for about half of the total increase. Krugman and Venables (1995, p. 877) also conclude that 'growing integration with the South is at best a minor factor in the economic woes of the North'.

Trade cannot fully explain the problems (unemployment, falling wages) of unskilled workers in the North, more particularly in the United States. First, if trade does lead to a fall in real wages of the unskilled in the North, then prices in the sectors using unskilled labour should also fall, but no such pattern can be observed (see Bhagwati and Dehejia, 1994; Lawrence and Slaughter, 1993). On the contrary, the 'international price of skill-intensive goods has fallen over the past decade or so relative to the price of (low-skill) labour-intensive goods, which would go against a trade-based explanation of rising inequality (UNCTAD, 1995a, p. 133). Furthermore, only 20–30 per cent of the US workforce is engaged in the traded goods sector, making it doubtful that what happens there would dominate the trends in the labour market as a whole. Freeman (1993) argues that the answer to the problem of low-skilled workers in the United States has to be sought primarily in the non-traded goods sector.

Second, the share of developing-country exports to the OECD countries is quite small: non-oil imports into the United States from low-wage countries account for just 2.8 per cent of GDP; the main impact of trade on employment would thus appear to be that which occurs within the OECD countries rather than that of trade with the ESEA newly industrializing economies

(NIEs). The United States continues to import mainly from the industrialized countries with similar skills and wage structures (see Krugman and Lawrence, 1994). It is noted that a good deal of loss of employment in the UK textiles and clothing industries has been due to imports from such countries as Italy, Germany and the United States (Dicken, 1992). For the European Union countries, the biggest adverse effect on employment results from a very large trade deficit with Japan.

Third, the fall in manufacturing employment in the OECD countries may have been due more to recession and slow growth in these countries, and to a reduction of exports to developing countries (in the 1980s), than to rising manufactured exports from developing countries (UNCTAD, 1995a). Finally, where imported manufactures from developing countries do not substitute for domestic products in the developed countries, they need not lead to a decline in domestic employment in these countries.

Thus the direct overall employment effect in the OECD countries of trade with NIEs is likely to be small. In such industries as textiles and clothing and leather products and footwear, developing countries have been able to increase their exports to the industrialized countries quite significantly. From the early 1980s to the early 1990s import penetration in these industries rose from around 8 per cent to 16 per cent (UNCTAD, 1995a, p. 142). These are also the industries in which job losses in the North are significant. The impact on labour demand and employment at the low-skill end of the spectrum is probably substantially greater, and may thus play a significant role in the prospects for low-skill workers. The indirect effect on certain industries and geographical areas of OECD firms being induced to invest in labour-saving technology and rationalize production appears to have been significant (Dicken, 1992).

The bulk of the increase in manufactured exports from developing countries has been accounted for by two groups of NIEs in South-East Asia: (1) the 'gang of four' (namely Hong Kong, Korea, Singapore and Taiwan) and (2) the second-tier NIEs (China, India, Indonesia, Malaysia, the Philippines and Thailand). Observers in the North believe that the competitive advantage of these countries lies in abundant unskilled labour and lower labour costs (sometimes dubbed 'unfair' trade and competition). However this cannot be the entire explanation as many of these countries (with the exception of India and Indonesia) are now suffering from increasing labour shortages and rising real wages. Other important factors in explaining their success in exports include increased FDI, product and technology upgrading, industrial diversification and rapid productivity growth (see below).

What about the impact of increased FDI flows on employment in the South and the North? There are two reasons why transnational enterprises invest abroad: (1) to replace exports by production abroad when they face tariff and other barriers, and (2) to search for lower costs in order to improve competitiveness. Production abroad may mean loss of production and employment at home, especially if production abroad does not generate any demand for inputs from the home country and the goods produced abroad are reexported to the home country rather than to the rest of the world. The net effect on employment in the home country (mostly industrialized countries in the North) will depend on whether the substitution effects of FDI on domestic investment and exports more than compensate for its complementary effects (UNCTAD, 1995a, p. 153).

At the global level, transnational enterprises (the main channel of FDI) employ barely 2 per cent of the economically active population. In the 1980s and 1990s the numbers employed may have increased as a result of the internationalization of services. However the increase in FDI in the late 1980s mainly took the form of mergers and acquisitions, which may not involve a net employment creating effect (Parisotto, 1993).

THE IMPACT OF TECHNOLOGY

Those who do not accept a trade-related explanation of the unemployment and falling wages of low-skilled workers in the North blame rapid technological change, particularly the use of information technology. But technological change both creates and destroys jobs. Rapid growth in employment is occurring in both North and South in business services (for example consultancy, design, software and data processing) and financial services (see Freeman *et al.* 1995). There seems to be no clearcut evidence that the net employment effect of the IT revolution has been negative in the North, where it has been mainly concentrated (Eatwell, 1995; Singh, 1995). No significant positive impact of the IT revolution has yet been detected in terms of growth of output or total factor productivity (the so-called productivity paradox). If the technology revolution were the source of increasing unemployment, then one would expect labour productivity to accelerate as labour displacement occurred. The figures for industrialized countries, however, show a slowdown in the growth of labour productivity during the last decade compared with the 1960s (Table 7.8). One must either conclude that 'revolution' is in fact too strong a term for the economic impact of the changes in information technology or, as believed by many students of technological change, that the major labour productivity effects will come only when the revolution is well underway, since their full impact will be delayed until institutional adjustments have been made. These adjustments are being hindered by the rigidity of the Fordist mass production system and efficiency-reducing forms of oligopoly (Oman, 1994). Other factors may also have been at work, such as the decline in innovative activity since 1970, especially in the United States, where R&D

Table 7. 8   Productivity growth in OECD countries (percentages)

	USA	Japan	EU	OECD
Total factor productivity[1]				
1961–70[2]	2.5	6.1	3.3	3.3
1971–80	0.6	1.8	1.7	1.3
1981–90	0.8	1.8	1.4	1.2
1991–95[3]	0.4	−0.3	0.9	0.5
Labour productivity				
1961–70[2]	2.6	9.2	5.4	4.8
1971–80	0.9	3.7	3.1	2.3
1981–90	1.1	2.9	2.2	1.8
1991–95[3]	0.6	0.7	1.5	1.0
Capital productivity				
1961–70[2]	2.3	−2.8	−0.9	0.0
1971–80	0.1	−3.9	−1.2	−1.1
1981–90[3]	0.1	−1.4	−0.1	−0.3
1991–95[3]	−0.1	−3.4	−0.4	−0.8

Notes:
1. Measured as a weighted average of the growth in labour and capital productivity, with the sample period averages for capital and labour shares as weights.
2. 1962 for Japan.
3. 1994 for Japan.
Source: OECD (1997).

expenditure has fallen (Eatwell, 1995; Thurow, 1992). It might, therefore, be that unemployment in the North would have been higher had labour productivity risen faster (see Chapter 1).

Regardless of the outcome on the labour productivity front, there is little doubt that technological change has affected the composition of labour demand in favour of skilled workers, and is thus a natural suspect in the declining relative (and sometimes absolute) wages of less skilled workers. The employment consequences of globalization will also derive in part from organizational innovations at the firm, interfirm and industrial levels that are often associated with technological innovation. Flexible specialization and more innovative patterns of organizing tasks and job functions may lead to structural unemployment in both developing and industrialized countries.

The developing countries have thus far participated far less extensively in the information revolution than has the industrial world, and most of the developing-country participation occurred in a handful of NIEs, mainly those of East Asia. The experience of this region contrasts with that of the OECD countries and all other developing regions: high technology importation and absorption has led to rapid growth in labour productivity. According to the World Bank (1993b), rapid growth in physical and human capital has accounted for two thirds of the region's growth, the remaining one third being explained by increases in efficiency or total factor productivity. Total factor productivity growth in East Asian countries during 1960–89 is estimated as follows: Taiwan, 3.7; Hong Kong, 3.6; Japan, 3.4; Korea, 3.1. Such growth has also tended to be above average in South-East Asia: Thailand, 2.5; Indonesia, 1.2; Malaysia, 1.1; and Singapore, 1.2 – all of which greatly exceed the estimates for Latin America (0.1) and Sub-Saharan Africa (−0.99) (ibid, p. 64).

The ESEA experience also shows that the adoption of high technology can, under at least some circumstances, lead to or be consistent with a rapid growth of employment, while also contributing to international competitiveness. Freeman *et al.* (1995) show that even when investment and employment shifted to countries such as China, the decline in manufacturing employment in Hong Kong and Taiwan was more than offset by a rise in employment in services.[7] Unlike in ESEA, employment has not grown rapidly in Latin America and the Caribbean, nor in South Asia (see Chapter 4). UNECLAC (1995a) time series data show that urban unemployment increased in Argentina, Brazil, Colombia, Panama and Peru between 1980 and 1994. It declined somewhat only in Bolivia, Chile, Costa Rica, Honduras, Mexico and Paraguay. The widening wage and income gaps, together with the modest growth of employment in this region, may be due to the fact that at low levels of technology technical change can be substantial and thus labour displacing. However in the case of OECD countries with an already fairly high degree of capital intensity, further technical changes may lead to no more than incremental changes in technology, which would be less labour displacing.

Globalization has been facilitated by developments in communications technology and by open markets for goods and capital. However labour markets are not characterized by the same degree of openness as the product, capital and financial markets. In several sectors, employment in the countries of the North has declined while rising in the South, especially in the rapidly growing economies of ESEA and to a lesser extent Latin America. It remains a moot point whether these gains and losses resulting from globalization have been equitably distributed among countries and regions.

The net effect of globalization on employment will thus depend on many factors, notably the capacity of the economies to absorb information technology, organizational innovations, the speed and direction of technological change, and industrial restructuring in both domestic and global industries. The employment impact of globalization, as noted above, can differ markedly by type of worker. Both skilled and unskilled employment are likely to grow quickly under conditions of rapid economic growth, as demonstrated by the experience of ESEA. In practice, however, economic growth during the past decade has been slow in most regions, except Asia, particularly East Asia.

Slow economic growth and reduced demand in the OECD countries may be far more important explanations of high unemployment rates than either globalization or technological change (see Eatwell, 1995). Be this as it may, the duality of labour markets and the lack of labour mobility, particularly of unskilled labour, suggest that social policy is not keeping pace with globalization. The result is a mismatch between jobs and available skills and people's job expectations.

There are wide variations in the development and use of information technology between different regions. This is reflected in expenditure on R&D as a proportion of GNP (Table 7.9) and in the data on the use of communications technology (Table 7.10). Among the developing countries, the R&D ratios are lowest in Africa and highest in Asia. For the Asia–Pacific region, average growth in IT investment during 1984–90 was 10–25 per cent per annum (Kraemer and Dedrick, 1994). Rapid investment growth is not peculiar to East Asian NIEs: in India investment growth is reported to be over 22 per cent per annum, though from a smaller base. Similar data for Africa are difficult to procure, but Moussa and Schware (1992) report wide variations in computer spending (including complementary investment in software, training, parts, service and maintenance) as a percentage of GDP within Africa in 1988. Computer spending is much higher in Francophone Africa than either West Africa or South Africa.

East Asia (excluding China) and Latin America use more information technology than do South Asia and Sub-Saharan Africa (Table 7.10). Information technology (combined with an increase in imports of labour-intensive goods, particularly from Asia) has been blamed for growing economic inequalities in many industrial countries. But such a tendency is clearly avoidable. Take the case of Korea during the past 20 years. This

Table 7.9   Research and development expenditure as a share of GNP, by region (percentages)

	1970	1980	1990
World	2.04	1.85	2.55
Developed countries	2.36	2.22	2.93
Europe	1.70	1.81	2.21
North America	2.59	2.23	3.16
Developing countries	0.32	0.52	0.64
Africa	0.33	0.30	0.29
South, East and South-East Asia	1.02	1.41	2.08
Western Asia	0.31	0.97	0.76
Latin America and the Caribbean	0.30	0.44	0.40

Sources: UNESCO, *Statistical Yearbook: Expenditure and Experimental Development* (various years); UNCTAD (1994).

Table 7.10   Use of communications technology, by region

	Radios (per 1000 persons)	TVs (per 1000 persons)	Telephone lines (per 100 persons)	Fax machines (per 100 persons)
Sub-Saharan Africa	144	23	1	–
South Asia	87	33	0.8	–
East Asia	212	38	2.1	–
East Asia exc. China	680	156	24.2	–
Latin America & the Caribbean	345	162	6.5	0.1
Industrial countries	1048	533	37.2	1.7
World	349	151	9.9	–

Source: UNDP (1996), p. 211.

period has seen a rapid introduction of the new information technologies, supported by a powerful science and technology base. It has coincided with a rapid increase in the importance of small and medium enterprises (SMEs) in the economy. Much of this increase is accounted for by the growth of sub-contracting by large firms to smaller ones (see Berry, 1997c). Throughout the period Korea has not suffered any increase in inequality, but rather an improvement.

CONCLUDING REMARKS

Taking a longer view, the experience of the ESEA economies (particularly Hong Kong, Korea, Japan and Taiwan) shows that growth and equity can be achieved simultaneously in a situation of high levels of trade (globalization), rapid technological change and limited job creation in the public sector. In all of these countries SMEs play an important role in manufacturing, export activities and the economy in general. All have a relatively equitable income distribution. And of course all have competed very successfully in world markets and grown rapidly.

Theory and records suggest that both rapid technological change and rising trade ratios can, by themselves, increase levels of inequality, but that outcome can be avoided if the variance of wages and labour productivity is not too great. Likewise the involvement of SMEs in export activities, directly or indirectly, through subcontracting or other links with exporters can help to prevent such an outcome when trade is substantial and growing. For this to happen across a wide range of industries, large firms must have confidence in and be willing to work with SMEs, as is the case in the ESEA economies mentioned above. These large-scale links are less established in Latin America, as noted emphatically by Japanese businesses, advisers and observers. For SMEs to make their full contribution under these conditions, the technological and human capital gaps between them and the larger firms must be of modest proportions. When this is the case, the dissemination of new information technologies should occur quickly and neither the variance of productivities nor the inequality of earnings should become too large.

Even when these conditions are reasonably well satisfied there may still be some danger of distribution becoming more unequal, since under rapid technological change so many firms – large and small – will be raising labour productivity that it may require a high level of investment and rate of growth to keep labour demand high.

The employment impact of globalization, as noted above, can be both positive and negative. Both skilled and unskilled employment is likely to grow rapidly in conditions of rapid economic growth, as has been demonstrated by the experience of ESEA. However, in practice growth during the past decade has been slow in most regions except East Asia. Slow growth and reduction in demand in the OECD countries may be far more important factors than technological change in explaining high unemployment rates.

This volume, like most studies of globalization, has focused more on the growth of trade in goods and services than on the increasing financial flows and interconnections. The recent financial crisis in South-East Asia reminds us that this aspect of globalization should not be forgotten. At the time of writing, there is a significant concern that the region's growth may slow down over a period while the problems are addressed. It lays to rest any simplistic idea that the pitfalls associated with globalization apply only in certain regions of the world. It may suggest that the net benefits to a free flow of capital will be modest, if indeed positive at all, in much of the Third World. Short-term flows cannot become the basis of solid long-term investment and growth. The arguments for some degree of control on short-term flows are strengthened with each new experience of this sort. Yet it is clear that as with the rules governing trade, the developing countries have little clout in the deliberations. It is to be hoped that this condition is at least somewhat modified in future so that the main sources of danger for these countries can be taken more seriously.

APPENDIX 7.1 GROWTH RATES OF EXPORTS OF GOODS AND NON-FACTOR SERVICES, GDP AND EXPORT/GDP RATIO BY, REGION 1970–94

	1970–80			1980–90			1990–94		
	GDP	Exp.	Exp./GDP	GDP	Exp.	Exp./GDP	GDP	Exp.	Exp./GDP
Low- and middle-income economies, by region	5.2	3.9	−1.2	3.1	7.3	4.1	1.9	n.a.	n.a.
Sub-Saharan Africa	3.8	2.8	−1.0	1.7	1.8	0.1	0.9	2.1	1.2
East Asia	6.9	9.5	2.4	7.9	9.7	1.7	9.4	12.7	3.0
South Asia	3.5	3.6	0.1	5.7	6.1	0.4	3.9	13.1	8.9
Latin America & Caribbean	5.4	−0.1	−5.3	1.7	5.4	3.6	3.6	6.3	2.6
Low-income	4.3	3.3	−1.0	5.8	5.7	−0.1	6.2	10.4	4.0
India	3.4	4.3	0.9	5.8	5.9	0.1	3.8	13.6	9.4
China	5.5	8.7	3.0	10.2	11.5	1.2	12.9	16.0	2.7
Other	4.4	1.9	−2.4	2.9	2.5	−0.4	1.4	3.0	1.6
Middle-income	5.5	4.0	−1.4	2.2	n.a.	n.a.	0.2	n.a.	n.a.
Lower middle-income	5.1	n.a.	n.a.	2.2	n.a.	n.a.	n.a.	−2.3	n.a.
Upper middle-income	5.9	2.2	−3.5	2.2	7.1	4.8	3.4	7.8	4.3
High-income	3.2	5.4	2.1	3.2	5.1	1.8	1.7	3.4[1]	1.7
World	3.6	4.0	0.4	3.1	5.3	2.1	1.8	3.9[2]	2.1

Notes:

1. Estimate based on World Bank data for the major high income countries, weighted by their 1992 dollar exports (World Bank, 1996a, p. 209).

2. Estimate based on the figure for high-income countries described in 1 and an estimate for the low- and middle-income group' based on World Bank data (1996a, p. 209) and estimates for the two missing categories, 'Europe and Central Asia' and 'Middle East and North Africa'. With the lower and upper limit estimates we used, this figure would range from 1.8 to 2.3.

Sources: World Bank (1994, 1995a, 1996a).

Notes

1. Current price export/GDP ratios for the world rose in the 1970s but not in the 1980s (Table 7.1), while the ratio in constant prices did not rise significantly in the 1970s but has risen at a little over 2 per cent per year since then. Thus for the world as a whole it is appropriate to date the recent surge of globalization from the 1980s. The increase in the ratio was due exclusively to the developing countries however, since the rate of increase actually slowed for the high-income countries in the 1980s, while that of the low and middle-income countries rose from –1.2 per cent to 4.1 per cent (see Appendix 7.1).

2. The export to GDP ratio is a somewhat misleading point of comparison between countries of unequal size, and hence between regions whose member countries are of different average sizes. The small size of many Sub-Saharan African countries no doubt contributes to the high export ratio.

3. The shares of manufactured exports for South Asia and East Asia (East and South-East Asia, according to our definition in this volume) call for some comment. The data supplied by the World Bank and presented in Table 7.2 seem to underestimate the East Asian shares (see the much higher shares based on the World Bank data base, which are more consistent with the country estimates presented in Chapter 5). The estimates are probably biased downwards by the big weight of China and Indonesia. The shares for Latin America presented in Table 3.2 are much higher than those given here; this probably reflects a different definition of 'manufactured'.

4. Comparable data for individual countries of South Asia are presented by Khan in Chapter 4.

5. The human development index is defined by the UNDP as a composite measure of human progress based on three elements: national income, life expectancy and educational attainment (for details see UNDP, 1990).

6. Their empirical tests are, however, not at all convincing. They use four components (the ratio of FDI to GDP, the share of manufactures in exports, the country's credit rating, and tariffs) to form an index of integration, but only one of these is a policy variable. Unsurprisingly this index is positively correlated with GDP growth and other macroeconomic performance variables. What this implies for policy instruments within the government's control is less clear.

7. A positive correlation is considered to exist among the countries of Asia and the Pacific between investment in information technology and growth in GDP and GDP per worker (see Kraemer and Dedrick, 1994), but the methodology of this study is suspect and should not be taken as refuting the 'productivity paradox' within the Asia–Pacific region.

8 Directions for Future Research

A.S. Bhalla

This volume has considered the benefits and costs of globalization – of free trade and of FDI – for both the North and the South. Our main concern has been the developing countries, whose integration into the global economy has been fraught with greater adjustment costs especially during the transition period.

Free trade does not automatically lead to higher growth and income equalization. In Chapter 1 Streeten notes that adjustment to changing comparative advantage means that 'trade policy becomes a policy for tramps', and that it imposes constant dislocation and hardship on people. These costs of dislocation need to be weighed against the extra income that results from international trade. Acceptance that there are both costs of and benefits from free trade implies that it will have to be *managed* so that the costs are minimized or reduced. International agreement on the management of the global economy may be another means of reducing the pressures of globalization. Whether the WTO is up to this task remains to be seen.

Controversy continues to surround the process of globalization. Protagonists argue that globalization is good for growth; antagonists, on the other hand, suggest that the adjustment costs of integration into the global economy can be too high, and that poverty and inequalities have grown during the accelerated globalization of the 1980s and 1990s (see Chapters 3–6). We conclude that the protagonists may be overstating their case, both for the *speed* of globalization and for the *positive* impact that it has on individual economies.

Lack of agreement on the consequences of globalization on growth and marginalization arises from the usual problem of identifying causal factors when a number of forces are at work simultaneously. Together with globalization, information technology is advancing rapidly and is reinforcing globalization, as we have noted in this volume (see Chapters 1–3 in particular). Domestic policies have an important influence on growth, poverty and marginalization, independently of globalization. As we noted in the Introduction, often one cannot be certain whether globalization is the cause or the effect of liberalization and domestic policy changes. Similarly one cannot be sure, or at least not on the basis of the available empirical evidence, whether the rising incidence of poverty, for example in South Asia, Latin America and Africa, is due mainly to the process of globalization or mainly to domestic policies. A number of causal factors interact and reinforce each other. The separate effect of each is often difficult to detect, especially in the absence of disaggregated empirical evidence.

The polemics in the literature on globalization arise in part because of this problem of identification. It also reflects the fact that globalization has been a continuous process of change that is still evolving. Under the circumstances, one cannot invoke a *counterfactual* to help isolate the effects during the pre-globalization and post-globalization periods. This volume has argued that waves of globalization in the form of trade liberalization and direct investment have been occurring over a long period (see Chapter 1, in particular). To represent the 1960s and 1970s as a pre-globalization period, as some do, is misleading. The 1980s and 1990s simply witnessed an acceleration of a wave that started in the early postwar period and was preceded by a major wave in the nineteenth and early twentieth centuries.

Lack of agreement on the impact of globalization is also due to the absence of good micro-level research based on disaggregated and detailed data. In this volume we have made a beginning by providing a quantitative picture of poverty, growth and unemployment during the 1980s and 1990s. A good deal more research is needed before any definitive conclusions can be drawn about the positive and negative effects of globalization.

Below we discuss a few promising areas of research of a microeconomic and policy-oriented nature, which will hopefully narrow the gap between theory and reality.

GLOBALIZATION, GROWTH AND PRODUCTIVITY

The protagonists of globalization argue that it is good for growth. However, actual evidence reveals that the growth rates of most countries and regions, with the exception of Asia (particularly East and South-East Asia), have been considerably slower in the 1980s and 1990s than in the 1960s and 1970s. Rigorous, empirical, country-specific and country-comparative research is needed to explain why this is so. If growth does not accelerate with globalization, the incidence of poverty becomes greater, as is shown in Chapters 4 and 5 of this volume.

The determinants of investment are not yet well understood. Khan (Chapter 4) shows that investment rates were quite high during the import-substitution phase in South Asia. In this subregion, despite its various inefficiencies, the import-substitution strategy provided a strong incentive to invest. It is argued that the weakness of the growth impulse from globalization in the region arises from the failure to create an alternative system of incentives to attain or maintain a high investment rate. The infrastructure in South Asia is woefully inadequate compared with that in East and South-East Asia. This may in part explain the failure of the South Asian countries to attract high levels of foreign direct investment (FDI). And in the absence of FDI, international competitiveness is difficult to achieve in some industries. East and South-East Asia have escaped this vicious circle by attracting FDI and channelling it skilfully through approriate incentives and strategic industrial policies for technological modernization. Latin America's case parallels that of South Asia in that the high rate of investment under ISI has not continued under the new strategy.

One key research question, therefore is what incentives are needed during the era of globalization to stimulate greater investment and thereby accelerate growth? Is lack of FDI a major constraint on growth? What role does total factor productivity (TFP) play in explaining the high growth rates in East and South-East Asia? The experience of OECD countries with declining TFP rates (see Chapter 7) suggests that this factor may be as important as the inadequate political structures and lack of good governance noted in Chapter 4.

A related research issue is the link between exports and FDI under export orientation and globalization compared with that under import substitution. Are FDI inflows essential for developing countries to increase their exports? It has been argued that exports and FDI were substitutes under import substitution but are complements under globalization. 'Tariff jumping', encouraged in a situation of high tariff barriers, may now be less important because of the current decline in average national tariff levels. The above hypothesis deserves further empirical testing.

While FDI may be good for growth, it may also involve some adverse effects on host countries, for example manipulation or distortion of consumer preferences, lack of technological spillovers due to restrictions imposed by transnationals on the export or R&D activities of their subsidiaries (see Chang, 1996), and the introduction of excessively capital-intensive technologies and high salaries, which together limit employment generation in the host countries (see Chapter 7). Research evidence on the effects of capital inflows (FDI, financial flows, loans and so on) into developing countries is much less abundant than that on the effects of trade. In the 1960s FDI and TNCs were considered by most developing countries to be of questionable value. Today the pendulum has swung to the other extreme and FDI often seems to be considered a panacea for all ills.

Empirical investigations are needed to determine the pros and cons of the role of FDI, financial flows and TNCs under the current global conditions. To what extent do movements of short-term capital cause macroeconomic instability, exchange rate appreciation and decline in exports and the overall rate of growth? What are the efficiency and distributional effects of financial liberalization? What are the implications for developing countries of monopoly/oligopoly power in the global financial markets? (See Berry *et al.*, 1996.)

GLOBALIZATION AND INEQUALITY

Very little research has been done on the relation between growing income inequality and specific economic reforms and technological change. At present not much is known about the precise effects of trade, FDI and financial flows and increasing international competition on the allocation of resources between and within countries, on efficiency and growth and on inequalities and unemployment.

Inequality between Nations

Consider first the inequalities between North and South. Recent research has concentrated on the impact of trade on North–South income inequalities and the distribution of jobs (see Freeman, 1993, 1995; Krugman and Lawrence, 1994; Lawrence and Slaughter, 1993; Wood, 1994, 1997). Chapters 1 and 7 note the considerable controversy surrounding the impact of exports from developing countries on the labour market in the North. The role of technological change and the extent to which it is contributing to the growing income gap between countries also remains rather unclear. Uneven dispersion and utilization of information technology would tend to influence the dispersion of wages between skilled and unskilled labour. If the benefits of new information technology are being exploited by the more developed of developing countries and larger enterprises, does it suggest a widening of these gaps both within the South and between North and South?

Further empirical research of a disaggregated nature can throw adequate light on the relative importance of different factors behind the growing inequality between the North and some parts of the South. It is also worth exploring whether the North–South dichotomy is still meaningful with the rapid integration of East and South-East Asia into the global economy.

Critics of globalization argue that integration into the world economy divides the world into rich and poor countries, with the rich gaining at the expense of the poor. This hypothesis needs detailed empirical testing. Krugman and Venables (1995) present a simple model in which regional differentiation is driven by an interaction between scale economies and transport costs. They present a two-stage analysis under which a decline in transport costs in the first phase of global integration may lead to the rich countries gaining at the expense of the poor. However in the second stage, when integration accelerates and transport costs decline further, benefits to the rich countries in the form of increased income may be eroded and the poor countries' income may start to grow at the expense of the rich countries. Thus the first phase is one of divergence and the second is one of convergence in incomes and economic structures. No empirical validation of the above model has yet been provided.

Much theory assumes complete globalization under which all factors of production – both labour and capital – are freely mobile. In practice such globalization is not taking place; free flows of capital are not accompanied by freer flows of labour and the integration of labour markets. The simple theory thus fails to provide a reliable prediction of the impacts of globalization. It is possible that the existing international inequalities in the distribution of income are being aggravated by the *incomplete* nature of globalization!

Inequality within Nations

The effects of trade liberalization and globalization on inequality within nations have remained relatively unexplored. In Chapter 2 of this volume, James refers to the issue and speculates that the gainers from globalization are large-scale, foreign-owned, urban-based firms rather than small-scale rural ones. This hypothesis needs to be empirically tested for different countries and regions. Clearly it is less likely to hold in countries with a high degree of linkage between large and small firms.

Research should thus be directed towards the causal factors underlying inequality within nations. In what ways and to what extent do trade liberalization and the spread of information technology contribute to wage and income inequalities within developing countries. How does globalization influence firms, workers, consumers and producers? Does it lead to a reduction in product prices, which would be welfare enhancing and favourable to consumers? Which social groups – rural or urban, high income or low income – are likely to benefit?

The relationship between poverty and income distribution in the context of globalization deserves further analysis. In Chapters 4 and 5 Khan notes that the incidence of poverty (measured by the headcount indices), which had shown a steady decline during the 1970s and 1980s, has increased in countries such as India and China during the 1990s, the period of accelerated globalization. The incidence of poverty in India increased after the introduction of economic reforms. This coincidence of liberalization and poverty increase is explained by a rise in the relative price of food and a reduction in the gap between domestic and world food prices as a consequence of trade liberalization. Are there other explanations for this increase in the incidence of poverty? Do trade liberalization, inflows of FDI and economic reforms largely explain the increase in poverty, or do domestic agricultural policies, for example, also have a role to play?

GLOBALIZATION AND EMPLOYMENT

The impact of trade liberalization on employment in the North has been the subject of many studies, as noted above, but far fewer studies have been conducted on the direct and indirect effects of trade liberalization, FDI and global financial flows on employment generation in developing countries. Globalization is likely to have a significant influence on the global distribution of jobs and the nature and quality of employment (see Chapter 7). The comparative advantage of developing countries could, in principle, be enhanced through increasing global competition if their low labour costs could be combined with relatively high worker skills. But it is often argued that the advent of new information technologies and their use in industrial countries in such labour-intensive industries as textiles and clothing may erode the comparative advantage and export competitiveness of developing countries. At present there is no conclusive evidence to suggest that the location of some of these industries will shift markedly back to the North. However if such trade reversal were to occur in the future, developing countries could lose billions of dollars of export income a year, and thereby employment.

Global competition can have a net negative effect on traditional jobs, especially since it is mainly the modern and large-scale manufacturing sectors, and to a lesser extent services, that are being globalized (see below). Such competition would then exert a downward pressure on wages and social security for workers in the organized or formal sectors of both industrial and developing countries. The question is whether fuller employment can be achieved at a wage level that is high enough to stimulate demand appreciably and sustain it over time.

Research on the impact of globalization on employment requires analysis of the following:

- The impact on relative factor prices and the costs of capital and labour.
- The employment-intensity of export products (additional employment generation through exports requires not only labour-intensive growth but also labour-intensive exports).
- The role of FDI in explaining levels and composition of trade and the direct and indirect employment effects that it produces.
- The determinants of competitive advantage of countries, for example human resource base, cost/price advantage and ability to absorb new information technology.

GLOBALIZATION AND SMALL ENTERPRISES

In principle, trade liberalization and freer imports of finished goods and raw materials can have both favourable and adverse effects on small and medium enterprises (SMEs). The effects may be beneficial if such trade liberalization improves these enterprises' access to scarce material inputs, capital equipment and technology. On the other hand, the effects may be adverse if finished goods are imported at below-cost prices (dumping) with which the SMEs cannot compete. In Chapter 3 Berry notes that small and medium enterprises may be especially vulnerable in the short run to accelerated import competition resulting from trade liberalization and globalization. These enterprises are generating a good deal of employment, so if they disappear in the face of foreign competition, an important source of employment generation will be lost. A decline in the demand for the products of SMEs may also occur through a shift in the consumption pattern towards imported goods and away from domestic goods. In Asia, Sri Lanka's liberalization experience suggests that such a shift in the consumption pattern has occurred, that the SMEs have been unable to compete in price terms because of dumping, and that the large firms have benefited from the liberalization of raw material imports and forced a number of small enterprises out of business (see ILO–ARTEP, 1987; Osmani, 1987).

Research is accordingly needed on the impact of trade liberalization on industrial structures in developing countries. Does globalization benefit only large-scale industry, which has initial advantages of economies of scale and export orientation? What has been the mortality rate of SMEs during the wave of liberalization in the 1980s and 1990s? Can this mortality be explained by increasing global competition and the withdrawal of protection from these enterprises? If it is true that globalization favours large industry, will it widen the gap between the modern and non-modern or informal (generally small-scale) sectors? What implications will this have for wage and income inequalities within developing countries?

GLOBALIZATION AND TECHNOLOGY

This volume has emphasized the two-way relationship between globalization and technology. First, technology is one of the main driving forces behind globalization. In turn, globalization of the world economy is transforming the way in which technology is generated and diffused. In Chapter 2 James notes two opposing tendencies – the dispersion of R&D and its concentration by transnationals in their home country. The globalization of technology can be defined in several ways, including (1) the exploitation of national innovations in global markets, (2) the sharing of costs and risks of industrial research across national borders by public and business institutions and (3) the generation of innovations across countries (see Archibugi and Michie, 1997a). While there is agreement on (1) and (2), controversy surrounds (3).

Globalization of Technology?

It is generally believed that transnationals are globalizing R&D to take advantage of economies of scale, since information technology enables worldwide control of R&D and sourcing of scientific and technological knowledge (see Cantwell, 1995). It is also argued that the spread of information technology and globalization are enabling the transnational corporations to disperse their activities worldwide to cater for the global market, rather than regional or national host-country markets. On the other hand many writers (Freeman, 1995; Patel, 1995; Patel and Pavitt, 1991) argue that the globalization of R&D is not taking place on any appreciable scale. Patel (1995) shows that the bulk of the patented inventions of over 500 of the world's largest enterprises took place in the firms' home countries. Tentative estimates show that the 'R&D activities of the US companies outside the United States amount to less than 10 per cent of the total, whilst those of the Japanese companies are much lower – less than 2 per cent' (Freeman, 1995, p. 17). Some of these R&D activities outside the United States and Japan are in other industrialized countries. Thus developing countries may not benefit from the location of this research.

One of the reasons for the above controversy is the lack of empirical industry-specific and product-specific studies, particularly with regard to the implications of technology globalization for host developing countries (see Chapter 2). At present it is not clear how this phenomenon will change the nature of innovations by transnationals in developing countries. Are these transnationals concentrating more on 'global' products to cater for the global markets than on domestic products? If so, what implications does this strategy have for R&D and product development within developing countries? Are these countries likely to be excluded from the benefits of the technology innovation and generation process? Our understanding of how globalization affects the nature and location of innovations is still rather rudimentary.

The Role of National Technology Policies

What is the precise role of national technology policies in a globalized economy? Many authors argue that despite globalization, technology remains largely country-specific and is conditioned by national skills, capabilities and cultural characteristics. On the other hand the increasing role of transnational corporations in R&D for global products, as noted above, might suggest a decline in the relevance of national technology policies. It is argued that the benefits of government-supported innovation in industry are likely to be transferred to other countries under globalization. Hence, there may be little incentive for a national technology policy to promote national innovations. This may be one of the reasons why many industrial countries are now shifting their emphasis from the generation of technology to the regulation of intellectual and industrial property rights in order to guarantee sufficient returns from existing technology in international markets (see Archibugi and Michie, 1997a, p.17).

With increasing globalization and domination by transnational corporations, national technological capabilities may become less important than capabilities at the *firm level* to compete internationally. Increasing competition in the international markets seems to be inducing firms to put a higher premium on quality than on profitability, price and cost. The role of an industrial and technology policy in future will therefore be more in the nature of government incentives to firms to introduce quality-enhancing innovations. Despite techno-globalism, infrastructure, education, communications and university–industry partnerships are some of the areas in which national government action will continue to be essential.

Global Markets and Innovations

It is not clear whether technological innovations are more likely or less likely to occur under the integrated and global market structures resulting from the process of globalization. According to the neoliberal view, a competitive environment in national and international markets will induce innovation. Government intervention is assumed to lead to greater inefficiencies than those resulting from market imperfections. However the historical experience of many developing countries (for example Korea and Taiwan) shows that a significant amount of innovation also took place during import-substituting industrialization under protective environments. How and to what extent competitive market forces spur innovation will, *inter alia*, depend on the nature of the industry and the market structure. Some industries are more globalized than others, and may thus suffer from greater global competition. Increasing knowledge-intensity of production is also raising firms' production costs and uncertainty (Mytelka,1994).

GLOBALIZATION AND GOVERNMENT POLICY

Several chapters in this volume (particularly Chapters 1 and 3) argue that globalization combined with *laissez faire* may be especially harmful to developing countries. Under certain circumstances, globalization may be accompanied by greater government and public services rather than less. In Chapter 1 Streeten argues that, contrary to expectations, a positive relationship between government size and globalization (in terms of trade and FDI ratios) may occur as a result of pressures to compensate those social groups who are hurt by globalization. In addition governments may have to spend more on public goods such as education and infrastructure when global competition becomes fierce.

Thanks to globalization, both developing and developed countries are becoming less and less in control of their macroeconomic policies. For example freer flows of finance and capital and open capital markets imply that the fiscal operations of governments are becoming increasingly interdependent, with significant effects on interest rates in many countries. Furthermore the growing power of global corporations and their freedom to move capital and production freely across national boundaries is limiting the control of the nation state over its industrial policy. Hence, there is a growing urgency to harmonize national government policies. These policies need to be aligned with the foreign investment strategies of the corporate world and the changing external conditions of aid and trade. This calls for institutional innovations to match economic and technological ones.

The issue of the government's role in the generation of and access to new information technology, particularly in the context of countries weakly integrated into the global economy, is a fruitful area for further research. Despite globalization, some role for strategic government intervention and public policy may be necessary for the adaptation, development and diffusion of new technologies. Public policy is likely to play a crucial role in creating a suitable environment for this purpose. Furthermore an initial assessment of a country's existing technological capabilities at different levels is essential to determine the scope for leapfrogging. This task cannot be done by private firms. While micro-decisions are made by these firms on the basis of some notion of choice and feasibility, it is up to the central mechanism to examine how these micro-systems fit into a macroeconomic framework that will provide a basis for investment and consumption planning (Enos, 1991).

In contrasting the neoliberal and neo-Schumpeterian approaches to high technology policy for industrial development, Schmitz and Cassiolato (1992) note that far less attention has been paid to market failures than to government failures. The recent experience of industrialized countries shows that markets continue to remain ineffective in compensating for technology-induced unemployment.

It is clear that, in the process of globalization, the corporate strategies of transnational and global firms towards R&D and technology development and transfer will increasingly determine the nature and scope of technological innovations. In developing countries, however, private expenditure on R&D remains very small and the bulk of R&D is supported by public funds. But with public funds declining in developing countries under globalization and structural adjustment programmes, the process of innovation in developing countries may actually slow down. The experience of many countries, especially in Africa and Latin America, shows how serious indebtedness can limit the scope of investment in new technologies. Yet such investment is an important prerequiste for successfully meeting the challenge of globalization.

Bibliography

AFRICAN DEVELOPMENT BANK (1995) *African Development Report* (Abidjan: African Development Bank).

AGOSIN, M.R. and D. TUSSIE (1993) 'Trade and Growth: New Dilemmas in Trade Policy – An Overview,' in M.R. Agosin and D. Tussie (eds), *Trade and Growth – New Dilemmas in Trade Policy* (London: Macmillan).

AHMED, I. (ed.) (1992) *Biotechnology: A Hope or a Threat?* (London: Macmillan).

AKYÜZ, Y. (1995) 'Taming International Finance', in J. Michie and J. Grieve Smith (eds), *Managing the Global Economy* (Oxford: Oxford University Press).

ALARCON, D. (1993) 'Changes in the Distribution of Income in Mexico During the Period of Trade Liberalization', Riverside, unpublished PhD dissertation, University of California–Riverside.

ALCORTA, L. (1992) 'The Impact of New Technologies on Scale in Manufacturing Industry: Issues and Evidence', United Nations University (UNU) Institute for New Technologies (INTECH) Working Paper no. 5 (Maastricht).

ALTIMIR, OSCAR (1982) *The Extent of Poverty in Latin America*, World Bank Staff Working Paper (Washington, DC: The World Bank).

ALTIMIR, OSCAR (1994) 'Income Distribution and Poverty Through Crisis and Adjustment', *CEPAL Review*, no. 52.

AMJAD, RASHID and A.R. KEMAL (1996) 'Macroeconomic Policies and Their Impact on Poverty Alleviation in Pakistan', ILO Southeast Asia and the Pacific Multidisciplinary Advisory Team, Manila (draft manuscript awaiting publication).

AMSDEN, ALICE (1979) *Asia's Next Giant* (New York: Oxford University Press).

AMSDEN, ALICE (1989) *Asia's New Giant: South Korea and Late Industrialization* (New York: Oxford University Press).

AMSDEN, ALICE (1993) 'Structural Macroeconomic Underpinnings of Effective Industrial Policy: Fast Growth in the 1980s in Five East Asian Countries', UNCTAD Discussion Papers Series no. 57 (Geneva: UNCTAD).

ANTONELLI, C. (1991) *The International Diffusion of Advanced Telecommunications: Opportunities for Developing Countries* (Paris, OECD).

ANTONELLI, C., P. PETIT and G. TAHAR (1992) *The Economics of Industrial Modernization* (London: Academic Press).

ARCHIBUGI, D. and J. MICHIE (eds) (1997a) *Technology, Globalization and Economic Performance* (Cambridge: Cambridge University Press).

ARCHIBUGI, D. and J. MICHIE (1997b) 'Technological Globalisation and National Systems of Innovation: an Introduction', in Archibugi and Michie, ibid.

ASIAN DEVELOPMENT BANK (1993, 1996) *Key Indicators of Developing Asian and Pacific Countries* (Manila: Oxford University Press for ADB).

ASIAN DEVELOPMENT BANK (ADB) (1994) *Asian Development Outlook 1994* (Manila: Oxford University Press for ADB).

AXELROD, R. (1984) *The Evolution of Cooperation* (New York: Basic Books).

BAGACHWA, M.S.D., T.O. ADEBOYE and O.A. BAMIRO (1995) 'Effects of Reforms on Technology Capability in Sub-Saharan Africa: A Conceptual Framework', African Technology Policy Studies Network (ATPS) Working Paper no. 1 (Nairobi: ATPS).

BAILY, MARY ANN (1977) *Technology Choice in the Brick and Men's Leather Shoe Industries in Colombia* (New Haven, Conn.: Yale University, Economic Growth Center).

BAIROCH, P. (1993) *Economics and World History-Myths and Paradoxes* (Hemel Hempstead: Harvester Wheatsheaf).

BAIROCH, P. and R. KOZUL-WRIGHT (1996) 'Globalization Myths: Some Historical Reflections on Integration, Industrialization and Growth in the World Economy', UNCTAD discussion papers no. 113, March (Geneva: UNCTAD).

BALASUBRAMANYAM, V.N., M. SALISU and D. SAPSFORD (1996) 'Foreign Direct Investment and Growth in EP and IS Countries', *Economic Journal*, January.

BALISACAN, ARSENIO (1996) 'Philippines: Policy Reforms and Poverty Alleviation', manuscript (Manila: ILO Southeast Asia and the Pacific Multidisciplinary Advisory Team), table 13.

BANGLADESH BUREAU OF STATISTICS (BBS) (1996), *Monthly Statistical Bulletin*, March (Dhaka: BBS).

BARBER, BENJAMIN (1995) *Jihad vs. McWorld* (New York: Random House).

BERGER, SUZANNE and RONALD DORE (eds) (1996) *National Diversity and Global Capitalism* (Ithaca: Cornell University Press).

BERRY, A. (1992) 'Firm (or Plant) Size in the Analysis of Trade and Development', in Gerald Helleiner (ed.), *Trade Policy, Industrialization and Development: New Perspectives* (Oxford: Clarendon Press).

BERRY, ALBERT (1997a) 'The Inequality Threat in Latin America', *Latin American Research Review*, vol. 32, no.2.

BERRY, A. (ed.) (1997b) *Poverty, Economic Reforms and Income Distribution in Latin America* (Boulder, CO: Lynne Rienner).

BERRY, A. (1997c) 'SME Competitiveness: The Power of Networking and Subcontracting', Working Paper (Washington, DC: Interamerican Development Bank).

BERRY, A., S. HORTON and D. MAZUMDAR (1996) 'Globalization, Adjustment, Inequality and Poverty', background paper for UNDP Human Development Report 1997 (Toronto: Department of Economics, University of Toronto).

BERRY, ALBERT and DIPAK MAZUMDAR (1991) 'Small-Scale Industry in East and Southeast Asia: A Review of the Literature and Issues', *Asian-Pacific Economic Literature*. September. (vol. 5, no. 2).

BERRY, ALBERT, MARIA TERESA MENDEZ and JAIME TENJO (1997) 'Growth, Macroeconomic Stability and the Generation of Productive Employment in Latin America', in A.R. Khan and M. Muqtada (eds), *Employment Expansion and Macroeconomic Stability under Increasing Globalization* (London: Macmillan).

BERRY, ALBERT and JAIME TENJO (1997) 'Trade Liberalization, Labour Reform and Income Distribution in Colombia', in Albert Berry (ed.), *Poverty, Economic Reforms, and Income Distribution in Latin America* (Boulder, CO: Lynne Rienner).

BEST, M. (1990) *The New Competition: Institutions of Industrial Restructuring* (Oxford: Basil Blackwell).

BHADURI, A. and D. NAYYAR (1996) *The Intelligent Person's Guide to Liberalization* (New Delhi: Penguin).

BHAGWATI, J. (1978) 'Anatomy of Consequences of Exchange Control Regimes', in National Bureau of Economic Research (NBER), *Studies in International Economic Relations*, vol. 1, no. 10.

BHAGWATI, J. (1993) *India in Transition: Freeing the Economy* (Oxford: Clarendon Press).

BHAGWATI, J. (1994) 'Free Trade: Old and New Challenges', *Economic Journal*, March.

BHAGWATI, J. and V. DEHEJIA (1994) 'Trade and Wages of the Unskilled: Is Marx Striking Again?', in J. Bhagwati and M. Klosters (eds), *Trade and Wages* (Washington, DC: American Enterprise Institute).

BHAGWATI, J. and T.N. SRINIVASAN (1993) *Indian Economic Reforms* (New Delhi: Ministry of Finance).

BHALLA, A.S. (1996) *Facing the Technological Challenge* (London: Macmillan).

BHALLA, A.S. and P. BHALLA (1997) *Regional Blocs: Building Blocks or Stumbling Blocks?* (London: Macmillan).

BHALLA, A.S. and DILMUS JAMES (eds) (1988) *New Technologies and Development: Experiences in "Technology Blending"* (Boulder, CO: Lynne Rienner).

BHALLA, A.S. and N. JÉQUIER (1988a) 'Telecommunications for Rural Development', in Bhalla and James, ibid.

BINSWANGER, HANS and VERNON W. RUTTAN (1978) *Induced Innovation* (Baltimore, MD: Johns Hopkins University Press).

BOURGIGNON, FRANÇOIS and CHRISTIAN MORRISSON (1989) *External Trade and Income Distribution* (Paris: OECD).

BRAGA, CARLOS A. PRIMO (1996) 'The Impact of the Internationalization of Services on Developing Countries', *Finance and Development*, March.

BRUNDENIUS, C. and B. GORANSSON (eds) (1993) *New Technologies and Global Restructuring* (Los Angeles, CA: Taylor Graham).

BRUTON, HENRY (1985) 'On the Production of a National Technology', in J. James and S. Watanabe (eds), *Technology, Institutions and Government Policies* (London: Macmillan).

BULMER-THOMAS, V. (1996) *The New Economic Model in Latin America and Its Impact on Income Distribution and Poverty* (New York: St. Martin's Press).

CANTWELL, J. (1995) 'The Globalization of Technology: What Remains of the Product Cycle Model?', *Cambridge Journal of Economics*, February.

CARD, DAVID E. and ALAN B. KRUEGER (1995) *Myth and Measurement: The New Economics of the Minimum Wage* (Princeton, NJ: Princeton University Press).

CARTER, M.R., B.L. BARHAM and D. MARSBAH (1996) 'Agricultural Export Booms and the Rural Poor in Chile, Guatemala and Peru', *Latin American Research Review*, vol. 31, no. 1.

CASTELLS, M. and L. TYSON (1988) 'High-Technology Choices Ahead: Restructuring Interdependence', in J. Sewell *et al.* (eds) *Growth, Exports and Jobs in a Changing World Economy* (New Brunswick: Transaction Books).

CENTRE FOR POLICY DIALOGUE (1995) *Experiences with Economic Reform: A Review of Bangladesh's Development* (Dhaka: University Press).

CHANG, HA-JOON (1996) 'Globalization, Transnational Corporations, and Economic Development–Can the Developing Countries Pursue Strategic Industrial Policy in a Globalising World Economy?, paper presented at the Economic Policy Institute Conference on 'Globalisation and Progressive Economic Policy' (Washington, DC: 21–3 June.

CHESNAIS, F. (1988) 'Multinational Enterprise and the International Diffusion of Technology', in G. Dosi, C. Freeman, R. Nelson, G. Silverberg and L. Soete (eds), *Technical Change and Economic Theory* (London: Pinter).

CHESNAIS, F. (1995) 'Some Relationships Between Foreign Direct Investment, Technology, Trade and Competitiveness', in J.Hagedoorn (ed.), *Technical Change in the World* (Aldershot: Edward Elgar).

CHINA, STATE STATISTICAL BUREAU (SSB) (1996) *China Statistical Yearbook* (Beijing: SSB).

Collected Writings of John Mayard Keynes (1982) vol. XXI (1933) Activities, 1931–39 (London: Macmillan).

204   *Bibliography*

COLLIER, P. (1995) 'The Marginalization of Africa', *International Labour Review*, vol. 134, nos. 4–5.

CORBO, VITTORIO (1988) 'Problems, Development Theory, and Strategies of Latin America', in Gustav Ranis and T. Paul Schultz (eds), *The State of Development Economics: Progress and Perspectives* (Oxford: Basil Blackwell).

CORNIA, G.A., R. VAN DER HOEVEN and T. MKANDAWIRE(eds) (1992) *Africa's Recovery in the 1990s* (London: Macmillan).

CORREA, C. (1996) *Implications of Property Rights for the Access to and Use of Information Technologies in Developing Countries*, (Geneva: UNCTAD).

CORTES, MARILUZ, ALBERT BERRY and ASHFAQ ISHAQ (1987) *Success in Small and Medium-Scale Enterprises: The Evidence from Colombia* (New York: Oxford University Press).

CULPEPER, ROY (1993) *Resurgence of Private Capital Flows to Latin America: The Role of American Investors* (Ottawa: The North–South Institute).

DAVIS, S. and J. HALTIWANGER (1991) 'Wage Dispersion Between and Within U.S. Manufacturing Plants, 1963–86', *Brookings Economic Papers* (Washington, DC: The Brookings Institution).

DEMERY, LIONEL, BINAYAK SEN, and TARA VISWANATH (1995) 'Poverty, Inequality and Growth', draft (Washington DC: World Bank Economic and Social Policy Department, March).

DIAZ-ALEJANDRO, CARLOS F. (1985) 'Goodbye Financial Repression, Hello Financial Crash', *Journal of Development Economics*, Sept.–Oct.

DICKEN, P. (1992) *Global Shift: The Internationalisation of Economic Activity*, 2nd edn (London: Guilford Press).

DORE, RONALD (1996) 'Ralf Dahrendorf, Quadrare il Cerchio, Comment', typescript.

DUCATEL, KEN and IAN MILES (1992) 'Internationalization of IT Services and Public Policy Implications', *World Development*, December.

EASTERLY, W., M. KRAMER, L. PRITCHETT and L. SUMMERS (1993) 'Good Policy or Bad Luck: Country Growth Performance and Temporary Income Shocks', *Journal of Policy Modelling*, vol. 32.

EATWELL, J. (1995) 'The International Origins of Unemployment', in J. Michie and J. Grieve Smith (eds), *Managing the Global Economy* (Oxford: Oxford University Press).

EATWELL, J. (1996) 'International Capital Liberalisation:an Evaluation: A Report to UNDP', SSA no. 96–049, April.

ECONOMIST, THE (1996) 'Trade and Wages', 7 December.

ECONOMIST, THE (1997) 'Asia's Economic Crisis–How Far is Down?', 15 November.

ENOS, J.L. (1991) *The Creation of Technological Capability in Developing Countries* (London: Pinter).

ESCANDON, JOSÉ F. (1981) 'Analisis de los Factores que han Determinado el Desarrollo de la Pequeña Empresa en Colombia: Una Interpretatcion Historica', *Coyuntura Economica*, vol. 11, no. 3.

EVANS, P. and P. TIGRE (1989) 'Going Beyond Clones in Brazil and Korea: A Comparative Analysis of NIC Strategies in the Computer Industry', *World Development*, November.

FAINI, RICCARDO, FERNANDO CLAVIJO and ABDEL SENHADJI-SEMLALI (1992) 'The Fallacy of Composition Argument: Is it Relevant for LDCs' Manufactured Exports?', *European Economic Review*, vol. 36.

FAIRCHILD, LORETTA G. (1979) 'Performance and Technology of U.S. and National Firms in Mexico', in James H. Street and Dilmus D. James (eds),

Technological Progress in Latin America: The Prospects for Overcoming Dependency (Boulder, CO: Westview Press).

FARRELL, M.J. (1987) 'Information and the Coase Theorem', *Journal of Economic Perspectives*, Fall.

FEENSTRA, R.C. and G.H. HANSON (1995) 'Foreign Investment, Outsourcing and Relative Wages', in R. Feenstra, G. Grossman and D. Irwin (eds), *Political Economy of Trade Policy: Essays in Honour of Jagdish Bhagwati* (Cambridge, Mass.: MIT Press).

FELIX, DAVID (1995) 'Financial Globalization vs. Free Trade: The Case for the Tobin Tax', UNCTAD Discussion Papers no. 108, November (Geneva: UNCTAD).

FISHLOW, ALBERT (1994) 'Economic Development in the 1990s', *World Development*, December.

FORSYTH, DAVID J.C. (1985) 'Government Policy, Market Structure and Choice of Technology in Egypt', in J. James and S.Watanabe (eds), *Technology, Institutions and Government Policies* (London: Macmillan).

FRANK, ANDRÉ GUNDER (ed.) (1969) *Capitalism and Underdevelopment in Latin America* (New York: Monthly Review Press).

FRANSMAN, M. (1991) 'Biotechnology-Generation, Diffusion, and Policy: An International Survey', United Nations University Institute for New Technologies (UNU/INTECH) working paper. (Maastricht: INTECH).

FREEMAN, C. (1973) 'A Study of Success and Failure in Industrial Innovation,' in B.R. Williams (ed.), *Science and Technology in Economic Growth* (London: Macmillan).

FREEMAN, C. (1995) 'The "National System of Innovation" in Historical Perspective', *Cambridge Journal of Economics*, February.

FREEMAN, C. and J. HAGEDOORN (1995) 'Convergence and Divergence in the Internationalization of Technology', in J. Hagedoorn (ed.), *Technical Change and the World Economy* (Aldershot: Edward Elgar).

FREEMAN, CHRISTOPHER, and BENGT-AKE LUNDVALL(eds) (1992) *Small Countries Facing the Technological Revolution* (London: Pinter).

FREEMAN, C. and L. SOETE (1994) *Work for All or Mass Unemployment: Computerised Technical Change into the 21st Century* (London: Pinter).

FREEMAN, C., L. SOETE and U. EFENDIOGLU (1995) 'Diffusion and the Employment Effects of Information and Communication Technology', *International Labour Review*, vol. 134, nos. 4–5.

FREEMAN, R. (1993) *Is Globalization Impoverishing Low Skill American Workers?* (Cambridge, Mass.: Harvard University Press).

FREEMAN, R. (1995) 'Are Your Wages Set In Beijing?', *Journal of Economic Perspectives*, Summer.

FRÖBEL, F., J. HEINRICHS and O. KREYE (1980) *The New International Division of Labour* (Cambridge: Cambridge University Press).

GARRETT, GEOFFREY (1995) 'Capital Mobility, Trade and the Domestic Politics of Economic Policy', *International Organization*, vol. 49, no. 4 (Autumn).

GARRETT, GEOFFREY and PETER LANGE (1995) 'Internationalization, Institutions, and Political Change', *International Organization*, vol. 49, no.4 (Autumn).

GASSMAN, H.P. (1991) 'Information Technology Developments and Implications for National Policies', *Futures*, vol. 23, no. 10.

GRUNWALD, J. and FLAMM, K. (1985) *The Global Factory: Foreign Assembly in International Trade* (Washington, DC: The Brookings Institution).

GURU-GHARANA, K.K. (1996) 'Macroeconomic Policies and Poverty in Nepal', report prepared for the ILO South Asia Multidisciplinary Advisory Team (Kathmandu: Nepal Foundation for Advanced Studies).

HAGEDOORN, J. and J. SCHAKENRAAD (1990) 'Inter-firm Partnerships and Co-operative Strategies in Core Technologies', in C. Freeman and L. Soete (eds), *New Explorations in the Economics of Technical Change* (London: Pinter).

HAMERMESH, D. (1993) *Labour Demand* (Princeton, NJ: Princeton University Press).

HANNA, N., S. BOYSON and S. GUNARATNE (1996) 'The East Asian Miracle and Information Technology, Strategic Management of Technological Learning', World Bank Discussion Papers no. 326 (Washington, DC: World Bank).

HANNA, N. and V. DUGONJIC (1995) 'Why a National Strategy for Exploiting Information Technologies?', *Information Technology for Development*, Advanced Technology Assessment System, issue no. 10, Autumn, (Geneva: UNCTAD).

HANNA, N., K. GUY and E. ARNOLD (1995). 'The Diffusion of Information Technology', World Bank Discussion Papers, no. 281 (Washington, DC: World Bank).

HARRIS, RICHARD D. (1992) 'New Theories of International Trade and the Pattern of Global Specialisation', in Gijsbert van Liemt (ed.), *Industry on the Move* (Geneva: ILO).

HARRIS, R.G. (1993) 'Globalization, Trade and Income', *Canadian Journal of Economics*, November.

HARRISON, GLEN, THOMAS RUTHERFORD and DAVID TARR (1995) 'Quantifying the Outcome of the Uruguay Round', *Finance and Development*, December.

HAYAMI, YUJIRO and VERNON W. RUTTAN (1971) *Agricultural Development: An International Perspective* (Baltimore, MD: Johns Hopkins University Press).

HELLEINER, G.K. (ed.) (1994) *Trade Policy and Industrialization in Turbulent Times* (London: Routledge).

HELLEINER, G.K. (1995) 'Trade, Trade Policy and Industrialisation Reconsidered', UNU/WIDER World Development Studies 6 (Helsinki, October).

HELLEINER, G.K. (1996) *Linking Africa with the World: A Survey of Options* (Nairobi: African Economic Research Consortium, January).

HENDERSON, G. (1989) *The Globalization of High Technology Production* (London: Routledge).

HIRSCHMAN, ALBERT O. (1958) *The Strategy of Economic Development* (New Haven, CT: Yale University Press).

HIRST, P. and G. THOMPSON (1996) *Globalization in Question* (Cambridge: Polity Press).

HOWLAND, M. (1995) 'Information Technology and the Location of Data Entry and Processing Services', in UNCTAD, *Information Technology for Development*, Advanced Technology Assessment System, issue no. 10, Autumn (Geneva: UNCTAD).

INTERAMERICAN DEVELOPMENT BANK (IDB) (1996) *Economic and Social Progress in Latin America–1996 Report* (Washington, DC: IDB, November).

INTERNATIONAL FINANCE CORPORATION (IFC) (1995), 'Trends in Private Investment in Developing Countries 1990–94', Discussion Paper no. 28 (Washington, DC: IFC).

INTERNATIONAL LABOUR OFFICE (ILO) (1995a) *World Employment 1995: ILO Report* (Geneva: ILO).

INTERNATIONAL LABOUR OFFICE (1995b) *Promoting Employment – Report of the Director-General*, International Labour Conference, 82nd Session (Geneva: ILO).

ILO–ARTEP (Asian Employment Programme) (1987) *Structural Adjustment: By Whom, For Whom* (New Delhi: ILO–ARTEP, March).

ILO–JASPA (1989) *African Employment Report 1988* (Addis Ababa: ILO–JASPA).

ILO–JASPA (1995) *Africa Employment Report 1994* (Addis Ababa: ILO–JASPA).

ILO–PREALC (1980) *Elasticidad de sustitucion: Evaluacion critica e implicaciones para politicas de empleo en America Latina*, Series Documentos de trabajo/192 (Santiago: ILO– PREALC).

INTERNATIONAL MONETARY FUND (IMF) (1996) *World Economic Outlook* (Washington, DC: IMF, May).

INTERNATIONAL TELECOMMUNICATIONS UNION (ITU) (1993) *African Telecommunication Indicators* (Geneva: ITU).

INTERNATIONAL TELECOMMUNICATIONS UNION (1996) *African Telecommunications Indicators* (Geneva: ITU).

JAMES, J. (1985) 'The Employment and Income Distributional Impact of Microelectronics: A Prospective Analysis for the Third World', ILO World Employment Programme, Working Paper no. 153 (Geneva: ILO).

JAMES, J. (1993) 'New Technologies, Employment and Labour Markets in Developing Countries', *Development and Change*, July.

JAMES, J. (1994) 'Microelectronics and the Third World', in C. Cooper (ed.), *Technology and Innovation in the Global Economy* (Aldershot: Edward Elgar).

JAMES, J. and A.S. BHALLA (1993) 'Flexible Specialisation, New Technologies and Future Industrialization in Developing Countries', *Futures*, July–August.

JAMES, J. and S. WATANABE (1985) *Technology, Institutions and Government Policies* (London: Macmillan).

JENSEN, MIKE (1996) 'Bridging the Gaps in Internet Development in Africa', mimeo, IDRC Development Gaps Study (Ottawa: IDRC, 31 August).

JESPERSON, EVA (1992) 'External Shocks, Adjustment Policies and Economic and Social Performance', in G.A. Cornia, R. van der Hoeven and T. Mkandawire (eds), *Africa's Recovery in the 1990s* (London: Macmillan).

KAPLINSKY, R. (1990) *The Economies of Small: Appropriate Technology in a Changing World* (London: Intermediate Technology Publications).

KATZ, JORGE, M. (ed.) (1987) *Technology Generation in Latin American Manufacturing Industries* (London: Macmillan).

KEYNES, M. (1933) 'National Self-Sufficiency', *Yale Review*, Summer.

KHAN, A.R. (1990) 'Poverty in Bangladesh: A Consequence of and a Constraint on Growth', *The Bangladesh Development Studies*, September.

KHAN, A.R. (1994) *Overcoming Unemployment* (Geneva: ILO and UNDP).

KHAN. A.R. (1996a) 'A Quarter Century of Economic Development in Bangladesh: Successes and Failures', paper presented at 'Bangladesh at 25' Conference at Columbia University South Asian Centre, New York, December.

KHAN, A.R. (1996b) 'Globalization and Urban Employment: Some Issues in Asian Perspective', paper prepared for the UNDP/Habitat Round Table, Marmaris, Turkey, 19–21 April.

KHAN, A.R. (1996c) 'The Impact of Recent Macroeconomic and Sectoral Changes on the Poor and Women in China', manuscript (Bangkok: ILO East Asia Multidisciplinary Advisory Team).

KHAN, A.R. (1996d) 'Employment, Growth and Liberalization: China's Growth in a Globalizing World Economy', manuscript (Bangkok: ILO/EASMAT).

KHAN, A.R. (1997) *Philippines: Employment in a Globalizing and Liberalizing World* (Manila: ILO Southeast Asia and the Pacific Multidisciplinary Advisory Team).

KHAN, A.R. and M. HOSSAIN (1989) *The Strategy of Development in Bangladesh* (London: Macmillan).

KITSON, M. and J. MICHIE (1995) 'Trade and Growth: A Historical Perspective', in J. Michie and J. Grieve Smith (eds), *Managing the Global Economy* (Oxford: Oxford University Press).

KOLATA, GINA (1996) 'With Major Math Proof, Brute Computers Show Flash of Reasoning Power', *The New York Times*, 10 December, Section C1.

KOREA LABOR INSTITUTE (1992) *Foreign Labor Statistics* (Seoul: Korea Labor Institute).

KRAEMER, K.L. and JASON DEDRICK (1994) 'Payoffs From Investment in Information Technology: Lessons from the Asia-Pacific Region', *World Development*, December.

KRUGMAN, P., J. ALM, S. COLLINS and E. REMOLONA (1992) *Transforming the Philippines Economy* (Manila: National Economic Development Authority UNDP).

KRUGMAN, P. and R. LAWRENCE (1994) 'Trade, Jobs and Wages', *Scientific American*, April.

KRUGMAN, P. and A.J. VENABLES (1995) 'Globalization and the Inequality of Nations', *Quarterly Journal of Economics*, November.

LAL, K. (1996) 'Information Technology, International Orientation and Performance: A Case Study of Electrical and Electronic Goods Manufacturing Firms in India', *Information Economics and Policy*, September (North-Holland).

LALL, SANJAYA (1987) *Learning to Industrialize: The Acquisition of Technological Capability in India* (London: Macmillan).

LALL, SANJAYA (1992) 'The Role of Technology in Economic Development', in Simón Teitel (ed.), *Towards a New Development Strategy for Latin America* (Washington, DC: Interamerican Development Bank).

LALL, SANJAYA (1993) 'Understanding Technology Development', *Development and Change* October.

LALL, SANJAYA (1995a) 'Industrial Strategy and Policies on Foreign Direct Investment in East Asia', *Transnational Corporations*, December.

LALL, SANJAYA (1995b) 'Employment and Foreign Investment: Policy Options for Developing Countries', *International Labour Review*, vol. 134, nos. 4–5.

LALL, SANJAYA et al. (1994) Technology and Enterprise Development in Ghana under Structural Adjustment (London: Macmillan).

LAWRENCE, R. (1996) *Single World, Divided Nations? International Trade and OECD Labour Markets* (Paris: The Brookings Institution and OECD Development Centre).

LAWRENCE, R. and M. SLAUGHTER (1993) 'Trade and US Wages: Great Sucking Sound or Small Hiccup', Brookings Papers on Economic Activity, Microeconomics, vol. 2 (Washington, DC: Brookings Institution).

LEE, J.S. (1994) 'The Role of the State in Economic Restructuring and Development: The Case of Taiwan', Occasional Paper Series no. 9403 (Taipei: Chung-Hua Institution for Economic Research).

LEVY, BRIAN et al. (1994) 'Technical and Marketing Support Systems for Successful Small and Medium-Size Enterprises in Four Countries', World Bank, Policy Research Department Working Paper 1400 (Washington, DC: World Bank, December).

LIPTON, M. (1985) 'The Prisoner's Dilemma and Coase's Theorem: A Case for Democracy in Less Developed Countries', in R.C.O. Matthews (ed.), *Economy and Democracy* (New York: St Martin's Press).

MADDISON, ANGUS (1989) *The World Economy in the Twentieth Century* (Paris: OECD Development Centre).

MADDISON, ANGUS (1995) *Monitoring the World Economy* (Paris: OECD).

MAIZELS, A. (1963) *Industrial Growth and World Trade* (Cambridge: Cambridge University Press).

MAIZELS, A. (1994) 'The Continuing Commodity Crisis of Developing Countries', *World Development*, November.

MARCELLE, G. (1996) 'Creating an African Women's Cyberspace', paper presented at the International Workshop on the Information Revolution and Economic and Social Exclusion in Developing Countries, Maastricht, UNU-INTECH, 23–5 October.

MARTIN, W. and L. ALAN WINTERS(eds) (1995) 'The Uruguay Round and the Developing Countries', World Bank Discussion Papers no. 307 (Washington, DC: World Bank).

MAZUMDAR, D. (1993) 'Labour Markets and Adjustment in Open Asian Economies: Korea and Malaysia', *World Bank Economic Review*, September.

MEDHI, KRONGKAEW (1996) 'Macroeconomic Policies and Poverty: the Thai Experience', manuscript (Bangkok: ILO East Asia Multidisciplinary Advisory Team).

MEDHI, KRONGKAEW et al. (1992) 'Rural Poverty in Thailand: Policy Issues and Responses', *Asian Development Review*, vol. 10.

MELLER, PATRICIO (1992) *Adjustment and Equity in Chile* (Paris: OECD Development Centre).

MINISTERIO DE AGRICULTURA Y DEPARTAMENTO NACIONAL DE PLANEACION (1990) *El Desarrollo Agropecuario en Colombia, Informe Final: Mision de Estudios del Sector Agropecuario* (Bogota: Editorial Presencia).

MODY, A. and C. DAHLMAN (1992) 'Performance and Potential of Information Technology: An International Perspective', *World Development*, December.

MODY, ASHOK, RAJAN SURI and JERRY SANDERS (1992) 'Keeping Pace with Change: Organizational and Technological Imperatives', *World Development*, vol. 20, no. 12.

MORLEY, SAMUEL A. (1995) *Poverty and Inequality in Latin America: The Impact of Adjustment and Recovery in the 1980s* (Baltimore, MD: Johns Hopkins University Press).

MORLEY, SAMUEL A. and GORDON W. SMITH (1979) 'Adaptation by Foreign Firms to Labour Abundance in Brazil', in James H. Street and Dilmus D. James (eds), *Technological Progress in Latin America: The Prospects for Overcoming Dependency* (Boulder, CO: Westview Press).

MOSLEY, P. (1996) 'Globalization and Liberalization in Sub- Saharan Africa: Implications for Growth and Poverty', in UNCTAD, *Globalization and Liberalization: Effects of International Economic Relations on Poverty* (Geneva: UNCTAD).

MOUSSA, A. and R. SCHWARE (1992) 'Informatics in Africa: Lessons from World Bank Experience', *World Development*, December.

MOYO, L. (1996) 'Information Technology Strategies for Africa's Survival in the Twenty-First Century: IT All Pervasive', *Information Technology for Development*, vol. 7.

MYTELKA, L. (ed.) (1994) *South–South Cooperation in Global Perspective* (Paris: OECD Development Centre).

NAYYAR, D. (1995) 'Globalization: The Past in Our Present', presidential address to the seventy-eighth annual conference of the Indian Economics Association, Chandigarh, 28–30 December.

NELSON, RICHARD R. (1968) 'A Diffusion Model of International Productivity Differences', *American Economic Review*, vol. 59, no. 3.

NUN, JOSÉ (1969) 'Superpoblación Relativa, Ejército Industrial de Reserva y Masa Marginal', *Revista Latinoamericana de Sociología*, vol. 5, no. 2.

OECD (1992) *Technology and the Economy – The Key Relationships* (Paris: OECD).

OECD (1993) *Science, Technology and Industry (STI) Review*, no. 13 (December).

OECD (1994) *The Jobs Study – Evidence and Explanations*, Parts I and II (Paris: OECD).

OECD (1997) 'Globalization and Linkages to 2020: Challenges and Opportunities for OECD Countries', Linkages II Study, draft prepared by the OECD Development Centre, Paris, 3 March.

OMAN, C. (1994) *Globalisation and Regionalisation: the Challenge for Developing Countries* (Paris: OECD).

OMAN, C. (1996) 'The Policy Challenges of Globalization and Regionalization', OECD Development Centre Policy Brief, no. 11 (Paris: OECD).

O'ROURKE, K., A. TAYLOR and J. WILLIAMSON (1996) 'Factor Price Convergence in the Late Nineteenth Century', *International Economic Review*, August.

O'SIOCHRÚ, S. (1993) 'Global Sustainability, Telecommunications and Science and Technology Policy', a report for the FAST Programme, Brussels.

OSMANI, S.R. (1987) 'The Impact of Economic Liberalisation on the Small-Scale and Rural Industries of Sri Lanka', in R. Islam (ed.) *Rural Industrialisation and Employment in Asia* (New Delhi: ILO–ARTEP).

PACK, H. and L. WESTPHAL (1986) 'Industrial Strategy and Technological Change: Theory vs. Reality', *Journal of Development Economics*, vol. 22, no. 1.

PARISOTTO, A. (1993) 'Direct Employment in Multinational Enterprises in Industrialized and Developing Countries in the 1980s: Main Characteristics and Recent Trends', in P. Bailey, A. Parisotto and G. Renshaw (eds), *Multinationals and Employment* (Geneva: ILO).

PATEL, P. (1995) 'Localised Production of Technology for Global Markets', *Cambridge Journal of Economics*, February.

PATEL, P. and K. PAVITT (1991) 'Large Firms in the Production of the World's Technology: An Important Case of "Non-globalisation"', *Journal of International Business Studies*, vol. 22.

PEREZ, C. (1985) 'Micro-electronics, Long Waves and World Structural Change: New Perspectives in Developing Countries', *World Development*, vol. 13, no. 3.

PEREZ, C. (1992) 'New Technologies and Development', in Freeman and Lundvall, *Small Countries*, op. cit.

PEREZ, C. (1994) 'Technical Change and the New Context of Development', in Mytelka, *South–South Cooperation*, op. cit.

PERLMAN, JANICE E. (1976) *The Myth of Marginality: Urban Poverty and Politics in Rio de Janeiro* (Berkeley, CA: California University Press).

PINTO, ANIBAL (1965) 'Concentracion del progreso tecnico y de sus frutos en el desarrollo latinoamericano', *El Trimestre Economico* (Mexico: Fondo de Cultura Economica, January–March).

POLANYI, KARL (1944) *The Great Transformation* (Boston, Mass: Beacon Press).

PREBISCH, RAUL (1950) *The Economic Development of Latin America and its Principal Problems* (New York: United Nations).

RAMANI, S. (1996) 'National Infrastructure Required to Promote Information Technology (IT) Applications', paper presented at the International Seminar on the Information Revolution and Economic and Social Exclusion in Developing Countries, Maastricht, UNU-INTECH, 23–5 October.

RAO, MOHAN (1995) 'Globalization: A View from the South', Amherst, University of Massachusetts, mimeo.

RASIAH, RAJAH (1996) 'Globalization and Liberalization in East and South East Asia: Implications for Growth, Inequality and Poverty', in UNCTAD, *Globalization and Liberalization: Effects of International Economic Relations on Poverty* (Geneva: UNCTAD).

RAVALLION, M. and B. SEN (1994) *When Methods Matter: Towards a Resolution of the Debate Over Bangladesh's Poverty Measures* (Washington, DC: World Bank).

REDDY, P. and J. SIGURDSON (1994) 'Emerging Patterns of Globalisation of Corporate R&D and Scope for Innovative Capability Building in Developing Countries', *Science and Public Policy*, vol. 21, no. 5.

ROBBINS, D. (1995a) 'Earnings Dispersion in Chile After Trade Liberalization', mimeo (Cambridge, Mass.: Harvard University).

ROBBINS, D. (1995b) 'Schematic Summary of Findings for Country Wage and Employment Structure Studies', mimeo (Cambridge, Mass.: Harvard University).

ROBBINS, D. (1996) 'Evidence on Trade and Wages in the Developing World', OECD Development Centre Technical Paper no. 119 (Paris: OECD, December).

RODRIK, DANI (1996) 'Why Do More Open Economies Have Bigger Governments?', NBER Working Paper no. 5537 (Cambridge, Mass.: NBER, February, Revised March).

RODRIK, DANI (1997) *Has Globalization Gone Too Far?* (Washington, DC: Institute for International Economics, April).

RUGGIE, JOHN G. (1995) *At Home Abroad, Abroad at Home: International Liberalization and Domestic Stability in the New World Economy*, Jean Monnet Chair Papers (Florence: The Robert Schuman Centre at the European University Institute).

SAMUDRAM, MUTHI (1996) 'Macroeconomic Policies and Poverty: The Malaysian Experience', manuscript (Bangkok: ILO East Asia Multidisciplinary Advisory Team).

SCHMITZ, H. and J. CASSIOLATO (1992) *Hi-Tech Industrial Development – Lessons From The Brazilian Experience in Electronics and Automation* (London: Routledge).

SCHWARE, R. and S. HUME (1995) 'The Global Information Industry and the Eastern Caribbean', in UNCTAD, *Information Technology for Development*, Advanced Technology Assessment System, no. 10 (Autumn) (Geneva: UNCTAD).

SHARMA, S. and D. DHAKAL (1995) 'Causal Analyses Between Exports and Economic Growth in Developing Countries', *Applied Economics*, vol. 26.

SILBER, SIMAO DAVI (1987) 'Aggregation and the Theory of International Trade', *Anais, XV Encontro Nacional da ANPEC*, vol. 1 (Salvador, Brazil).

SINGH, AJIT (1995) 'Institutional Requirements for Full Employment in Advanced Economies', *International Labour Review*, vol. 134, nos 4–5.

SODERSTON, B. (1980) *International Economics*, 2nd edn (London: Macmillan).

SOLOW, ROBERT M. (1990) *The Labour Market as a Social Institution* (Cambridge, Mass.: Basil Blackwell).

SOUTH CENTRE (1996) *Liberalization and Globalization: Drawing Conclusions for Development* (Geneva: South Centre).

SPINANGER, D. (1992) 'The Impact on Employment and Income of Structural and Technological Changes in the Clothing Industry', in G. Van Liemt (ed.), *Industry on the Move* (Geneva: ILO).

STATE DATA ANALYSIS SYSTEM FOUNDATION (SEADE) (1995) *Yearbook* (São Paulo: SEADE).

STEWART, FRANCES (1995) 'Biases in Global Markets: Can the Forces of Inequity and Marginalisation be Modified?', in Mahbub ul Haq, Richard Jolly, Paul Streeten and Khadija Haq (eds), *The UN and Bretton Woods Institutions: New Challenges for the Twenty-First Century* (London: Macmillan).

STIGLITZ, JOSEPH E. (1987) 'On the Microeconomics of Technical Progress', in Katz, *Technology Generation*, op. cit.

STOKEY, N. (1994) 'Free Trade, Factor Returns, and Factor Accumulation', mimeo (Chicago, Ill.: University of Chicago).

STREET, JAMES H. and DILMUS D. JAMES(eds) (1979) *Technological Progress in Latin America: The Prospects for Overcoming Dependency* (Boulder, CO: Westview Press).

STREETEN, PAUL (1989) 'International Cooperation', in Hollis Chenerey and T.N. Srinivasan, *Handbook of Development Economics*, vol. 2 (Amsterdam: North Holland).

STREETEN, PAUL (1993) 'Markets and States: Against Minimalism', *World Development*, August.

SUGANYA, HUTASERANI and SOMCHAI JITSUCHON (1988) 'Thailand Income Distribution and Poverty Profile and their Current Situations', Thailand Development Research Institute's year-end Conference Proceedings, Pattaya, December.

SUNKEL, OSVALDO (1973) 'The Pattern of Latin American Dependence', in Victor Urquidi and Rosemary Thorp (eds), *Latin America in the International Economy* (London: Macmillan).

SUSSMAN, G. (1991) 'The Transnationalization of Philippine Telecommunications: Postcolonial Continuities', in G. Sussman and J.A. Lent (eds), *Transnational Communications: Wiring the Third World* (Newbury Park: Sage).

TEITEL, SIMÓN (1992) *Towards a New Development Strategy for Latin America* (Washington, DC: Interamerican Development Bank).

TENDULKAR, S.D., K. SUNDARAM and L.R. JAIN (1996) 'Macroeconomic Policies and Poverty in India 1966–67 to 1993–94', manuscript (New Delhi: ILO South Asia Multidisciplinary Advisory Team).

THUROW, L. (1992) *Head to Head – The Coming Economic Battle Among Japan, Europe and America* (New York: William Morrow).

TOKMAN, VICTOR E. (1989) 'Urban Employment Problems: Research and Policy in Latin America', in Bernard Salome (ed.), *Fighting Urban Unemployment in Developing Countries* (Paris: OECD Development Centre).

UCHITELLE, LOUIS (1996) 'What Has the Computer Done for Us Lately?', *The New York Times Week in Review*, Sunday 4 December, Section 4.

UNITED NATIONS (1992) *World Investment Report*, New York, Transnational Corporation and Management Division.

UNITED NATIONS (1993, 1994, 1995), *International Trade Statistics Yearbook* (New York: UN).

UNITED NATIONS (1996) *World Economic and Social Survey* (New York: UN).

UNITED NATIONS CENTRE FOR TRANSANTIONAL CORPORATIONS (UNCTC) (1992) *World Investment Report* (New York: UNCTC).

UNITED NATIONS CONFERENCE ON TRADE AND DEVELOPMENT (UNCTAD) (1984, 1991, 1993) *Handbook of International Trade and Development Statistics* (Geneva: UNCTAD).

UNITED NATIONS CONFERENCE ON TRADE AND DEVELOPMENT (1994, 1995a, 1996) *World Investment Report* (Geneva: UNCTAD).

UNITED NATIONS CONFERENCE ON TRADE AND DEVELOPMENT (1995b) *Trade and Development Report* (Geneva: UNCTAD).

UNITED NATIONS DEVELOPMENT PROGRAMME (UNDP) (1990, 1993, 1995, 1996) *Human Development Report* (New York: Oxford University Press).

UNITED NATIONS ECONOMIC COMMISSION FOR AFRICA (UNECA) (1994–5), *Economic and Social Survey of Africa* (Addis Ababa: UNECA).

UNITED NATIONS ECONOMIC COMMISSION FOR AFRICA (1996) *Framework to Build Africa's Information and Communication Infrastructure* (Addis Ababa: UNECA).

UNITED NATIONS ECONOMIC COMMISSION FOR LATIN AMERICA AND THE CARIBBEAN (UNECLAC) (1995a) *Statistical Yearbook for Latin America and the Caribbean* (Santiago: UNECLAC).

UNITED NATIONS ECONOMIC COMMISSION FOR LATIN AMERICA AND THE CARIBBEAN (1995b) *Economic Survey of Latin America and the Caribbean 1994–95* (Santiago: UNECLAC).

UNITED NATIONS ECONOMIC COMMISSION FOR LATIN AMERICA AND CARIBBEAN (1996a) *Economic Panorama of Latin America 1996* (Santiago: UNECLAC).

UNITED NATIONS ECONOMIC COMMISSION FOR LATIN AMERICA AND THE CARIBBEAN (1996b) *Preliminary Overview of the Economy of Latin America and the Caribbean* (Santiago: UNECLAC).

UNITED NATIONS EDUCATIONAL, SCIENTIFIC AND CULTURAL ORGAN-IZATION (UNESCO) (various years), *Statistical Yearbook: Expenditure and Experimental Development* (Paris: UNESCO).

UNITED NATIONS INDUSTRIAL DEVELOPMENT ORGANIZATION (UNIDO) (1993) *African Industry in Figures* (Vienna: UNIDO).

UNITED NATIONS INDUSTRIAL DEVELOPMENT ORGANIZATION (1996) *The Globalization of Industry: Implications for Developing Countries Beyond 2000* (Vienna: UNIDO, December).

UNITED NATIONS RESEARCH INSTITUTE FOR SOCIAL DEVELOPMENT (UNRISD) (1995) *States of Disarray: The Social Effects of Globalization* (Geneva: UNRISD).

UNITED STATES (1991) *Statistical Abstract of the United States* (Washington, DC: US Government Printing Office).

VAITSOS, CONSTANTINO V. (1974) *Intercountry Distribution of Income and Transnational Enterprises* (Oxford: Clarendon Press).

VAN LIEMT, GIJSBERT (ed.) (1992) *Industry on the Move* (Geneva: ILO).

VIDAL, GORE (1992) *Screening History* (Cambridge, Mass.: Harvard University Press).

WADE, ROBERT (1990) *Governing the Market: Economic Theory and the Role of Government in East Asian Industrialization* (Princeton, NJ: Princeton University Press).

WADE, ROBERT (1996a) 'Japan, the World Bank, and the Art of Paradigm Maintenance: *The East Asian Mircale* in Political Perspective', *New Left Review*, no. 217.

WADE, ROBERT (1996b) 'Globalization and its Limits: Reports of the Death of the National Economy are Greatly Exaggerated', in Suzanne Berger and Ronald Dore (eds), *National Diversity and Global Capitalism* (Ithaca, NY: Cornell University Press).

WATANABE, S. (1995) 'Microelectronics and the Third World Industries: An Overview', in UNCTAD, *Information Technology for Development*, Advanced Technology Assessment System, no. 10, Autumn (Geneva: UNCTAD).

WEISSKOFF, R. (1992) 'The Paraguayan Agro-Export Model of Development', *World Development*, vol. 20, no. 10.

WHEELER, D. and A. MODY (1988), *Risks and Rewards in International Location Tournaments: The Case of US Firms*, (Washington, DC: World Bank. (mimeo).

WILLIAMSON, JEFFREY (1995) 'The Evolution of Global Labour Markets since 1830: Background Evidence and Hypotheses', *Explorations in Economic History*, April.

WILLIAMSON, JEFFREY G. (1996a) 'Globalization and Inequality Then and Now: The Late 19th and Late 20th Centuries Compared', NBER Working Paper no. 5491, March.

WILLIAMSON, JEFFREY (1996b) 'Globalization, Convergence and History', *Journal of Economic History*, June.

WINSBURY, R. (1995) 'Who Will Pay for the Global Village? Funding the Buenos Aires Declaration', in UNCTAD, *Information Technology for Development, Advanced Technology Assessment System*, issue 10, Autumn, (Geneva, UNCTAD).

WOOD, A. (1994), *North–South Trade, Employment and Inequality: Changing Fortunes in a Skill Driven World* (Oxford: Clarendon Press).

WOOD, A. (1995) 'How Trade Hurt Unskilled Workers', *Journal of Economic Perspectives*, Summer.

WOOD, A. (1997) 'Openness and Wage Inequality in Developing Countries: The Latin American Challenge to East Asian Conventional Wisdom', *World Bank Economic Review*, January.

WOODALL, PAM (1996) 'A Survey of the World Economy', *The Economist*, 28 September.

WORLD BANK (1984, 1987, 1988–93a, 1995a–96a) *World Development Report* (New York: Oxford University Press).

WORLD BANK (1993b) *The East Asian Miracle* (New York: Oxford University Press).

WORLD BANK (1993c) *Global Economic Prospects and the Developing Countries* (Washington, DC: World Bank).

WORLD BANK (1993d) *Socioeconomic Time-series Access and Retrieval System (Stars)*, version 3.0 (Washington, DC: World Bank, May).

WORLD BANK (1995b) *Annual Report*, (Washington, DC: World Bank).

WORLD BANK (1995c) *Bangladesh: Recent Economic Developments and Priority Reform Agenda for Rapid Growth* (Washington, DC: World Bank).

WORLD BANK (1995d) *World Tables* (Baltimore, MD, and London: Johns Hopkins University Press).

WORLD BANK (1996b) *Global Economic Prospects and the Developing Countries* (Washington, DC: World Bank).

WORLD BANK (1996c) *Managing Capital Flows in East Asia* (Washington, DC: World Bank).

WORLD BANK (1996d) *Social Indicators of Development* (Washington, DC: World Bank).

WORLD BANK (1996e) *African Development Indicators* (Washington, DC: World Bank).

YOUNG, J. (1993) 'Computers in a Sustainable Society' Washington DC. World Watch Institute *Worldwatch paper* 115.

YU, T.S. (1994) 'Does Taiwan's Industrialization Have Its Own Paradigm?', Occasional Paper Series no. 9404 (Taipei: Chung-Hua Institution for Economic Research).

Author Index

215

Author Index

Subject Index